B
824.6     Bergmann, Gustav
.B4
1967      The metaphysics
          of logical posi-
          tivism

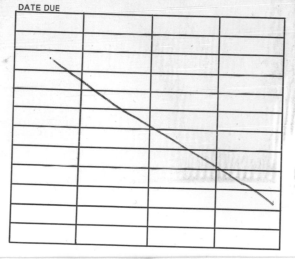

# THE METAPHYSICS OF
# LOGICAL POSITIVISM

# THE METAPHYSICS OF
# LOGICAL POSITIVISM

by

GUSTAV BERGMANN

THE UNIVERSITY OF WISCONSIN PRESS

MADISON, MILWAUKEE, AND LONDON

1967

Published by
The University of Wisconsin Press
Madison, Milwaukee, and London

U.S.A.: Box 1379, Madison, Wisconsin 53714
U.K.: 26–28 Hallam Street, London W.1

Printed in the United States of America
Library of Congress Catalog Card Number 54–5790

## PREFACE

THERE WAS a time when a philosopher had to write books, or at least one thick book, if he wished to obtain a hearing for what was then called his system. This age is of shorter breath. Today many philosophers are content to pursue their education in public by means of the papers they insert in learned journals. If such a one has reached middle age and is fortunate enough to have friends who encourage him, he is urged to publish a volume of essays. This is the case in which I find myself. I have for some time, and I fear quite recklessly, conducted my education in public; I have a few generous friends whose judgment I value; and I must confess that the mere thought of writing a book on first philosophy terrifies me. Some causes of this terror probably belong in the psychoanalyst's study; one reason I think bears public statement. As things now stand, no philosopher, at least no analytical philosopher, can reasonably start afresh. All he can hope to do is to throw some new light on a few points within the tradition to which he owes most of his views, or, perhaps, to add a new twist to the method practiced by its masters. Thus, if he submits to the rules of the book-writing game, he will be forced to say once more many things that have been said before and much better than he can possibly hope to say them. To do this, outside the seminar room, is to waste one's colleagues' time as well as one's own. As for our students, I believe it is our duty to send them first of all to the classics and to the great contemporary masters. So instructed, they, too, should be able to make sense of what is not exactly a textbook.

This is not a collection of my papers on first philosophy but a selection from them. Nor is the order in which they are arranged chronological. This requires some comment. The papers fall into three groups. Taken together, the first six, of most recent origin, provide an outline of the views I now hold. The second group consists of the next three, which are the earliest included in this volume. Together with three other still earlier ones which I have excluded, they form a unit centered around the realism phenomenalism issue. The excluded papers are "Pure Semantics, Sentences, and Propositions" (*Mind*, 53, 1944), "A Positivistic Metaphysics of Consciousness" (*Mind*, 54, 1945), "Undefined Descriptive Predicates" (*Philosophy and Phenomenological Research*, 8, 1947). I omit them because for the most part they merely say very badly what I have since said again, a little less badly, in the six essays of the first group. I mention them because there I first struck out on my own, trying to free myself from the influence of Carnapian positivism though not yet, alas, from its apparatus. Having said that much, as I believe I should, I wish to add, as I believe I also should, that this by now radical dissent has not at all affected either my gratitude or my admiration for Carnap. I still think of him as the outstanding figure in a major phase of the positivistic movement. The third group consists of all the remaining essays, some of them very short. These are in the main elaborations of themes struck in the first nine pieces. The arrangement within this last group represents a compromise between their subject matter and the order in which I remember having written them. The concluding essay differs from the rest. Quite nontechnical, it touches at least indirectly on my philosophy in that broader sense in which everyone who is not himself an analytical philosopher speaks of a man's philosophy. Thus it is, perhaps, not out of place at the end of a volume that is otherwise rather technical.

Aside from a few editorial changes I have left the papers as they were originally written. This means that, taken singly, most of them would benefit from expansion. Taken together, they should throw a good deal of light upon each other. It also means that some, particularly the earlier ones, contain passages which I could now improve and which do not, as they stand, completely jibe with the rest. But I fear that, if I started revising, I would soon reach the point where the only proper thing to do is what I dare not do, namely, write a metaphysical treatise. So I shall persist in my ways, not from either arrogance or laziness but because I cannot help it, hoping that I shall learn from the critics of this volume what improvements and clarifications are most needed so that I can try to provide them over the years in some future essays. But there is one matter on which I feel I ought to say a word now, since I know that it has bothered some of my friends. Consider an awareness whose content is referred to by 'This is a tree'. An awareness must be distinguished from its content. Yet, to be an awareness with a certain content and to be an awareness of a certain kind is one thing and not two. The predicate I proposed as a name of this kind is, in the illustration, ' 'This is a tree' '. The awarenesses that exemplify it are named by particulars. The distinction is, of course, but a variant of the familiar one between type and token; like the latter, it adds in most contexts nothing to the analysis. Having once called attention to it, I proceeded therefore immediately to neglect it, using such predicates as ' 'This is a tree' ' as if they were particulars. But I have come to think that there are contexts in which the distinction is helpful. However that may be, an accurate formulation will be found in the third essay.

A table indicating where the pieces originally appeared will be found at the end of the volume. The necessary permissions by publishers and editors have been granted and are gratefully acknowledged. One of the essays was at this writing still in press. The editor of the journal in which it was to appear has permitted me to withdraw it.

A careful subject index should help to bring out the continuity of theme and thought among the essays. By compiling such an index Professors May Brodbeck, of the University of Minnesota, and William H. Hay, of the University of Wisconsin, have further increased the large debt of gratitude which I owe them.

G.B.

*Iowa City*
*July 1, 1953*

# PREFACE TO THE SECOND EDITION

THE LOGICAL positivists, whether they knew it or not, were all either metaphysical materialists or phenomenalists. The former hold that there is nothing mental; the latter, that everything is mental. The contrast seems extreme, yet it really isn't. Perceiving, believing, remembering, and so on, are kinds of mental acts. Each such act means something; or, as one says, it intends something. This connection between a mind and whatever it happens to be about at the moment is unique. Intentionality is the essence of mind. Each act, or perhaps some constituent of it, is an intentional entity. Words are mere noises, material entities which do not in this fundamental sense mean anything, even though we use them to communicate what we mean and even though their images, either auditory or visual or kinaesthetic, are causally enmeshed with most of our thoughts. But, then, these images themselves are something we intend. The simples, often called sense data, out of which the phenomenalist builds his world, do not and cannot intend anything. Structurally, therefore, even though he calls them mental, they are like material entities. Or, to say the same thing differently, the phenomenalist's and the metaphysical materialist's are both one-level worlds. That is why, structurally, the contrast is not as great as it seems, just as, historically, some logical positivists found it quite easy to shift from one of these apparent extremes to the other. The realist's is a two-level world of minds and of bodies, in which the former are capable of intending the latter as well as themselves and each other.

The logical positivists of the Vienna Circle were my first teachers. Thus I was faced with an unpalatable choice. Dialectically, metaphysical materialism always seemed and still seems to me the greater evil. (Scientific materialism is but common sense.) So I began my philosophical career as a reluctant phenomenalist in the style of the Circle. Now I am, and have been for some time, a realist of the phenomenological variety. The break occurred in the early fifties, when I proposed an analysis of the act. This book, my first, a collection of essays originally published in 1954, reflects the struggles which led to that break. Much of it I now reject. Yet there are also many analyses, of issues and of movements, including pragmatism, logical positivism, and the so-called linguistic philosophy, which I still think are right.

Two of the essays introduce the act. Another, about semantics, mentions the meaning nexus which has come to play so great a role in my thought. The essay on the problem of relations in classical psychology first manifests what has since become one of my major concerns. The concluding piece, on ideology, has been well received by many social scientists.

By now logical positivism belongs to history. Yet it was a vigorous movement; some of its members were brilliant; its contribution to the philosophy of science remains most valuable. From the record of such a movement much can be learned. This book, in its own peculiar way, is part of the record. Thus, since it is still in demand although it has been out of print for some time, a new edition seems justified.

G.B.

*Iowa City, Iowa*
*October, 1966*

[x]

# CONTENTS

CONTENTS

## LOGICAL POSITIVISM *

LOGICAL POSITIVISM is a movement rather than a school, in the sense that those to whom the label is currently applied represent a broad range of interests and, on questions of common interest, often disagree with respect to what constitutes the right answer or about the proper method to arrive at it. Thus a systematic and critical account, preceded by a minimum of historical remarks, becomes preferable to a simple narrative. In the case of a far-flung, complex, and still very active movement, a report of this kind must to some extent reflect the opinions of the reporter; in a sense, it is merely a proposal as to what body of doctrine may reasonably be called Logical Positivism.

The difficulties one encounters in isolating a sufficiently comprehensive core of sufficiently detailed agreement are not unrelated to the circumstance that the writers who are, in fact, called Logical Positivists derive intellectually and, in most cases, also biographically from one of two centers, the Cambridge School of Analysis and the Vienna Circle. One might even say, though not without qualification, that what has come to be called Logical Positivism—the term appeared for the first time in 1930—is the result of the interaction that

* V. Ferm, ed., A History of Philosophical Systems (New York: Philosophical Library, 1950), pp. 471-82. Reprinted by permission.

[1]

took place between the two centers during a formative period of not much more than ten years, which, broadly speaking, coincides with the third decade of the century.[1] The qualification needed is this. As things now stand, most Continental positivists (though many of them now live and teach in the United States, I shall, for convenience, call them so) seem to have entered upon a retrogressive development away from epistemological analysis and toward a more or less naive realism. Logical Positivism, though enriched by the Continentals' continuing contributions to fields of their original interest (mathematical logic and the philosophy of science), thus appears today as the contemporary form of British empiricism.

All this is not to deny that *as long as one sticks to cautious generalities* all Logical Positivists could still agree that they (a) hold Humean views on causality and induction; (b) insist on the tautological nature of logical and mathematical truths; (c) conceive of philosophy as logical analysis, *i.e.*, as a clarification of the language which we all speak in everyday life; and (d) that such analysis leads to the "rejection of metaphysics" in the sense that, *e.g.*, the points at dispute among the *traditional* forms of idealism, realism, and phenomenalism could not even be stated, or, at least not be stated in their original intent, in a properly clarified language. Meager as such diplomatic formulae appear beside a large and often

---

[1] The beginning of this period is marked by the appearance, in both English and German, of Ludwig Wittgenstein's *Tractatus Logico-Philosophicus* (London, 1922); its peak by Rudolf Carnap's *Der Logische Aufbau der Welt* (Berlin, 1928), the work in which the author comes closest to the classical empiricist tradition; its end by Carnap's *The Logical Syntax of Language* (German: Vienna, 1934; English: New York, 1937) and Moritz Schlick's *Gesammelte Aufsaetze 1926-1936* (Vienna, 1938), which show him under the influence, not to say fascination, of Wittgenstein. Much of the later writings of the Continental group is contained in the eight volumes of the journal *Erkenntnis* (1930-39).

[2]

controversial literature, it is worth noticing that these four points can all be found in the *Tractatus;* two of them, (b) and (d), state, no matter how inadequately, Wittgenstein's decisive contribution, the "new turn" by which Logical Positivism distinguishes itself from the earlier empiricist philosophies which could not account for the peculiar truth claim of logic and mathematics and hovered uneasily between Humean scepticism and the traditional ontological positions. This new turn makes Wittgenstein, in the eyes of many, the dominant figure of the movement. Be that as it may, there is no doubt that the formative period of interaction began when both Cambridge and Vienna fell under the spell of the *Tractatus.* But Wittgenstein himself had already been in England and come into contact with G. E. Moore and Bertrand Russell. This brings us back to the differences between the two centers.

What happened at Cambridge [2] was the second phase of a revolution that had begun at the turn of the century. The first phase, led by G. E. Moore, had already replaced the "speculative" and "metaphysical" temper of British Hegelianism by an atmosphere of literal-minded "analysis" and cautious "empiricism." To be sure, Moore has always been a realist; nor did he ever accept the Humean denial of intuited connections between simple characters (which is probably one of the reasons why British positivists still strangely consider such truths as, say, the transitivity of temporal succession or the mutual exclusiveness of colors as analytic). Yet Moore's insistence that the task of philosophy is not either to prove or to disprove common sense but merely to make clear

[2] Most of the work of this group is to be found in the main English journals. A. J. Ayer's *Language, Truth and Logic* (London, 1936) and *The Foundations of Empirical Knowledge* (London, 1940) have almost the status of textbooks.

what it is that we know and how we know it when we assert such propositions as 'tables are real' or 'lions exist'—this insistence lies half-way between the old "metaphysics" and the "antimetaphysical" turn of the new. This continuity had important effects on the British positivists, many of whom are students of Moore. (The flavor of his incomparable style still lingers in their writings.) It led some of them to embrace a phenomenalism not unlike, in spite of Humean and Wittgensteinian overtones, the neutral monism of William James. Thus they are disturbed by the notion of unsensed sensa, whose paradoxical air they cannot resolve by the casuistic analysis of ordinary usage to which, under the influence of Moore, they tend to limit themselves. Others, combining Moore's technique with the Wittgensteinian contention that philosophers always attempt to say the unsayable, have taken to practicing some sort of grammatical psychotherapy. Thus, perhaps not all the effects of the British continuity are desirable. Yet it is probably this continuity that saved virtually all British positivists from the implicit materialism (physicalism [3]) which in Vienna led to the proclamation that philosophy was coextensive with the methodology of the special sciences, *i.e.*, that the meaningful core of *all* philosophical questions could be *completely* recovered through what has since become known as the operational analysis [4] of the spe-

---

[3] The prime mover behind this tendency was Otto Neurath, an important member of the Circle whose manifold activities and encyclopedic, if not always profound, interests defy classification. The programmatic pamphlet, *Wissenschaftliche Weltauffassung: Der Wiener Kreis* (Vienna, 1929) owes its existence to his initiative, social actionism, and reformist zeal.

[4] To understand why 'operational' is sometimes used in such phrases as 'operational analysis' and 'operational definition,' consider the definition of, say, length in terms of the laying-off of a yardstick. It is a so-called definition in use, *i.e.*, roughly, what it gives a synonym for, in terms already understood, is not 'length', but the simplest kind of sentence in

[4]

cial sciences in terms of physical objects and some of their immediately observable properties and relations. This "scientistic" radicalism of Vienna (which Schlick, the personal center of the group, never shared) had its causes. To simplify for the sake of suggesting a pattern, Vienna tried to achieve in one step what in England had been accomplished in two. For, with the exception of some relatively isolated figures, the heavy hand of Kantianism and Hegelianism still lay over German academic philosophy, particularly in the Protestant North; empiricism, ever since the *Materialismusstreit* and the days of the great Helmholtz, had found its best refuge, such as it was, among the method-conscious and mathematically inclined scientists. Thus one understands why the members of the Circle (and their associates in Berlin and Prague) drew most of their inspiration from the development of axiomatics (Hilbert), the anti-Kantian implications of relativity (Einstein), Poincaré's conventionalism, the rising American school of behaviorism in psychology and the social sciences, and most important, from *Principia Mathematica*.[5] Nor is it surprising that the break occurred

which 'length' occurs; the synonym given is a compound sentence describing the operations performed and the result obtained in ascertaining the length of an object. However, this does not mean that length is a product of, or in any other sense dependent on, these operations. To say anything of the sort is to take an instrumentalist position. Generally instrumentalism, which is essentially an idealistic metaphysics, and logical positivism, which stands in the tradition of British empiricism, are irreconcilable opposites. Attempts to engineer a *rapprochement*, made when the Continentals first came to America, were thus bound to fail.

[5] B. Russell and A. N. Whitehead, *Principia Mathematica*, 3 vols. (Cambridge, 1910-13, 2nd ed., 1925-27), frequently quoted as *PM*. During the first phase of the British development Russell's logical analyses parallel Moore's work. His influence on the Continental positivists is second only to Wittgenstein's. Russell himself, deeply committed to realism, has never accepted the positivistic turn, which he did so much to bring about. Yet he says, in *An Inquiry into Meaning and Truth* (New York, 1940), that he is "as regards method, more in sympathy with the logical positivists than with any other existing school."

[5]

in the Catholic South, never quite conquered by idealism, where Husserl (whose antipsychologism in logic and whose conception of philosophy as descriptive are relevant antecedents), Meinong (who stimulated Russell), and other students of Brentano cultivated logic and their own peculiar brand of Aristotelian "empiricism." Even Mach, whose phenomenalism was, except for Wittgenstein and Russell, the strongest single philosophical influence, owed much to this atmosphere in which he lived and taught.

Turning to a more systematic treatment, I explain first in what sense Logical Positivism is an empiricist philosophy and why it considers the analysis of language its principal tool. Consider the account a traveller ordinarily gives of a geographical region or an experimentalist's description of his apparatus. If one does not mind the trouble, one can, at least in a schematic manner or, as one also says, in principle, transcribe such an account so that (1) the transcript contains, besides grammatical particles, only a small number of "undefined" terms, also called undefined descriptive constants, and (2) everybody who understands these terms and the "grammar" of the language knows, after reading the transcript, what he would know had he read the original account. If given the "definitions" of the terms that occur only in the original, such a person could even reconstruct the latter. If one says 'simple ideas' in stead of 'undefined terms', one sees that, broadly speaking, this is but a linguistic version of Locke's basic vision, provided one extends—as one must, if the thing is to be philosophically significant—the claim for the possibility of such a linguistic "reconstruction" to the whole of our experience. But everything still depends on the choice of the undefined terms! To be an empiricist means to adopt an "empiricist meaning criterion" or "prin-

[6]

ciple of acquaintance," *i.e.*, to assert the sufficiency of a class of undefined terms that refer to the sort of thing philosophers call the phenomenally given in contradistinction to, say, physical objects. Logical Positivists are empiricists in this sense; and they also hold that the grammatical schema of *PM* is adequate for the purpose, which implies that all undefined descriptive constants (with whose referents we must be acquainted) are either proper names or predicates. (Again, this latter thesis, Russell's logical atomism, commits one to a Humean view on causality and induction, a frequency theory of probability and, as will be seen, a syntactical interpretation of the modalities.) On the other hand, empiricists need not restrict their basis, as Hume did without appreciating the need for both proper names and predicates, to (the names of) nonrelational sense data; leaving aside the niceties of precise formulation, all Logical Positivists would probably admit the necessity of including some relational predicates, *e.g.*, some spatial and temporal ones, among the undefined terms. (The new logic's emphasis on relations as well as Mach's and Meinong's preoccupation with the introspective irreducibility of some relational characters are here relevant antecedents.) Nor does an analysis that penetrates "down" to those very simple and, alas, very fragile givennesses philosophers call sense data have any particular virtue in itself. The point is, rather, that one needs it if one wants to answer the questions philosophers have asked about space, time, substance, and change, and also for that *partial* resolution of the realism thesis, which Berkeley anticipated in his theory of physical objects. So I must next say what I mean by the phrase 'resolution of the realism thesis' and why and under what conditions the linguistic turn is essential for this purpose. I shall begin by explaining

[7]

what is meant by an ideal language. An ideal language must be (1) *complete*, (2) *formally constructed*,[6] and (3) it must allow for the *resolution of all philosophical puzzles.*

Our natural languages, English, French, German, etc., are complete in the obvious sense that "everything" can be said in any one of them. The analyst's ideal language is not complete in this literal sense; in fact, it is not at all a language actually to be spoken but merely the blueprint or schema of one, complete only in the sense that it shows, in principle, the structure and systematic arrangement of all areas of our experience. To illustrate what this means, we do not, in designing such a schema, attempt to invent and catalogue names for all discriminable hues, brightnesses, pitches, tastes, etc.; we simply stipulate that a sufficient number of such predicates is to be included among its undefined terms. Similarly, when we retrace in such a schema Berkeley's analysis or, if you please, definition of a physical object, we are content with a reconstruction "in principle," leaving the rest to the scientific study of perception. In an obvious and obviously innocuous sense, the ideal language is thus a fiction. Yet the British positivists, probably under the influence of Moore's close adherence to idiomatic English and his suspicion of all systematizing, tend on the whole to reject it as unjustifiably speculative and, therefore, but another excrescence of the Teutonic furor. Many differences in

---

[6] Such a construction, also called syntactical, makes no reference whatsoever to the prospective use of the language or the "meaning" of its terms. Its first step (in the case of a written language) consists in choosing classes of geometrical shapes which are to serve as the *signs* or symbols of the language. In the second step one lays down the rules by which certain finite series of signs are singled out as *sentences*. Every other string of signs corresponds to what I have, in the text, called grammatical nonsense. Logic in the narrower sense is further interested in formally characterizing that subclass of the class of all sentences which corresponds to what we mean by tautological (analytic) truth.

[8]

formulation, as well as some which are not merely matters of formulation, stem, I believe, from this difference. Be that as it may, the idea, implicit in Russell's writings, was most vigorously taken up by the Continentals. Carnap, in particular, saw clearly that the grammatical schema of *PM*, supplemented with descriptive constants, was a likely candidate for the ideal language. No matter how mistaken otherwise, his book of 1928 [1] remains an impressive attempt at such a reconstruction (*Aufbau, Konstitution*) of the world.

With respect to the last of the three criteria for an ideal language, it turns out that *in* the *PM* language the traditional philosophical assertions cannot be stated, or, to say the same thing differently, that attempts to state them lead to grammatical nonsense. To show by an example how this works, it is sufficient to mention that, depending on their context, the forms of the idiomatic 'to be' appear in at least four different transcriptions corresponding to predication ('John *is* a man'), class inclusion ('a man *is* a mammal'), identity ('the father of John *is* the husband of Mary') and the existential clause ('there *is* an x such that . . . x . . .'). Taken together with the rule that the existential clause joined to a constant yields, not a sentence, but grammatical nonsense, this simple observation is enough to reject what the Viennese called metaphysical realism. However, this "resolution" of a traditional position is, so far, both *partial* and *negative*. To complete it, one must also, positively, identify the structural features of the ideal language that reflect those aspects of our experience on which the realists insisted when they engaged in the traditional dialectic with their idealistic and phenomenalistic opponents. Such a positive feature is, for instance, the occurrence of the all-clause and the existential

[9]

clause in the grammatical apparatus, which, together with the undefined temporal relations of the specious present, permits a treatment of the past, the future and, generally, "the unperceived," which is free from the echoes of "metaphysical" phenomenalism. This, of course, merely illustrates what must be done with respect to the realism issue, just as this issue itself, though historically rather central, serves merely to illustrate what must and can be done, negatively and, since they all have a common-sense core, positively for all philosophical positions or, as the Mooreans would rather have it, puzzles.

This raises the question how the claim of everything being expressible *in* the ideal language can be reconciled with a method of philosophizing by means of statements *about* it. One way out of this difficulty is to assert, with Wittgenstein, (1) that all "statements of empirical fact," *i.e.*, nontautological statements which fulfill our meaning criterion, can be transcribed into the ideal language, and (2) that even our own philosophy, strictly speaking, cannot be stated, that it merely "shows itself," so that the reader of this essay, for instance, insofar as it is not purely historical, must "throw away the ladder after he has climbed up on it." It is important to distinguish the principle involved in (2) from the question of a sufficiently broad conception of "empirical fact." The facts of awareness, for instance, and of moral and ethical experience were either ignored by most Logical Positivists—in this they followed James Mill, who taught that to be aware of something and to be aware of this awareness is one and the same thing; or they reconstructed them only partially, from without, as it were, within the framework of behavioristic science, thus rashly denying the status of empirical facts to the phenomenal givennesses in-

[10]

volved. To remedy such shortcomings which, as will be seen, can be done, is one thing; to face the principle involved in (2) is another. Now there is one thing, I believe, that can be done, not to avoid eventual withdrawal into Wittgensteinian silence, since at some time talk must come to an end, but at least to postpone it as long as something can perhaps still be said. This solution hinges on the second criterion, which requires that the ideal language be constructed formally. First, all one does in so constructing it is to lay down rules about geometrical designs; thus one stays safely in the realm of the speakable. (The mathematical niceties involved need not concern us.) Second, by constructing a pattern, without any explicit reference to its use, that can, in fact, serve as the ideal language, one makes sure that in exhibiting its structure one exhibits the basic structure of the world. If at this point I am told that this answer makes that basic structure itself "merely a matter of fact," I should counter that in so broad a sense everything is a fact and that my critic has, therefore, not said anything. If I am told that ultimately I must rely upon the significance of this geometrical treatment of language "to show itself," I would not argue.

I turn now to the discussion of two "metaphysical" tendencies, the one toward *logical constructionism*, the other toward *logical structuralism*, which Logical Positivists have not always avoided.

One who says that all "there is" are sense data and that a physical object, say, *e.g.*, a chair is a "construction" out of sense data, is, obviously, a traditional phenomenalist rather than a Logical Positivist. Yet some Logical Positivists, probably under the influence of Russell, come dangerously close to saying this. Thus it may pay to dispel the illusion. Since

[11]

what one asserts in denying that chairs are constructions is usually expressed by 'chairs exist', this can be done by analyzing the latter statement. The point, then, is that the transcription of this statement into the ideal language reads, roughly, 'there is something such that this something is a chair'. A little more accurately, in a sense data analysis this transcription contains, not one, but very many existential clauses; and the relational predicate, 'chair', whose referent these clauses assert to be exemplified, has a very complicated definition. However, this definition, though it contains existential clauses, does not involve "existence" in the sense of the argument between constructionists and realists. After all, no definition does. All one can say about a definition is, first, that it is grammatically correct and second, that it stays, like our Berkeleyan definition of 'chair', within the limits of the principle of acquaintance. On the other hand, the existential clause could not conceivably apply, either falsely or truly, to such a predicate as 'chair', since to apply it to a constant, whether defined or undefined, whether proper name or predicate, yields, not a sentence, but grammatical nonsense. All one can say is that correctly defined predicates are or are not "exemplified"; in this sense there is, of course, no reasonable doubt that chairs "exist." What goes for chairs and mermaids, who do not happen to "exist," goes also for densities, forces and all the other "abstract entities" of science. The old poser, whether they are "fictitious" or "real," simply never arises. (This is not to say that there are not certain questions as to how the entities of a scientific model theory, such as electrons, are to be accounted for. But then, this is a very technical matter within the philosophy (logical analysis) of science and, as such, devoid of properly philosophical import. All basic philosophical questions can be argued in terms of chairs and mermaids. Who believes otherwise is a victim of that unfortunate scientism so strong among most Continental positivists.)

The axioms of, say, Euclidean geometry are sometimes called the "implicit definitions" of the descriptive constants ('point', 'straight line', 'coincide', etc.) that occur in them. This means that somebody unfamiliar with points, lines, their coincidence, etc., or with any other empirical interpretation of the axiomatic system, may yet be said to be familiar with all of them in the sense that (1) he could, within the limits of inductive uncertainty, recognize one, and (2) he can derive, or check the derivation, of any geometrical theorem. The gist of logical structuralism is the extension of this idea to the whole of our experience. Its hope is to provide grounds for the view that while "the quale of our experience is subjective, private, ineffable, its form or structure is objective, public, communicable." The naivete of this short-cut to avoid the classical problems is patent. The main document of structuralism in the positivistic literature is Carnap's *Aufbau*.[1] Historically, structuralism echoes the old dichotomy of content and form and, from recent sources, Schlick's distinction between *Erkennen* and *Erleben*, and, also, Russell's between knowledge by acquaintance and by description. (For a consistent Logical Positivist there is, of course, no such thing as knowledge by description, in the sense that nothing needs to be added to what has been said about chairs, mermaids, and forces.) The intent of all this, particularly with Carnap and Russell, is quite clearly realistic. However, when structuralists insist that the "meaning" of an undefined predicate, say 'green', not exhausted by the ineffable quale, comprehends the laws of color, they fall, no matter how unconsciously, into the idealist-pragmatist

[13]

thought pattern. Insistence on the self-containedness of the given is the very foundation of all nonidealistic philosophy, positivist and realist alike.

With respect to the problem of tautological (analytical) truths (logic and arithmetic), which occupies a very prominent place in the literature, I can here only say that it is *possible* to characterize their transcriptions into the ideal language formally [6]—at least, this is the basic idea, whatever technical modifications it may have to undergo in the hands of the mathematical logicians. This *distinguishes* them from so-called statements of empirical fact, for which the formalist can only certify grammatical correctness. From the viewpoint here taken, the clarification of what we mean when we say that certain propositions express necessary or nonfactual truths *consists* in pointing at this possibility and this distinction. But it is readily seen that this answer does not appeal to the nontechnical, casuistic, and often psychologizing temper of the British positivists. Thus some of them, impressed by the arbitrariness of definitions *within* a language and by the importance of recognizing statements not ordinarily so recognized as definitions or conventions, have tended to speak of necessary truth as truth by definition or convention. This is not only inadequate in itself; it also blurs—as in the aforementioned case of the transitivity of temporal succession—the distinction between analytical truth (logical form) and the incidental grammatical form of idiomatic speech.

In ethics and aesthetics all Logical Positivists are, in a nontechnical sense of the term, relativists. Most Continentals are of the opinion that everything one can say on these subjects belongs, in principle, to the social sciences. The British, though more traditional in tone, follow by and large the same line. Sometimes these views are argued by means of a distinction between "cognitive" and "noncognitive," which is both irrelevant and spurious, since our givennesses do not come with these labels and since, as James observed, they are, in an obvious sense, all cognitive. However, there is no reason why one should not, as the facts seem to warrant, admit an undefined predicate with the root meaning of, say, 'good'. In a careful *Aufbau*, which avoids the genetic fallacy,[7] this is certainly compatible with the common sense core of relativism. But apparently most Logical Positivists fear that if they admit such characters are "there," they will also have to admit that something else is "out there," perhaps even in a "non-natural" manner. These fears are the wages of unexamined realistic residues.

With respect to the Self, the British positivists hold views very similar to those of Hume, James Mill, and William James. Most Continentals, with the typical foreshortening of perspective due to their scientism, are satisfied with that partial clarification of related issues that lies in a correct statement of behaviorism. Some others cling to the so-called double aspect theory, which is merely a statement of (scientific) common sense, not its analytical clarification. Recently, however, an attempt [8] has been made to include in the ideal language an undefined predicate of immediate awareness. This has three consequences. First, it does justice

[7] To explain this phrase, assume, for the sake of the argument, a scientific theory of the psychoanalytic type to be true. On what occasions we feel, say, moral disapproval depends causally, according to such a theory, on what other occasions in our early childhood we experienced or anticipated pleasure or pain. But this does not mean that what we now experience when we morally disapprove of something is either pleasure or pain, or their anticipation, or perhaps their memory. Who neglects this distinction commits the genetic fallacy.

[8] G. Bergmann, "A Positivistic Metaphysics of Consciousness," *Mind*, 54 (1945), 193-226, and "Professor Ayer's Analysis of Knowing," *Analysis*, 9 (June, 1949), 98-106, and also pp. 215-27 of this book.

to the phenomena which provide the ground for the "act" philosophies of Descartes, Locke, Brentano, and Moore. Second, one needs it to dispel completely the apparent phenomenalistic implications of a consistent empiricism. Third, in completing the ideal language, it strives, in its own way, toward the ideal of that "complete" description of the world which is, and always will be, the business of *philosophia prima et perennis*. But this, to be sure, is a far cry from the iconoclasm of the early positivists.

# SEMANTICS *

SEMANTICS is not a philosophical system; nor is there any group of philosophers or any philosophical movement whose work is semantical in a technical sense that requires a technical term. Thus one cannot speak of a philosophical semanticist or a semantical philosophy as one speaks, say, of a philosophical realist or an idealistic philosophy. Yet the opposite impression has been created by the frequency with which some philosophers as well as some students of other fields, traditionally and on historical grounds considered closely allied with technical philosophy, now use 'semantics' and 'semantical'. Perhaps this justifies a brief account of the different things different writers mean by these terms. It is well to realize, though, that if it is to be of any use to philosophers, such an account must state its own philosophical presuppositions. The standpoint here taken is that of Logical Positivism.[1] The bias this introduces is in practice much less pronounced than one might fear on principle. For many of the "semanticists" who have an explicit philosophical position are either Logical Positivists or rather close to Logical Positivism. Those who are not share at least some

* V. Ferm, ed., *A History of Philosophical Systems* (New York: Philosophical Library, 1950), pp. 483-92. Reprinted by permission.
[1] Explanations of ideas and terms to be found in the preceding article on Logical Positivism will not be repeated. Familiarity with that article is assumed.

[17]

traits of the positivistic temper. Their inclination is analytical rather than speculative; and they have a high regard for the significance, or potential significance, of behavior science on the one hand and of mathematical logic on the other.

The word 'semantics', derived from a Greek root signifying *sign,* has come to be used for certain studies of *language.*[2] Derivatively, studies that use the results of such investigations as *tools* for their own purposes are then also called semantical. In this derivative sense a good deal of philosophy has been semantical ever since the Platonic Socrates taught his disciples to speak precisely and to distinguish between the meanings of words. This emphasis on language, common to all analytical philosophy, has been particularly strong in British Empiricism, as anyone who glances through Locke's Essay can see for himself. But it is also true that Logical Positivism, the contemporary form of British Empiricism, attributes to one kind of linguistic study—the one which has been called *formal* [1]—a tool position of such centrality and excellence as has never been claimed before. However, Logical Positivism is not in any other sense a philosophy of language or a linguistic philosophy. What now sometimes goes by these names is a systematically impure mixture of anthropology, psychology, criticism, and philosophy proper.

The historian of philosophy is probably justified in connecting the linguistic turn of Logical Positivism with the rise of modern or mathematical logic, which began around the middle of the last century. From the viewpoint of the general historian of ideas this development is but part of a larger pattern. Our civilization as a whole has, during this

---

[2] Within philology, which in the broadest sense is also a semantical discipline, 'semantics' is the name for the study of the historical development of the meanings of words.

century, become increasingly language-conscious. Since I cannot spend much space on speculating about the broader social dynamisms which produced this result, I shall content myself with the hint that this language-consciousness of ours grew simultaneously with our ideology-consciousness. Whatever the social forces involved, the intellectual sources of this growth were, systematically speaking, scientific rather than philosophical or logico-mathematical. The central phenomenon there is the development of the social or, as I shall call them, behavior sciences which, modest as their present achievements are if compared with physics or even biology, have yet during this period reached a level that makes the idea of a real science of man something more than a utopia. The scientific study of linguistic behavior, that is, its adequate description and the search for its causes and effects in and on the group and the individual belongs to behavior science. It occupies by now a strategic position in psychology, anthropology, sociology, and, also, in such intellectual pursuits as literary criticism, to which these traditional divisions of behavior science are of auxiliary service. Semantics, in one sense of the term, is this science of language or, perhaps better, linguistic behavior. To avoid confusion I shall, in this sense, always speak of *scientific semantics*. (In view of the fundamental position of psychology among the traditional divisions of behavior science 'psychological semantics' would also be a good name.)

All Logical Positivists and virtually all scientific semanticists are behaviorists. The behaviorist insists that all the technical terms of his field are defined in terms that refer to what he himself, the scientist, immediately observes. To understand this, imagine a laboratory situation in which a subject S is, as one usually says, expected to discriminate between two shades of green. In describing this situation the behaviorist may, without further elaboration, say that *he* sees two different shades of green. But when he says, on the basis of what he observes, 'S *sees* two different shades of green', then he considers 'sees' as a technical term and, very roughly speaking, the whole sentence as the left side of its definition; the right side consisting of a statement of what he, the scientist, has observed.[3] The same procedure is followed in the case of "linguistic" behavior. Words spoken or written by his subjects are, to begin with, for the behaviorist just physical events. It is his business to define the conditions under which a noise or a gesture becomes a "word" or "sign"; what he means by saying that his subject "understands" a "language," that some "sentences" of this language "designate," and therefore "inform" his subjects about their physical environment, while others merely "express" or "direct" their "attitudes." To say the same thing differently, the words in this paragraph around which I put double quotes are all technical terms of behavior science. Or one could also say that the behavior scientist and his subjects do not, in principle, speak the same language.

No argument is needed to show that the actual resources

[3] This does not commit us to the opinion that S has no data or that it is "meaningless" to speak of them. Indeed, if our scientist were to say 'If I have two green data and S sees them (in the behavioristic sense of 'seeing'), *then* there are also two similar data (numerically different from mine and perceived by S)', his statement could be shown to satisfy the principle of acquaintance. But the behavioristic approach is desirable in the interest of reliability and objectivity in the ordinary, nonphilosophical sense of these terms. Nor does it impose any limitations on behavior science since all the evidence we can, *in fact,* ever have for what is asserted, in statements like the one just mentioned, by the clause following 'then' is asserted by clauses of the kind that precedes it. Behaviorism, in short, is a methodological not a philosophical position. And, as indicated by the phrase 'in fact', that I cannot have your data is upon this view not an analytical truth.

of a behavior science thus strictly conceived are as yet very limited and, for all we know, may always remain so. Certainly it would be foolish to reject, for *practical* purposes, less reliable knowledge which we possess about human behavior (though behaviorists in this case prefer to speak of prescientific insight). To admit this is one thing. To agree, as virtually all scientific semanticists do, that behavior science can, *in principle,* be behavioristically construed and, for all purposes of *methodological* analysis, must be so construed, is another thing. Yet this agreement has at least two far-reaching consequences. Assume, first, for the sake of the argument, that a scientific semanticist has succeeded in distinguishing between "factual" or "cognitive" sentences which "designate" *matters of fact* and others, called "non-factual" or "noncognitive" because they do not so "refer." It will be noticed that the phrase 'matters of fact', which I have italicized but not put between double quotes, belongs to the scientist's own language. His achievement presupposes, therefore, that he already knows what *he* means by matters of fact and is thus, rather obviously, completely irrelevant for what is meant by a philosophical analysis of this, philosophically speaking, very difficult phrase.[4] What has been shown in this case could be shown in all others. I conclude that scientific semantics has no direct philosophical import or significance whatsoever. The mistaken belief that this is not so can probably be traced to the interest Deweyan pragmatists (instrumentalists) have taken and still take in scientific semantics. For the tendency to substitute scientific (causal and genetic) for philosophical

[4] In other words, language analysis which is philosophically significant must be analysis from the standpoint of the speaker, that is, in the illustration given, of the scientist. Also, as has been shown in the article on Logical Positivism, it proceeds formally, not scientifically.

analysis and, even worse, to mistake the former for the latter is one of the hallmarks of instrumentalism.

Consider, second, the definitions which "semanticists" who are not themselves practicing scientists but "philosophical" writers [5] offer for the technical terms of scientific semantics. It is often said, e.g., that A is a "sign" of B if it promotes behavior that B would promote but that is not appropriate to A alone. Plausible as this sounds, it must not be taken too seriously. Or is the behavior promoted in me by 'murder' really always of the kind I would display when I witnessed murder? Generally, the very difficult job of framing adequate definitions for the terms of scientific semantics (and of finding the laws in which they occur) is better left to the practicing behavior scientist. For, if the principle of the thing has once been established, it is hard to see what value there is in anticipatory armchair science. All one does if one does this sort of thing is restate, sometimes rather pretentiously, common sense.

The *formal* study of language consists in the construction of artificial sign systems; as I explained in introducing the notion of the ideal language [1] such an artificial or formal language, also called *calculus*, is really but the grammatical schema or skeleton of a language and one must not in constructing it have explicit reference to anything but the shapes and arrangement of the signs themselves.[6] 'Formal semantics' would be a good name for this discipline; as it happens it is most commonly known as *logical syntax*. For-

[5] Probably the best-known work in this vein is C. W. Morris, *Signs, Language and Behavior* (New York, 1946), containing a good bibliography of what is by now a voluminous literature. Morris himself was originally a pragmatist.
[6] This, as has been seen, is also the condition upon which the actual similarity of such a calculus with our natural language (or, as one also says, its *interpretation*) is philosophically significant.

[22]

mal, pure, or, if you please, philosophical semantics is a branch of logical syntax. To explain what it deals with some preparatory remarks are needed.

A sign, its name, and what it is the name of are three different things. Commonsensical as it is, the distinction is fundamental and of far-reaching import. In idiomatic speech we neglect it. We say, *e.g.*, 'Paris is the capital of France' as well as 'Paris has five letters,' employing the same sign once as the name of the city, once as the name of this name. Or, as one also says, once we *use* it, once we *mention* it. We would do better if we wrote the second time ' 'Paris' has five letters', making 'Paris' and ' 'Paris' ' two different words.[7] In ordinary speech our understanding of the context saves us from the confusions which, on principle, must arise if one neglects such precautions. On the other hand, it should be clear that in constructing a calculus to be interpreted as containing these two sentences one must see to it that it contains two different signs; and, generally, that in a calculus an expression must be distinguished from that other expression that one wishes to interpret as its name. To make one obvious point, if we have a formal classification of signs in which the names of individual objects are called particulars while the names of characters are called universals, then the name of a universal is, of course, a particular, and so is the name of any word, expression, or sentence.[8] A related

---

[7] Single quotes are customarily used to mark the distinction. The single quotes after 'making' and the outer pair of such quotes after 'and' are due to the circumstance that the sentence in the text does not use but mentions what they surround.

[8] This is not quite correct since when we speak of a word we do not ordinarily mean any single one of its occurrences or *tokens,* whose name would be a particular, but all occurrences of a certain *type* (roughly, similar marks on paper, similar noises). The name of a word would then be a universal. However, the simplification I have introduced is harmless.

distinction is that between language and *metalanguage*. Just as the behavior scientist does not himself, in principle, use the language of his subjects, so the formalist does not in designing and discussing a calculus himself speak it—whatever it could mean to speak an artificial language. Rather, he speaks about it in, say, English; or, as one also says, English is his (syntactical) metalanguage. A mathematician could, *e.g.*, invent a rule that coordinates to each sentence of a calculus a number depending only on the shapes and the arrangement of its signs; he could then use these numbers, which are of course English words, instead of proper names, as in prisons numbers are used instead of proper names, when he speaks in his English metalanguage about the sentences of the calculus. Such a rule has in fact been invented, for *PM* and related calculi, by the mathematician K. Goedel. Mathematicians, who are not primarily concerned with philosophical accuracy, have been misled by Goedel's rule into saying that calculi containing expressions (number signs) which can be interpreted as numbers contain the names of their own sentences. This is inaccurate for at least three reasons. First, the number signs of the calculus must be distinguished from the (English) numbers which the logician, like the prison warden, uses instead of proper names. Second, in philosophically interesting calculi number signs are never particulars, as they would have to be if they were proper names. Third, and most important, there is no reason whatsoever why a calculus that contains number signs should also contain sentences that could be interpreted as '. . . designates (is the name of) . . .', where the first blank is filled by a number and the second by the (English) interpretation of a sentence of the calculus.

The prime concern of logical syntax has long been (1) to

[24]

construct calculi which contain for *every* English sentence (including arithmetical identities) which we consider intuitively as a tautological (analytical) truth [9] a corresponding sentence; and (2) to characterize formally the class of *all* these sentences. It was Goedel who showed, in a justly celebrated paper that appeared in 1931, that if one insists on certain ways of carrying out this characterization the problem (2) is insoluble. His proof makes use of sentences which, *with the inaccuracy pointed out in the last paragraph,* can be interpreted as saying about themselves that they possess a certain syntactical property, that is, to repeat, a property that depends only on the shapes and the arrangement of their signs.

*Formal semantics* is the syntactical construction of calculi that can be interpreted as containing the word 'true', some expression of "naming," such as 'designates' as it occurs in ' 'Peter loves Mary' designates Peter loves Mary' and, therefore, also the names of at least some of its expressions, say, *e.g.,* of its sentences. If one succeeds in constructing such a calculus, then one has, upon the positivistic view of philosophical analysis, the proper tool for the resolution or, if you please, reconstruction of the philosophical issues that revolve around truth, designation, and related ideas. Among these notions truth is, no doubt, the one that troubled philosophers most. For a philosophical analysis of truth three points are of primary importance.

1. Since truth is predicated of sentences and since the names of sentences are particulars *in* the calculus, 'true' will be a predicate *in* the calculus that takes particulars as

---

[9] Since 'true' will presently be used precisely, it should be noted that 'true' and 'analytically true' are not technical terms of the syntacticist. All he does is design definitions that reflect formally what is meant intuitively by the latter term.

[25]

its subjects. 'True', in a philosophically relevant sense of the term, is, therefore, not a syntactical property of the sentences of a calculus. In other words, the main task of formal semantics is not to "define truth" by finding a formal characterization of all true sentences but, rather, to frame, within the calculus it constructs, a definition of 'true'. The point needs emphasis because the mathematician Tarski,[10] who in a sense founded the discipline of formal semantics, preoccupied as he was with mathematical rather than with philosophical issues, conceived of truth as a syntactical property. This was particularly unfortunate because philosophers, who did not really understand him, thought Tarski had proved "that the words 'true' and 'false', as applied to the sentences of a given language, always require another language, of higher order, for their adequate definition." [11] All that can be proved is that if one considers truth as a syntactical property of the sentences of a calculus, then this calculus is either inconsistent or it cannot contain a predicate that could, *with the inaccuracy pointed out in the discussion of Goedel's rule,* be interpreted as 'true'. The proof proceeds, analogously to Goedel's, by constructing, within the calculus, a sentence that may, *with the same inaccuracy,* be interpreted as saying about itself that it is false and which has, therefore, been *mi*staken for a formal reconstruction of the famous Liar paradox ('I am now lying'—If the speaker does not lie, then he lies; if he lies, then he does not lie).

---

[10] A. Tarski, *Der Wahrheitsbegriff in den formalisierten Sprachen.* (This monograph appeared in Polish in 1933, in German translation in the Polish journal *Studia Philosophica* in 1936.) R. Carnap's *Introduction to Semantics* (Cambridge, 1942) suffers philosophically from the author's dogmatic realism, technically from the tendency to subsume syntax under semantics.

[11] Quoted from B. Russell, *An Inquiry into Meaning and Truth* (New York, 1940), p. 75.

2. One of the reasons why it is philosophically absurd to consider truth as a syntactical property is that one can assert a sentence to be true if and only if one knows (a) what it says or means and (b) whether what it says is the case (which, of course, is a matter of fact, not of words, syntax, or what have you). Philosophers refer to this piece of common sense as the correspondence view of truth. Realists, grounding this view in their peculiar conception of objective fact, sometimes claim that Logical Positivists cannot consistently adopt it. It seems thus desirable to reconstruct formally the common-sense core of the correspondence view. To do this one has to construct a calculus in which, say, the sentence ' 'Peter loves Mary' is true if and only if ('Peter loves Mary' designates Peter loves Mary) and (Peter loves Mary)' and all similar sentences are analytic. In the sentence just mentioned the clause in the first parenthesis corresponds to condition (a) above, the second to condition (b).

3. Since truth is a matter of thought or language and since, in contradistinction to idealistic views, the object of thought is not in any way affected by being thought about, it seems desirable to distinguish truth and designation from such "natural" properties and relationships as, say, greenness and fatherhood. Casting about for a formal expression of this idea one finds that in calculi similar to *PM* [12] one can formally distinguish between so-called *descriptive* signs and expressions on the one hand and so-called *logical* ones on the other. *E.g.*, 'green' and 'is the father of' belong to the first category, 'and', 'not' and 'transitive' to the second.

It follows that the philosophically most interesting task of

[12] The *PM* schema being the only likely candidate for the ideal language, it is not necessary to consider other calculi. Carnap was apparently the first to recognize the philosophical significance of the formal distinction between logical and descriptive expressions.

formal semantics is solved if one can supplement the schema of *PM* by a logical sign of designation and, in terms of it and in agreement with the condition in 2, define a predicate 'true'. This, it turns out, is not at all difficult.[13]

Though it is not necessary for an adequate definition of truth, one may attempt to refine the formalization of designation so that the calculus also contains sentences that can be interpreted as, say, ' 'Peter' designates Peter' or ' 'green' designates green'. In calculi which do not have a certain property known as extensionality, such attempts meet with difficulties first pointed out by G. Frege as early as 1892. Carnap [14] has recently undertaken a systematic treatment of such questions. Investigations of this kind may be of some formal interest; their philosophical significance is doubtful. If, *e.g.*, one were to explore "what there is" by trying to determine what "entities" can be "named" in a calculus that embodies certain features of the ordinary usage of 'name' and 'naming', he would, it seems to me, grievously overestimate the philosophical import of this usage. At any rate, I do not see what insight one could gain in this way that could not also be gained by a syntactical study of the (non-linguistic) part of the ideal language.

It appears, then, that aside from its usefulness for a

---

[13] Formally this can be done as follows: 1. *PM* (unramified) is supplemented by descriptive constants and it is stipulated that only closed expressions are sentences. 2. For each sentence there is a particular obtained by surrounding the sentence with single quotes. 3. The sign '*Des*' is added with the proviso that all substitution instances of '*x Des p*' are sentences. 4. All sentences '' . . .' *Des* . . .', all sentences obtained from these through rewriting of bound variables, and the negations of all other substitution instances of '*x Des p*' are added to the primitive sentences. 5. '*true* (*x*)' is defined by '(E *p*) (*x Des p . p*)'. Contexts containing '*Des*' are not extensional.

[14] R. Carnap, *Meaning and Necessity* (Chicago, 1947). For an incisive criticism see G. Ryle's review in *Philosophy*, 24 (1949), 69-76.

positivistic statement of the correspondence view and, perhaps, aside from some problems of intrinsic mathematical interest, formal semantics is philosophically not important. The same, it has been seen, holds for scientific semantics, again aside from questions that are of intrinsic scientific interest. I conclude, therefore, that the current rage for "semantics" is but a passing moment in the history of philosophical thought.

# LOGICAL POSITIVISM, LANGUAGE, AND THE RECONSTRUCTION OF METAPHYSICS *

1. *Introduction.* A philosophical movement is a group of philosophers, active over at least one or two generations, who more or less share a style, or an intellectual origin, and who have learned more from each other than they have from others, though they may, and often do, quite vigorously disagree among themselves. Logical positivism is the current name of what is no doubt a movement. The common source is the writings and teachings of G. E. Moore, Russell, and Wittgenstein during the first quarter of the century. However, two of these founding fathers, Moore and Russell, do not themselves belong to the movement. The logical positivists have also greatly influenced each other; they still do, albeit less so as the disagreements among them become more pronounced. There is indeed vigorous disagreement, even on such fundamentals as the nature of the philosophical enterprise itself. The very name, logical positivist, is by now unwelcome to some, though it is still and quite reasonably applied to all, particularly from the outside. Reasonably, because they unmistakably share a philosophical style. They

* This essay appeared in English in *Rivista Critica di Storia della Filosofia,* 8 (1953), 453-81. Reprinted by permission.

all accept the linguistic turn Wittgenstein initiated in the *Tractatus*. To be sure, they interpret and develop it in their several ways, hence the disagreements; yet they are all under its spell, hence the common style. Thus, if names in themselves were important, it might be better to choose linguistic philosophy or philosophy of language. In fact, these tags are now coming into use. But they, too, like most labels, are misleading. For one, the concern with language is nothing new in first philosophy or, if you please, epistemology and metaphysics. Certainly all "minute philosophers" have shared it. For another, there is strictly speaking no such thing as the philosophy of language. Language may be studied by philologists, aestheticians, and scientists such as psychologists or sociologists. To bring these studies thoughtfully together is well worth while. Customarily, such synoptic efforts are called philosophy. There is no harm in this provided they are not mistaken for what they are not, namely, technical philosophy. Rather than being philosophers of language, the positivists, who are all technical philosophers, are therefore philosophers through language; they philosophize by means of it. But then, everybody who speaks uses language as a means or tool. The point is that the positivists, newly conscious of it, use it in a new way.

The novelty is, I believe, radical. Even the greatest innovators never do more, can do no more, than add one or two features to the tradition, perhaps submerge one or two others. The tradition as a whole persists. Features is a vague word. I had better speak of new questions and methods; for they, not the answers we give, matter. The logical positivists neither added nor submerged a single major question. Their characteristic contribution is a method. This may mean radical novelty; it does, I believe, in their

[31]

case. There is a sense, though, in which the linguistic turn has not even produced startlingly new answers. The answers the positivists give to the old questions, or those which most of them give to most, are in some respects very similar to what has been said before within the empiricist stream of the great tradition. On the other hand, both questions and answers are so reinterpreted that they have changed almost beyond recognition. At least, alas, beyond the recognition of many. Many of the logical positivists themselves, like other innovators before, even thought that they had disposed of the tradition. Some still believe it. I think there is merely a new method, though one that is radically new, of approaching the old questions.

This is not a historical paper. I wish to speak as a philosopher. Thus, while I am aware of how much I owe to others, I can only speak for myself. Nor is my intent primarily critical. Yet, such is the dialectical nature of philosophy that we cannot either in thinking or in writing do without that foil the ideas of others provide. This makes us all critics as well as, in a structural sense, historians. Thus, while it is my main purpose, or very nearly so, to explain one kind of logical positivism, I shall, almost of necessity, discuss all others. They fall into two main divisions. The one is made up by the ideal linguists, the other by the analysts of usage, more fully, of correct or ordinary usage. The ideal linguists are either *formalists* or *reconstructionists*. The outstanding formalist is Carnap. What the reconstructionists hope to reconstruct in the new style is the old metaphysics. Clearly, from what has been said, I am a reconstructionist. There is, third, the *pragmatist* variety. These writers, we shall presently see, are best counted with the ideal linguists. Usage analysis flourishes above all at Oxford and Cambridge. These philosophers are also known as, fourth, the therapeutic positivists or *casuists*. One variant of this view deserves to be distinguished. For want of a better term I shall, with a new meaning, resuscitate an old one, calling this view, fifth, *conventionalist*. This wing is led by Ryle.

The expositor's position determines, as always, his strategy. The argument will center around reconstructionism. But since I believe the method to be neutral in that it may be used by all and any, I shall set it off as clearly as I can from the specific conclusions to which it has led me. Not surprisingly, these conclusions, or answers to the old questions, lie within the empiricist tradition, if it is conceived broadly enough to include the act philosophies of Moore and Brentano. The debt to Hume and the phenomenalists in general is, naturally, tremendous. One clever Englishman recently proposed the equation: Logical Positivism is Hume plus mathematical logic. He has a point, though by far not the whole story. But whatever these specific conclusions may be, I can hardly do more than hint at a few of them. This must be kept in mind throughout. I have, of course, discussed them elsewhere. Here, however, they serve mainly as illustrations, *pour fixer les idées*, for even in philosophy abstractness cannot without disadvantage be pushed beyond certain limits.

2. *The linguistic turn.* What precisely the linguistic turn is or, to stay with the metaphor, how to execute it properly is controversial. That it must be executed, somehow or other, is common doctrine, flowing from the shared belief that the relation between language and philosophy is closer than, as well as essentially different from, that between language and any other discipline. What are the grounds of this belief and how did it arise?

[33]

*First.* There is no experiment on whose outcome the predictions of two physicists would differ solely because the one is a phenomenalist, the other a realist. Generally, no philosophical question worthy of the name is ever settled by experimental or, for that matter, experiential evidence. Things are what they are. In some sense philosophy is, therefore, verbal or linguistic. But this is not necessarily a bad sense. One must not hastily conclude that all philosophers always deal with pseudoproblems. Those who thus stretch a point which is telling enough as far as it goes, are overly impressed with the naïve "empiricism" of the laboratory. Most of them are formalists. Scientism and formalism, we shall see, tend to go together. *Second.* Philosophers maintain in all seriousness such propositions as that time is not real or that there are no physical objects. But they also assure us that we do not in the ordinary sense err when, using language as we ordinarily do, we say, for instance, that some event preceded some other in time or that we are perceiving physical objects such as stones and trees. Outside their studies, philosophers themselves say such things. Thus they use language in two ways, in its ordinary sense and in one that is puzzling to say the least. To decide whether what they say as philosophers is true one must, therefore, first discover what they say, that is, precisely what that peculiar sense is. The inquiry is linguistic. It starts from common sense, for what else is there to start from. These points were pressed by G. E. Moore. His emphasis on ordinary usage and common sense reappears, of course, in the British branches of the movement. The common-sense doctrine also influenced the reconstructionists. It is worth noticing, though, that in the form in which all these positivists have adopted it, the doctrine is not itself a philosophical proposition. Rather, it helps to set their style, assigning to philosophy the task of elucidating common sense, not of either proving or disproving it. In this form the common-sense doctrine also represents at least part of what could be meant by saying, as both Husserl and Wittgenstein do, that philosophy is descriptive. *Third.* This point stands to the second in a relation similar to that between morphology and physiology or, perhaps, pathology. We have seen that philosophers, using language in their peculiar sort of discourse, arrive at such propositions as that there are no physical objects. Taken in their ordinary sense, these propositions are absurd. The man on the street, however, who uses the same language never ends up with this kind of absurdity. We also know that the conclusions one draws depend on the grammatical form of the statements that express the premises. We notice, finally, that sometimes two statements, such as 'Peter is not tall' and 'Cerberus is not real', exemplify the same grammatical form though they say really quite different things. We conclude that philosophers come to grief because they rely on grammatical form. What they should trust instead is the logical form of statements such as, in our illustration, 'Peter is not tall' and 'There is no dog that is three-headed, etc.'. Consistently pursued, the notion of logical form leads to that of an ideal language in which logical and grammatical form coincide completely. Both notions took shape when Russell answered several philosophical questions, some about arithmetic, some about just such entities as Cerberus, by means of a symbolism. There is one more suggestion in all this, namely, that in an ideal language the philosopher's propositions could no longer be stated so that he would find himself left without anything to say at all. 'Peter exists', for instance, has no equivalent in Russell's symbolism, Peter's existence showing itself, as it

[35]

were, by the occurrence of a proper name for him. Ontology is, perhaps, but an illusion spawned by language. So one may again be led to think that all philosophy is verbal in a bad sense. The suggestion seduced the formalists as well as those who later became usage analysts. It even seduced Wittgenstein. The reconstructionists reject it. According to them, philosophical discourse is peculiar only in that it is ordinary or, if you please, commonsensical discourse about an ideal language.

Ordinary discourse about an ideal language is, indeed, the reconstructionist version of the linguistic turn. But a statement so succinct needs unpacking. Precisely what is an ideal language? I cannot answer without first explaining what syntax is.

3. *Syntax.* Signs or symbols may be artificial, that is, expressly devised, or they may have grown naturally. In either case they do not say anything by themselves. We speak by means of them; we "interpret" them; having been interpreted, they "refer." Syntax deals only with some properties of the signs themselves and of the patterns in which they are arranged. This, and nothing else, is what is meant by calling syntax formal and schemata syntactically constructed formal languages. It would be safer to avoid any term that suggests interpretation, such as 'language', 'sign', or 'symbol'. I shall simply speak of syntactical schemata and their elements. Or one could use a prefix to guard against confusion, calling the elements f-signs, for instance, 'f' standing for 'formal'. In this section, where I discuss only f-notions, I shall suppress the prefix. Later on I shall occasionally take this precaution. In themselves, signs are physical objects or events. Written signs, and we need not for our purpose consider others, are instances of geometrical shapes. Syntax

is thus quite commonsensical business. It is, so to speak, a study in geometrical design. But philosophers are not geometricians. They do not invent and investigate these schemata for their own sake, as mathematical logicians often do, but with an eye upon their suitability for serving, upon interpretation, as the ideal language. Making this claim for any one schema, the geometrician turns philosopher, committing himself to a philosophical position. This is why I insisted that the method as such is neutral. Yet, to introduce neutrally the syntactical notions or categories (f-categories!) which I shall need would be tediously abstract and is, at any rate, quite unnecessary for my purpose. So I shall, instead, introduce them by describing that particular schema which I judge to be, with one later addition, that of the ideal language. Broadly speaking, it is the schema of Russell's *Principia Mathematica.* Very broadly indeed; and I shall have to speak broadly throughout the rest of this section, simplifying so sweepingly that it amounts almost to distortion, though not, of course, as I judge it, to essential distortion.

The construction of the schema proceeds in three steps. First one selects certain shapes and kinds of such as its elements or signs. Then certain sequences of shapes are selected or, if you please, defined as its sentences. Order, as the term sequence implies, enters the definition. Finally a certain subclass of sentences, called analytic, is selected. Turning to some detail, relatively speaking, I shall, in order to fix the ideas, add in parentheses some prospective interpretations from our natural language. *First.* The elements are divided into categories. Though based on shape and nothing else, the divisions are not nominal in that the definitions of sentence and analyticity are stated in their terms. Signs are either

[37]

logical or descriptive. Descriptive signs are either proper names ('Peter'), or predicates and relations of the first order ('green', 'louder than'), or predicates and relations of higher orders ('color'). Logical signs are of two main kinds. Either they are individually specified signs, connectives ('not', 'and', 'if then') and quantifiers ('all', 'there is something such that'). Or they are variables. To each descriptive category corresponds one of variables, though not necessarily conversely; to proper names so-called individual variables (such phrases as 'a certain particular'), to predicates predicate variables (such phrases as 'a certain property'), and so on. *Second.* Sentences are either atomic or complex. Atomic sentences are sequences of descriptive signs of appropriate categories ('Peter (is) green', 'John (is) taller than James'). Complex sentences contain logical signs ('John (is) tall *and* James (is) short', '*There is something such that* it (is) green'). *Third.* In defining analyticity arithmetical technics are used; in the sense in which one may be said to use such technics who, having assigned numbers to people on the basis of their shapes, called a company unlucky (f-unlucky!) if the sum of the numbers of its members is divisible by 13. A sentence is said to follow deductively from another if and only if a third, compounded of the two in a certain manner, is analytic. ('$p$' implies '$q$' if and only if 'if $p$ then $q$' is analytic.) The definition of analyticity is so designed that when a descriptive sign occurs in an analytic sentence, the sentence obtained by replacing it with another descriptive sign of the same category is also analytic. (In 'Either John is tall or John is not tall', the terms 'John' and 'tall' occur vacuously.) Two such sentences are said to be of the same "logical form"; analyticity itself is said to depend on "form" only, which is but another way of saying that it can be characterized by means

[38]

of sentences which contain none but logical signs. This feature is important. Because of it, among others, f-analyticity can, as we shall see, be used to explicate or reconstruct the philosophical notion of analyticity which, unfortunately, also goes by the name of formal truth. Unfortunately, because the f-notion of logical form which I just defined needs no explication. The philosophical notion, like all philosophical ones, does. To identify the two inadvertently, as I believe Wittgenstein did, leads therefore to disaster. But of this later.

The shapes originally selected are called the undefined signs of the schema. The reason for setting them apart is that many schemata, including the one I am considering, provide machinery for adding new signs. To each sign added corresponds one special sentence, called its definition, the whole construction being so arranged that this sentence is analytic. This has two consequences. For one, the definitions of the language which, in some sense, the schema becomes upon interpretation, are all nominal. For another, interpretation of the undefined signs automatically interprets all others. Defined signs whose definitions contain undefined descriptive signs are themselves classified as descriptive.

4. *Ideal language and reconstruction.* To interpret a syntactical schema is to pair its undefined signs one by one with words or expressions of our natural language, making them "name" the same things or, if you please, "refer" equally. An interpreted schema is in principle a language. In principle only, because we could not speak it instead of a natural language; it is neither rich nor flexible enough. Its lack of flexibility is obvious; it lacks richness in that we need not specify it beyond, say, stipulating that it contains color predicates, without bothering which or how many. Thus, even an interpreted schema is merely, to use the term in a

[39]

different sense, the "schema" of a language, an architect's drawing rather than a builder's blueprint. The ideal language is an interpreted syntactical schema. But not every such schema is an ideal language. To qualify it must fulfill two conditions. *First,* it must be complete, that is, it must, no matter how schematically, account for all areas of our experience. For instance, it is not enough that it contain schematically the way in which scientific behaviorists, quite adequately for their purpose, speak about mental contents. It must also reflect the different way in which one speaks about his own experience and, because of it, of that of others; and it must show how these two ways jibe. *Second,* it must permit, by means of ordinary discourse about it, the solution of all philosophical problems. This discourse, the heart of the philosophical enterprise, is the reconstruction of metaphysics. So I must next explain how to state, or restate, the classical questions in this manner and, if they can be so stated, why I insist that this discourse is, nevertheless, quite ordinary or commonsensical though, admittedly, not about the sort of thing the man on the street talks about. Making the range of his interests the criterion of "common sense" is, for my taste, a bit too John Bullish.

Consider the thesis of classical nominalism that there are no universals. Given the linguistic turn it becomes the assertion that the ideal language contains no undefined descriptive signs except proper names. Again, take classical sensationism. Transformed it asserts that the ideal language contains no undefined descriptive predicates except nonrelational ones of the first order, referring to characters exemplified by sense data which are, some ultrapositivists to the contrary notwithstanding, quite commonsensical things. I reject both nominalism and sensationism. But this is not the point. The point is that the two corresponding assertions, though surely false, are yet not absurd, as so many of the classical theses are, as it is for instance absurd to say, as the sensationists must, that a physical object is a bundle of sense data. Obvious as they are, these two illustrations provide a basis for some comments about the reconstruction in general.

*First.* I did not, either affirmatively or negatively, state either of the two classical propositions. I merely mentioned them in order to explicate them, that is, to suggest what they could plausibly be taken to assert in terms of the ideal language. For the tact and imagination such explication sometimes requires the method provides no guarantee. No method does. But there is no doubt that this kind of explication, considering as it does languages, is quite ordinary discourse. Yet it does not, by this token alone, lose anything of what it explicates. To say that a picture, to be a picture, must have certain features is, clearly, to say something about what it is a picture of. I know no other way to speak of the world's categorial features without falling into the snares the linguistic turn avoids. These features are as elusive as they are pervasive. Yet they are our only concern; that is why the ideal language need be no more than a "schema." I just used the picture metaphor, quite commonsensically I think, yet deliberately. For it has itself become a snare into which some positivists fell, not surprisingly, since it is after all a metaphor. Of this later. *Second.* A critic may say: "Your vaunted new method either is circular or produces an infinite regress. Did you not yourself, in what you insist is ordinary discourse, use such words as 'naming' and 'referring'? Surely you know that they are eminently philosophical?" I have guarded against the objection by putting quotation marks around these words when I first used them. The point is that

[41]

I did use them commonsensically, that is, in a way and on an occasion where they do not give trouble. So I can without circularity clarify those uses that do give rise to philosophical problems, either by locating them in the ideal language, or when I encounter them in a philosophical propostion which I merely mention in order to explicate it, or both, as the case may be. But the critic continues: "You admit then, at least, that you do not, to use one of your favorite words, explicate common sense?" I admit nothing of the sort. The explication of common sense is circular only as it is circular to ask, as Moore might put it, how we know what in fact we do know, knowing also that we know it. *Third*. The critic presses on: "Granting that you can without circularity explicate the various philosophical positions, say, realism and phenomenalism, I still fail to see how this reconstruction, as you probably call it, helps you to choose among them." I discover with considerable relief that I need no longer make such choices. With relief, because each of the classical answers to each of the classical questions has a common-sense core. The realist, for instance, grasped some fundamental features of experience or, as he would probably prefer to say, of the world. The phenomenalist grasped some others. Each, anxious not to lose hold of his, was driven to deny or distort the others. From this squirrel cage the linguistic turn happily frees us. Stated in the new manner, the several "cores" are no longer incompatible. This is that surprising turn within the turn which I had in mind when I observed that the old questions, though preserved in one sense, are yet in another changed almost beyond recognition. To insist on this transformation is one thing. To dismiss the classical questions out of hand, as some positivists unfortunately do, is quite another thing. *Fourth*. The method realizes the old ideal of a philosophy

[42]

without presuppositions. Part of this ideal is an illusion, for we cannot step outside of ourselves or of the world. The part that makes sense is realized by constructing the schema formally, without any reference to its prospective use, strict syntacticism at this stage forcing attention upon what may otherwise go unnoticed. But the critic persists: "Even though you start formally, when you choose a schema as the ideal language you do impose its "categories" upon the world, thus prejudging the world's form. Are you then not at this point yourself trading on the ambiguity of 'form', as you just said others sometimes do?" One does not, in any intelligible sense, choose the ideal language. One finds or discovers, empirically if you please, within the ordinary limits of human error and dullness, that a schema can be so used. Should there be more than one ideal language, then this fact itself will probably be needed somewhere in the reconstruction; equally likely and equally enlightening, some traits of each would then be as "incidental" as are some of Finnish grammar. More important, all this goes to show that the reconstructionist's philosophy is, as I believe all good philosophy must be, descriptive. But it is time to relieve the abstractness by showing, however sketchily, the method at work.

5. *Three issues.* The common-sense core of *phenomenalism* is wholly recovered by what is known as the principle of acquaintance. (Later on I shall restore the balance by reconstructing what I think is the deepest root of realism. Realism, to be sure, has others, such as the indispensability of the quantifiers, which permit us to speak of what is not in front of our noses. But these roots run closer to the surface.) The word principle is unfortunate; for description knows no favorites. The feature in question is indeed a principle only in that quite a few other explications are found

to depend on it. What it asserts is that all undefined descriptive signs of the ideal language refer to entities with which we are directly or, as one also says, phenomenally acquainted. Notice the difference from sensationism. Relational and higher-order undefined predicates are not excluded. The indispensability of at least one of these two categories is beyond reasonable doubt. Nor does the principle exclude undefined descriptive signs that refer to ingredients of moral and aesthetic experience. If ethical naturalism is explicated as the rejection of such terms, then one sees that a reconstructionist need not be an ethical naturalist. I, for one, am not.

The ideal language contains proper names, the sort of thing to which they refer being exemplified by sense data; 'tree' and 'stone' and 'physical object' itself are, broadly speaking, defined predicates, closer analysis revealing that the "subjects" of these predicates do not refer to individual trees and stones. That this amounts to a partial explication of the substantialist thesis, accepting a small part of it and rejecting the rest, is fairly obvious. Another aspect of the matter raises two questions. Definitions are linguistic constructions, more precisely, constructions within a language. How detailed need they be? What are the criteria for their success? To begin with the second question, consider the generality 'No physical object is at the same time at two different places'. Call it S and the sentence that corresponds to it in the ideal language S'. Since 'time' and 'place' in S refer to physical time and place, the descriptive signs in S' are all defined. Their construction is successful if and only if S' and a few other such truths, equally crucial for the solution of philosophical problems, follow deductively from the definitions proposed for them in conjunction with some other generalities containing only undefined descriptive signs, which we also know to be true, such as, for instance, the sentence of the ideal language expressing the transitivity of being phenomenally later. The construction is thus merely schematic, in the sense in which the ideal language itself is merely a schema. The building stones from which it starts in order to recover the sense in phenomenalism are so minute that anything else is patently beyond our strength. Nor, fortunately, is it needed to solve the philosophical problems. To strive for more is either scientism or psychologism, scientism if one insists on definitions as "complete" as in the axiomatization of a scientific discipline, psychologism if one expects them to reflect all the subtlety and ambiguity of introspective analysis. Formalists tend to scientism; usage analysts to psychologism.

*Analyticity* is not a common-sense notion. However, the differences that led philosophers to distinguish between analytic and synthetic propositions are clearly felt upon a little reflection. There is, first, a difference in certainty, one of kind as one says, not merely of degree. Or, as it is also put, analytic truth is necessary, synthetic truth contingent. Certainty is a clear notion only if applied to beliefs. Besides, what is sought is a structural or objective difference between two kinds of contents of belief. There is only this connection that, once discovered, such a structural difference will be useful in explicating the philosophical idea of certainty. Second, analytic (tautological) truths are empty in that they say nothing about the world, as 'John is either tall or not tall' says nothing. Third, there is even in natural languages the difference, often though not always clear-cut, between descriptive (not f-descriptive!) words such as 'green' and logical (not f-logical!) ones such as 'or'. Analyticity depends only on the logical words and on grammatical "form." Fourth, descriptive

[45]

words seem to refer to "content," to name the world's furniture, in a sense in which logical words do not. These, I believe, are the four felt differences which philosophers, including many positivists, express by calling analytical truths necessary, or formal, or syntactical, or linguistic. Without explication the formula courts disaster; its explication has four parts, all equally important. First, our knowledge that all "content" variations of analytic "form" ('George is either tall or not tall', 'James is either blond or not blond', etc.) are true is, in the ordinary sense, very certain. But no claim of a philosophical kind for the certainty of this knowledge can be the basis of our explication; it can only be one of its results. Second, the notions of analyticity and of logical and descriptive words correspond to perfectly clear-cut f-notions of the ideal language. Third, the specific arithmetical definition of f-analyticity in the ideal language (that is, in the simplest cases, the well-known truth tables) shows in what reasonable sense analytical truth is combinatorial, compositional, or linguistic. Fourth, arithmetic, the key to this definition, is itself analytic upon it. Taken together these four features amply justify the philosophers' distinction between what is either factual or possible (synthetic) and what is necessary (analytic), between the world's "form" and its "content." But if they are taken absolutely, that is, independently of this explication, then the phrases remain dangerously obscure. Greatest perhaps is the danger of an absolute notion of form as a verbal bridge to an absolute notion of certainty. Nothing is simpler, for instance, than to set aside syntactically a special class of first-order predicates, subsequently to be interpreted by color adjectives, and so to define f-analyticity that 'Nothing is (at the same time all over) both green and red' becomes analytic. Only, this kind of f-analyticity would

[46]

no longer explicate the philosophical notion. Ours does. But that it does this is not itself a formal or linguistic truth.

*Ontology* has long been a favorite target of the positivistic attack. So I shall, for the sake of contrast, reconstruct the philosophical query for what there is. The early attacks were not without grounds. There is, for one, the absurdity of the classical formulations and, for another, the insight, usually associated with the name of Kant, that existence is not a property. In Russell's thought, this seed bore double fruit. On the one hand, when 'Peter' is taken to refer to a particular, 'Peter exists' cannot even be stated in the ideal language; his "existence" merely shows itself by the occurrence of a proper name in the schema. On the other hand, such statements as 'There are no centaurs (centaurs do not exist)' or 'There are coffeehouses in Venice' can be expressed in the ideal language, in a way that does not lead to absurdity, by means of quantifiers, which are logical signs, and of defined predicates, whose definitions do not involve the "existence" of the kinds defined. This is as it should be. Ontological statements are not ordinary statements to be located within the ideal language; they are philosophical propositions to be explicated by our method. Logical signs, we remember, are felt not to refer as descriptive ones do. This reconstructs the classical distinction between existence and subsistence. Ontology proper asks what exists rather than subsists. So the answer to which we are led by our method seems to be a catalogue of all descriptive signs. Literally, there can be no such catalogue; but one would settle for a list of categories, that is, of the kinds of entities to which we refer or might have occasion to refer. But then, every serious philosopher claims that he can in his fashion talk about everything. So one could not hope to reconstruct the various ontological

[47]

theses by means of a list of all descriptive signs. The equivalent of the classical problem is, rather, the search for the undefined descriptive signs of the ideal language.[1] I used this idea implicitly when I explicated nominalism and phenomenalism. To show that it is reasonable, also historically, consider two more examples. Take first materialism or, as it now styles itself, physicalism or philosophical behaviorism. Interpreted fairly, even this silliest of all philosophies asserts no more than that all mental terms can be defined in a schema whose undefined descriptive predicates refer to characters exemplified by physical objects. Quite so. I, too, am a scientific behaviorist. Only, the materialist's schema is, rather obviously, incomplete and therefore not, as he would have to assert, the ideal language. Russell, on the other hand, when he denied the existence of classes, meant, not at all either obviously or sillily, no more than that class names are defined signs of the ideal language.

6. *Wittgenstein.* Historically, Wittgenstein's *Tractatus* is the source of reconstructionism. Systematically, having at least four grave defects, it is merely an anticipation. Each of these defects has influenced the course of the movement.

There is, first, Wittgenstein's famous ineffability thesis. Taken by itself, even an interpreted syntactical schema is mute. Literally, it does not speak about or refer to anything; we speak or refer by means of it. Of course, one may guess, as François Champollion once did or very nearly did, what a syntactical schema could be made to say; but this is a different story. Yet, Wittgenstein's formula that language cannot speak about itself is misleading in two ways. For one, it

---

[1] One could argue that this conception of ontology is anticipated in the *Tractatus* (2.01, 2.02, 2.027). But I was not aware of that when I first proposed it.

may be taken to assert that one cannot or must not construct syntactical schemata which upon interpretation refer to themselves. Natural languages do in this perfectly harmless sense speak about themselves. It is true, though, and this is probably one of the contributory causes of many confusions, that in natural languages such discourse sometimes produces paradoxes, particularly and not surprisingly if one neglects the distinction between an expression and its name. In the ideal language this need not be the case. The precautions its syntactical construction requires in order to avoid those neat paradoxes to which the mathematicians have first called our attention may be safely left to the mathematicians. This is not a philosophical problem. Nor was Wittgenstein, I believe, overly impressed by it. He used his formula to reject all philosophy as a futile attempt to talk about the ineffable. This is his version, well suited to the streak of mysticism that was in him, of the linguistic turn. But then again, it shows how close to the reconstructionist idea he really was. He did in fact propose an ideal language; only, he forbade *de jure* all discourse about it, that Moorean discourse, if I may so call it, which is the heart of the philosophical enterprise. *De facto*, as Russell observed, he managed to say a good deal about his ideal language, in a style as terse as it is often obscure, and certainly anything but Moorean.

Second, Wittgenstein's notions of form and analyticity are absolute, in the sense I explained and rejected. Consider, for instance, his assertion that every "possible world," whatever its "content," would yet be of the same "logical form" as ours, which implies, among other things, that '$p$ or not-$p$' is in all possible worlds "necessarily" true. The point is that without some such explication as I have given the expressions within double quotes remain problematic. Or, to put the same thing

[49]

differently, Wittgenstein uses them, in what should be ordinary discourse about the ideal language, philosophically. Take the relevant explication of 'possible'. What is thus possible is what is expressed by a sentence which is synthetic upon that notion of analyticity that fits our world. The circularity is obvious. Even worse, one can so explicate the phrase 'possible world' that Wittgenstein is seen to be outright mistaken. Nothing keeps one from constructing a schema, in all other respects like ours, whose "logic" is, say, three-valued. To be sure, this is tediously abstract; conversely, to call such a schema a possible world is a very exuberant metaphor. For one would not know how to interpret it at all, even less how to interpret it so that it becomes the ideal language. But I, for one, do not wish to argue with those who insist that the world "could" be so, or could so change tomorrow, that this and only this schema could serve as ideal language. I never claimed to do more than to describe what I find, empirically as it were.

In contrast to this hypostatization of form, a strange weakening of the notion occurs at two places in the *Tractatus*. This is its third major defect. The dominant and, I think, correct doctrine is that what is formal or syntactical about such predicates as 'green', 'red', and 'square' is merely that they are predicates, more precisely, nonrelational predicates of the first order. Yet, Wittgenstein also maintains that some such sentences as 'nothing is (all over at the same time) both green and red' are analytic. 'Nothing is both green and square' is not even true. Since Wittgenstein himself exploits to the utmost the insensitivity of analytic form to content variation, the inconsistency is only too manifest. One of the causes of this curious slip is, perhaps, the confusion to which I have called attention before of the purely structural notion of analyticity with the essentially psychological one of certainty. It is indeed mere quibbling to insist that there is a difference in certainty among the two beliefs that nothing is both green and not green and that nothing is both green and red. But if one wishes to maintain that the second of these two propositions is analytic, then one is virtually forced to argue as the casuists argue. In his later life Wittgenstein became indeed the founding father of casuism. But of this presently. In the *Tractatus* the weakened notion of form appears once more, in a passage where space and time are counted part of the world's form, not with its content. This is a curious Kantian echo. Some spatial and temporal predicates must appear among the undefined descriptive signs of the ideal language. This is the core of the so-called relational theory of space and time. To put it succinctly, the world is not in space and time; space and time are in the world. Nor is it without interest in this connection that Wittgenstein was very fond of the metaphor of logical space, for the world is not suspended in logical space either. Or, if you please, everything is a fact, or merely a fact. Only, to say this is to say no more than that at night all cows are black. Philosophy is still the art of distinction.

There are, finally, what seem to be the grounds of Wittgenstein's ontology. I say seem because I believe that he himself was not aware, or not fully aware, of these grounds. An unexamined metaphysics, that is, one implicitly held, is for a philosopher the worst metaphysics of all. This is therefore where the fourth trouble lies. I, for one, share what I take to be Wittgenstein's none too explicit ontological views. But I also believe that if these views are held explicitly and on the right grounds then they do not occupy the strategic position which implicitly they have in his thought. In other words, if

[51]

I discovered that the reasoning that led me to them was fallacious or if the world were in this one respect different, I would not by this token alone have to modify or abandon any other of my opinions. Stated as I would state it, the thesis is that the undefined descriptive signs of the ideal language are all either proper names or first-order predicates, including relational ones. I have called this view elementarism in order to indicate that next to nominalism it is the least crowded of all ontologies. The hidden grounds on which Wittgenstein holds it are two. The first is not hard to find, particularly if one examines the traditional version which says that all there is are particulars and the characters they exemplify. Replace in this formula the deliberately jejune 'there is' by the conventionally unanalyzed 'exists', replace 'particulars' by 'particulars in space and time', and you will recognize the old Democritean suspicion against all "abstract" or "Platonic" entities, the rejection of anything not "in" space and time. Of course, 'in' is here merely a rudimentary metaphor, a particular being no more "in" the web of spatial and temporal relations, some of which it exemplifies, than it is "in" greenness if it is green or "in" pitch if it is a tone. Clearly, there is some connection between this root of Wittgenstein's elementarism and his views on space and time; and there is at least some vague affinity to the Democritean physicalism of most formalists. Nor is it without interest that, as I hope to show, elementarism plays a strategic role in Ryle's thought. Wittgenstein's second ground is more deeply hidden. Let me explain. So far I have not distinguished between naming and referring. Yet, Wittgenstein was impressed with the difference between the ways in which sentences and terms "refer." According to him, a sentence refers to a state of affairs; it does not name it, for what is there to be named in the case of, say, a false sentence? Proper names and undefined predicates, on the other hand, if they are introduced in accordance with the principle of acquaintance, do name something that is there. Adopting this usage, an elementarist might say that what exists is what can be named. Surely this is a very roundabout way of speaking and, like all such ways, may lead to perdition. At the moment this is not my point. The point is that this is where the picture metaphor, taken literally, creates pseudoproblems. A picture depicts trait by trait what it is the picture of. So do names. Language does not, otherwise it would be of no use. Yet, according to the metaphor which I believe guided Wittgenstein, language is a picture of the world. Of course, he was not so foolish as to do away with sentences. Nor was he, I think, overly impressed by the classical poser of negative propositions. But the fact remains that the only sentences that did not puzzle him were atomic ones such as 'this is green' or 'this is to the left of that'. Defined predicates and complex sentences, he felt, refer differently. The only complex sentences he really trusted were connective combinations, such as conjunctions and disjunctions, of atomic ones, because the truth tables had convinced him that connectives do not, as it were, pretend to name anything. So they are harmless and may pass. This, I believe, is the second ground of his elementarism. The overt motive was, and with some still is, to find a so-called meaning criterion, that is, to circumscribe what may be said in the ideal language. The picture metaphor is a poor guide in this undertaking. Nor is this really a new or separate problem. All we need to observe if we want to make sure that we understand what we say is syntax and the principle of acquaintance, the one when we form our sentences, the other when we choose their descriptive constituents.

[53]

7. *Further issues.* The ideal language contains such statements as 'There are coffeehouses in Venice' and 'There are physical objects'. This answers the criticism that whoever accepts the principle of acquaintance, since he is not able to say these things, cannot escape the absurdities of phenomenalism. Such critics hanker after the philosophical assertion that physical objects exist, that is, as I explicate it, they insist that the ideal language contain undefined descriptive signs referring to physical objects and their characters. This is a far cry from common-sense realism. Yet, realism has a deeper root, which we must first explicate and then reconstruct. Common sense rightly insists on the difference between 'This is a tree' and 'I know (see) that this is a tree'. Neither of these two statements being philosophical, they must both be located in the ideal language. The second raises the issue of acts or, as some positivists call them, propositional attitudes, knowing, remembering, doubting, and so on, in brief, the issue of awareness. This is essentially not a psychological question, though it is also psychologically undeniable that, first, an awareness, say, a knowing, is different from its content, say, that this is a tree; and, second, that some awarenesses, say, a knowing that this is a tree, are the contents of others. The specter of an infinite regress which Hobbes raised at this point against Descartes and which Brentano tried to lay by his notion of an *eigentuemliche Verflechtung* need not worry us. That is indeed a psychological affair; all we are called upon to produce is a schema of the act pattern, that is, of such sentences as 'I know that this is a tree'. Now I know no way of introducing the act verbs by definition, without using in these definitions at least one of them, that does not run into difficulties somewhere. Taking a hint from the psychologically inclined among the classical

phenomenalists, one might try, for instance, to define these characters in terms of some minute kinaesthetic qualities and similar fictions of a doctrinaire introspectionism. The trouble is that since these are fictions, the proposal violates the principle of acquaintance. Taken philosophically, it thus raises more questions than it can answer. It follows that the ideal language contains at least one undefined descriptive sign naming an act, say, awareness. What is the syntactical status of this sign? If one follows the lead of ordinary grammar, then what is needed is not only a new sign but a new syntactical category, since as they are used in our natural languages the act verbs correspond neither to predicates nor to proper names of the ideal language, for in our natural languages 'knowing that' is, without being a connective, a modifier of a whole sentence, the one which is called the dependent clause. To choose this course is to reintroduce many of the classical absurdities; also, it amounts to abandoning some of the clarifications we have achieved, for instance, as I cannot here explain in detail, the explication of analyticity. Fortunately, this course need not, nay, must not be chosen. The decisive insight is that an awareness, which is never identical with its content, is itself a particular. (This is indeed the deepest and most significant core of Berkeley's "nominalism.") The name of a particular, however, is a proper name and this makes the act verbs in the ideal language ordinary predicates. Are they then relational predicates? Or, to put the same thing differently, does the sentence which corresponds, on the ground floor of the ideal language, to our paradigm, read more nearly like 'I know that this is a tree' or like 'Knowing that this is a tree'? This is, of course, the issue of the Self. The second alternative is, I believe, correct. All I can say here is that while when I direct my gaze

[55]

inwards I do find knowings, I do, like Hume, find no such thing as a knower. This sort of Self is an illusion spawned by ordinary grammar. The empirical Self or, with the linguistic turn, the common-sense usage of the personal pronouns must and in principle can be reconstructed in a pattern that was invented by Locke. For the rest, I believe that the inability to cope with the act which most positivists have inherited from the classical phenomenalists is a very grave shortcoming. To have called attention to it is the other decisive contribution of Moore who, in this respect, owes a great debt to Brentano and, through him, to Locke. The issue lies indeed deeper than the realism-phenomenalism controversy; it appears already within the "phenomenally given" in the difference between 'This is a tree percept' and 'I am having a tree percept'. Sometimes one should speak metaphorically or metaphysically, lest one's soul shrivel; sometimes one must, if one wishes to be understood. Let me say, then, that without this correction the positivist's universe remains flat, with subject and object squeezed into one plane. This is a taint of either phenomenalism or materialism which the linguistic turn as such does not remove. But if the correction is made the way I propose then one does not need to abandon either elementarism or the syntactical schema of *Principia Mathematica,* for syntactically 'being aware' is just a predicate among predicates and the name of an awareness just a particular among particulars.

With respect to the act verbs this is as it ought to be, reflecting as it does the place which minds do have in the world. About the names of contents or, more precisely, kinds of contents, something more can be done provided one is not afraid, as we have seen one need not be, of languages which do in a sense speak about themselves. Let me explain. To say that the sentences of the ideal language correspond to actual or potential contents of awareness is but a reaffirmation of the principle of acquaintance which I express by calling these sentences the texts of mental states. To be a mental state of a certain kind is indeed the same as, or "means," to have a certain text. With this in mind, let us take our next cue from a device used in ordinary language whenever one wants to distinguish an expression from its name and ask whether we could not use ' "This tree is green' '[2] as a predicate that names in the ideal language the kind any particular awareness with this text exemplifies. Two things should be noticed. First, the device must not be introduced uncritically, since in this case the sign is not quite innocent of what it names. Second, if we introduce it at all, the ideal language should also contain the truism ' 'This is a tree' means this is a tree' and, at the same time, show that it is a truism. For, I repeat, to be an awareness of a certain kind and to have a certain text are not two things, but one. I believe that one can, not uncritically, add the quotes and a sign to be interpreted as 'means' to our schema; not uncritically, because a satisfactory argument can be made on purely syntactical grounds that the two new signs are logical and that the truism is analytic. This, by the way, is the addition to the syntactical schema of *Principia* which I mentioned much earlier. But let it be noticed that the inclusion of at least one undefined act predicate among its descriptive vocabulary, or the correction as I just called it, is quite independent of this addition to its logical apparatus.

Up to this point I have not once used either 'means' or 'meaning'. The cause of this is, of course, the ambiguity

---

[2] This is not a double quote, which is merely a stylistic device, but one "semantical" or single quote within another.

of the term and the conviction that it has been a rich source of confusion among positivists as well as among others. One of the connotations, the one with which I just used the term and the only one with which I shall use it, is purely linguistic; it does not strictly speaking refer to anything any more than does either 'or' or 'all'. Loosely speaking, it marks the "relation" between an expression and its name. This loose usage, we shall see, was very misleading. In another connotation or, if you please, in two others, I avoid the term, speaking instead of naming and referring. These I shall discuss presently. As for our addition to the syntactical schema, it also yields an explication of the philosophical notion of truth. By means of 'means' one can within the ideal schema define a predicate, to be interpreted as 'true', such that to state that a sentence is true is analytically equivalent to stating first what it means and then this meaning. This is the small nourishing kernel of the correspondence theory of truth, one of the strongholds of philosophical realism. I call it a small kernel because this truism, too, is a verbal affair. Aside from the help these explications afford in avoiding some errors, meaning and truth are indeed philosophically arid notions. Nor is this surprising. What could one possibly learn about the world from those sentences of the ideal language which, since they contain one or both of these terms, are essentially about language? Concerning further connotations of truth two comments will suffice. In ordinary discourse the term and its derivatives serve no purpose besides style and emphasis. Philosophically, there is also the unclear idea of verification. Some even consider a so-called verification principle a cornerstone of positivism. They argue that we know only what we have verified and, in a blend with the equally hazy notion of a meaning criterion, that we must not say what cannot at least in principle be verified. The trouble is, as with the meaning criterion, that this is not a new or separate problem. Having verified something is the same thing as to know it, or something else from which one infers it, as one knows what he sees or hears or is otherwise directly acquainted with.

8. *The pragmatists.* The pragmatist writers study language as it names or refers. Theirs is a scientific investigation, philosophical only in the peripheral sense of being for the most part speculative and anticipatory. A really worth-while science of linguistic behavior does as yet not exist, could not possibly exist as long as scientific psychology and sociology are in their present rudimentary state. Why, then, mention these studies at all? Why tag their authors with the name of a philosophical movement? Science sometimes aids the philosopher indirectly. It may help us to see that a certain question is scientific, not philosophical. (To extend this claim dogmatically to all philosophical questions is scientism.) Or it may help us to recognize that what we thought was one question of a philosophical nature is a tangle of several, one of them scientific. (The others may be philosophical or moral.) The tangle we must eventually unravel is meaning, its scientific component what I call naming or referring. This explains our interest. The label I use can also be justified. The authors who write on this subject and are also philosophers are either pragmatists or were at some time under the influence of pragmatism, particularly in its Deweyan or instrumentalist variety. Another influence upon them is formalism. The link between instrumentalism and formalism is scientism, that is, as I just explained, the belief that the sound core of any philosophical problem is always a scientific one and nothing else. This version of the rejection of all

[59]

philosophy is the very essence of instrumentalism, with psychology and sociology as the sciences destined to supplant metaphysics. Dewey is a philosopher only in that he supports this doctrine with an elaborate rationale which is in part genuinely philosophical and, curiously enough, in the Hegelian pattern.[3] This is why I think that the tag is not only justifiable but enlightening.

Imagine an anthropologist who just arrived on an inhabited island whose name begins with 'O'. He will soon discover that the sounds the natives make are of two kinds, one being distinguished by its causes as well as its effects. This interesting kind he calls o-words. Or, if you please, this is his definition of 'o-word'. But one must not forget that he does not proceed as arbitrarily as the syntacticist who makes "by definition" certain shapes the elements of his game. Only the name, if anything, of this class of sounds is arbitrary; membership in it depends on the causes and effects a sound has. Among these our anthropologist will, if he is wise, include mental states. (I mention this because most pragmatists make so much of their behaviorism. But the sound core of this doctrine is merely a way of speaking about minds. For scientific purposes though, I would be the first to insist, this is the only proper way, at least in principle.) The pattern of causal relations among o-words and other things is intricate and subtle; yet its essence can be stated very simply. The occurrence of a particular o-word, for instance, is in a characteristic fashion causally connected with thought and overt behavior concerning trees. To this connection our anthropologist refers when he says that the o-word o-means tree, or,

[3] For a brilliant analysis of the structure of pragmatism as well as of its influence and affiliations see the long essay by May Brodbeck in M. Brodbeck, J. Gray, W. Metzger, *American Non-Fiction 1900-1950* (Chicago, 1952).

synonymously, that it o-names or o-refers to trees. I, for one, shall again shun 'meaning', even with a prefix. O-reference, then, is nothing "logical" or "definitional"; it is a natural or empirical relation among o-words on the one hand and events, states of affairs, and all sorts of things on the other, in exactly the same sense in which being-to-the-left-of and being-louder-than are natural relations, only much more complex. In the ideal language 'o-refers' is a descriptive expression; this is why I call the relation natural or empirical. The expansion of this expression which contains only undefined descriptive signs is very long, this is why I call the relation complex. There are several philosophical lessons in this scientific fairy tale. They are all negative, as one would expect; yet they are important.

Much of our talk about language is not one bit different from the anthropologist's, though we do not, of course, use prefixes. Such discourse is, therefore, of the same kind as scientific discourse, which is not philosophical but merely an extension of common sense. It moves, to speak metaphorically, in a constituted universe in which no philosophical question ever needs to be asked and in which none can be answered. Let me explain why I again insist on this point. I have said before that I always use 'naming' and 'referring' commonsensically. If I wanted to express this in a manner which is now, after my story has served its purpose, merely ridiculous, I could say that the proper explication of the two words is always that of 'o-naming' and 'o-referring'. But it is far from ridiculous to point out that if one says, as I did, that language refers to events, states of affairs, and all sorts of things, one does not thereby embrace an ontology of events, states of affairs, and all sorts of things. For, obviously, this is a commonsensical or, if you insist, scientific use of the crucial phrases. One more comment should drive home the point that such discourse about language, useful though it may be heuristically, is yet philosophically irrelevant. Imagine that our anthropologist, being of a philosophical bent, attempts a classification of o-words that might not occur to everyone. He proposes to divide them into o-descriptive and o-logical ones. 'Descriptive' and 'logical' (not 'o-descriptive' and 'o-logical'!) are philosophical words that need explication. To learn or to discover for himself this explication our scientific friend must study philosophy. Having done this he may, if he wishes, by a simple process of translation, transfer the distinction, with all the roughness it has in natural languages, from his own to the native idiom. Frankly, I do not see much point in the exercise. What I do see is that if he does not know the explication, anthropology will not help him to find it.

It is time that I explain my preference for the letter 'O'. It stands for the first letter in 'object language'; for this is what the islanders' idiom is often called while the anthropologist is said to speak a metalanguage. Both terms are clumsy and unnecessary; but they are widely used; so I shall say a few words because of the bewilderment and the confusion they have caused. The plurality of natural languages is not relevant for our purposes. If one disregards it, then there is one and only one language, the natural language we all speak and understand. Using it, one may either speak "scientifically" about language or one may construct and interpret artificial sign systems. Cryptographers design such codes, as Ryle contemptuously calls them, and we have, for our very special purpose, designed the schema of one. Thus, if those two clumsy terms are to be used at all, then our natural language is the only metalanguage; the so-called ideal language is the object language of philosophical discourse. Also, language is, metaphorically speaking, a closed universe; it cannot literally contain another language. If for instance, a German teacher of French says ''chien' bedeutet Hund', then ''chien'' is literally the German name of the French word 'chien'. That is, of course, the origin of the quoting device. But to say all this is not to say that syntacticists cannot construct several sign systems and, still syntactically, relate them to each other in all sorts of manners. One must not be confused by the ways they have of speaking about their mathematical games.

Now, finally, the meanings of meaning, of which there are at least four. There is, first, the one I call meaning, a logical or linguistic relation between words and words. There is, second, the one I call naming or referring, a natural relation between words and things. Some of the classical philosophers use the term in a third sense for the contents of acts which are said to inexist intentionally in them. This is, so to speak, a metaphysical kind of referring, the appropriate metaphysics being that of direct realism. Explicating as we did the act and referring, we have, I submit, reconstructed the sound core of this classical position. Again, psychologists who inquire how the meaning is carried, either associatively or by some conscious representative such as an image when, say, a man hears a word and knows what it means, ask a purely scientific question. This is the fourth theoretically important meaning of meaning. The possibility of confusions among the four is only too obvious. Formalism, we shall see, fails to distinguish between the first two.

9. *Formalism.* Formalism is the end product of a combination of three attitudes. One is the rejection of classical philosophy common to virtually all early positivists, the other de-

votion to science, the third a great love for artificial sign systems. The three go well together. The argument that philosophical controversies cannot be decided experimentally, for instance, serves as a bridge between the first two; again, admiration of the physical sciences may tempt one to put too high a value on the new symbolic technics and thus in the end to pay for their coveted neatness and precision with vacuity. Carnap, the outstanding formalist, has always lived in this intellectual climate. Less than twenty-five years ago he was, nevertheless, as close to reconstructionism as anybody had ever been before except, perhaps, Wittgenstein. He was also the first to recognize the significance of that bit of arithmetic that is so important in the explication of analyticity. Later on, soon after he had moved to America, his formalism became more pronounced. Fully developed, formalism is an uneasy marriage between two extremes. The one, from which I take the name, is purely "formalistic." The other is a crude metaphysics implicitly held; this, I believe, is the price every philosophy that explicitly rejects metaphysics must pay.

To understand the formalistic side of formalism, consider the old question whether numbers exist. Russell both explicated and answered it admirably by interpreting number signs as defined logical expressions of the ideal language. This corresponds to the classical answer that numbers subsist. But the formalist now tells us again that the question itself is not a good question, that the only one we can and need ask and answer is whether a certain symbolism contains number signs; if it does, then numbers exist in this symbolism; if not, not. If this were all there is to philosophy, it would be about words and nothing but words. This is indeed the epiphany of the word.

[64]

The implicit metaphysics is an uncritical realism which manifested itself early in the formalists' concentration on artificial languages whose undefined descriptive terms are, broadly speaking, the names of physical objects and of some of the characters they exemplify.[3a] Except for mental terms and the more abstract ones of science and common sense, this is virtually the language of what I called a constituted universe. With respect to the concepts of science, the formalists' analytical achievement is brilliant and by now virtually noncontroversial. It is, of course, also quite independent of their specifically philosophical views. The mental terms they are content to define as the behavioristic psychologists do, within the sort of artificial language they prefer. This is their physicalism and their behaviorism. Thus they prevent themselves, by a typically scientistic foreshortening, from coming to grips with at least two large groups of philosophical issues, those raised by minds and those centering around the realism-phenomenalism controversy. Obviously, their artificial language is therefore not the ideal language. These, I hinted, are old weaknesses. In its most recent state formalism expands its artificial language into a "semantical system." All it gains is the opportunity for new errors and confusions.

Generously interpreted, a semantical system is the syntactical reconstruction, always within the limits of physicalism and behaviorism, of what our anthropologist had to tell us. So let us consider one of his characteristic sentences, say, ' 'tree' o-names tree'. The formalist transcribes it by ' 'tree' designates tree'. 'Designates', it will be noticed, is another word I have so far avoided. The formalist collapses into it the two radically different ideas I distinguish as mean-

[3a] For a detailed demonstration by one of my students of the realism implicit in Carnap's as well as in Schlick's views see L. Pinsky, "Positivism and Realism," to appear in *Mind*.

[65]

ing and referring. He opts for the linguistic connotation, meaning, when he says, as he does, what I would express by calling his artificial language syntactically constructed and 'designates' one of its logical signs. This latter illusion is probably enhanced by the "definitional" freedom we have in devising codes. He opts for the empirical connotation, referring, when he insists, as he also does, that in the paradigm ''tree'' and 'tree' refer to the *word* 'tree' and to trees respectively. So interpreted, a semantical system is merely an "axiomatization"' of behavior science and therefore, as I explained, without philosophical significance. As far as this future science is concerned, is it really likely to benefit from an axiomatization which axiomatizes nothing but, and that barely, the crude common sense any science must try to go beyond? One does not, after all, cut butter with a razor. There are, besides, the very real possibilities of present philosophical confusion. I select two, one a formalistic excess, the other a curiously naïve excursion into ontology.

One of the formalists' illusions seems to be that "semantics" avoids the "formalism" of "syntax." Of course, this is but the "formalistic" version of the old error that a sign system as such says anything. Analyticity is a syntactical notion. So it is in the following manner replaced by one supposedly superior. In terms of 'means', we remember, one can define the equally linguistic 'true'. The formalist, by means of the ambiguous 'designates', defines in his semantical system $L$ an equally ambiguous 'true'. This gives him in $L$ a sentence which I transcribe, a little cavalierly, as follows: 'This tree is green is true = Def. ('this tree is green' designates this tree is green) and (this tree is green). The expression in the first parenthesis on the right side he calls a "semantical rule" which he knows to be true provided only he understands L. The expression in the second parenthesis being a synthetic sentence, he does not, merely by understanding L, know whether it is true or false. Yet, he discovers, there are some cases where the second parenthesis does not bother. In this happy event he calls the quoted sentence on the left side L-true, this being the notion which is to supplant analyticity. Of course, these happy cases are exactly those in which the expression in the second parenthesis is analytic in L. It follows that to have a significant notion of L-truth one must first have a significant notion of analyticity in L. Far from having been disposed of, the problem has merely been pushed back one trivial step. Of course, the thing is not done quite that transparently, otherwise it would not have been done at all. But this is what it amounts to.[4]

Now for the excursion into ontology. Meaning, naming or referring, and analyticity are connected in the following three ways. First, construing 'meaning' as strictly as I think one must one cannot in the ideal language truly say ' 'Peter loves Mary' means Mary is loved by Peter'. No damage is done, however, since we can say instead: 'Peter loves Mary if and only if Mary is loved by Peter' is analytic. Second, one will wish to say, as one can without difficulty, that ' 'Morning star' means Evening star' is false but that 'Morning star' and 'Evening star' refer to the same thing. Third, one will wish to say, as one again can without difficulty, that ' 'Man' means featherless biped' is false because 'A thing is a man if and only if it is a featherless biped' is not analytic. If, however, one wants to express all these ideas by axiomatizing an ambiguous 'designates' and without even

---

[4] I argued this point quite technically by analyzing an error in Carnap's *Meaning and Necessity*. Unimportant in itself, this slip illustrates perfectly the basic misconception and could hardly have occurred without it. See *Mind*, 57 (1948), 494-95.

the notion of analyticity to fall back upon, then one has quite a mathematical problem on hand. So one may overestimate its solution and, guided by habits not wholly extinguished, interpret this solution philosophically. This Carnap has lately done by suggesting that what "exists" is what is designated. We remember the pattern, with a different word, from Wittgenstein. But we also remember that 'designates' stand ambiguously for 'o-refers' and that while our anthropologist did not make any ontological commitments by making words refer to all sorts of things, Carnap now does. The curious result is that propositions in the classical sense, the golden mountains once thought about, and all sorts of things are being returned to ontological status through this semantical back door. It was, I believe, Lord Acton who once made a penetrating remark to the effect that those who ignore the past may, at their own risk, have to relive it.

10. *Casuism.* Philosophy is the disease of which it is the cure.[5] This is the essence of casuism distilled into one sentence. The disease is metaphysics. The cure is ordinary discourse about ordinary language, the casuist's version of the linguistic turn. But this discourse is critical, not merely descriptive as the anthropologist's. One could even call it therapeutic, comparing one whom the casuist involves in philosophical conversation about a classical problem with a patient who has entered upon a cure. For if the treatment is successful then the patient will cease to worry about the problem because he has recognized that it is merely a puzzle, a pseudoproblem created by bad grammar. 'Worry' and 'puzzle' are indeed key words of this linguistic existentialism

---

[5] The phrase is Feigl's who is not a casuist but a disciple of Carnap and who used it in another context.

with a happy ending. This is where the other tag, therapeutic positivism, comes from.

The casuist, we see, shares the belief common to all
positivists that philosophical difficulties stem from bad grammar. Only, he embraces the extreme view that good grammar
dissolves, rather than solves, all classical problems and thus
completely disposes of philosophy. In this respect casuist and
formalist are alike. They part ways when the former rejects
the artificial languages which the latter uses to spot bad
grammar. How, then, does the casuist know good grammar
from bad? This is where his casuism comes in. I shall state
this part of the doctrine in four steps, more or less as if it
were an argument. First, the casuist is greatly impressed
with a fact I mentioned when I sketched the background
of the linguistic turn. The man on the street who uses
ordinary language to talk about what he ordinarily talks
about, though he may of course get into trouble, never gets
into the sort of trouble we know so well as philosophical
perplexity. Second, the meanings of words (I think I can
now safely speak of meaning) vary with the situations in
which we apply them and, which is perhaps the same thing,
with the verbal contexts into which we put them. The good
grammar or correct usage of a word, or of a connotation of
a word, consists of all the ways in which it can be combined
with others into sentences that do not yield philosophical
perplexity. This is the casuist's implicit conception of good
grammar. Usually, though, a few strategic sentences will
suffice to give us the right idea. Third, if a word has two
more or less distinct contexts, one may inadvertently transfer the grammar of the one to the other. This is bad grammar
of the sort that can lead to philosophical perplexity. In the
case of a gradual transition between contexts trouble may

[69]

arise when one forgets that while they are similar in some respects they are also in varying degrees unlike each other. Fourth, the cure is performed by exhibiting all these differences and transitions, gradual or abrupt as the case may be, and by pointing at the exact spot where the fateful slip occurred. We understand now why artificial languages don't appeal to the casuist. In constructing them, or at least in constructing them well, one does what he wants to do in his own way. Nor does he believe that there are any traffic rules or general philosophical propositions to keep us on the straight and narrow path of correct usage. All one can do is to do the job in each case exactly as the circumstances of the case require. This is where the tag, casuism, comes from. This stress on philosophy as an activity, this horror of philosophical propositions, is probably, as Ryle suggested, an attenuation of Wittgenstein's ineffability thesis. This, then, is the casuist doctrine. What are its weaknesses and its strengths?

There are some strengths. A casuist's distinctions may be part of the required explication. Induction is, I think, a case in point. From one who worries about the grounds of induction the casuist inquires whether he does not perhaps wonder how any number of instances can ever furnish the adequate reasons for a generalization. If the worrier agrees that this is what he is really worrying about, then he is told that one also speaks of adequate reasons where a deductive proof is in order but that this is surely not the sort of thing he is looking for. As it happens and as we have all long known, this is indeed a part of the required explication. Or take the metaphor that calls percepts images. The "grammar" of 'image' helps one to understand a good deal of what has been said for and against representative realism. In this case, though, the service is very modest, really not more than an old and familiar way of focusing the problem. Generally, the casuist's contribution may be, and often is, of some propaedeutic value. His basic weakness is that he stops too soon. Comparing the philosopher to a surgeon, one might say that the casuist sometimes exposes the delicate inner organ but that he never operates on it. I shall give two schematic illustrations, calling them schematic because I do not care to attribute them to anybody in particular; one to demonstrate how the casuist convinces himself that no operation is necessary; one to show how he, too, may become the victim of an implicit metaphysics. Some doubt that we can ever know what is in another's mind; some believe that we can and sometimes do know such things. My schematic casuist first tells the believer that he believes as he does because he has all the evidence *he* can possibly have, namely, the other's behavior. Next he tells the doubter that he doubts because, since he does not share the other's awareness, he does not have all the evidence *anyone* (which includes the other) could possibly have. Then he disposes of the problem of other minds by pointing out that the two argue at cross purposes since they do not use 'knowing' with the same grammar. I notice, first, the guileless use of 'possible' where it carries an eminently philosophical meaning. I notice, second, that the little play on 'he' and 'anyone' presupposes other minds, which in this case entails a circularity. And I notice, third, that while we may all without circularity agree on what we are directly acquainted with and that we are not so acquainted with other minds, it takes some doing to explicate on this basis what we mean when we say truly that we do sometimes know not only how the other behaves but, in a sense, also what is in his mind. This is of course

[71]

the problem or, if you please, the operation the surgeon must perform. Now for the illustration with the implicit metaphysics. Some casuists think they know from correct usage that we know something if we have a perfect reason to believe it and, also, that we know whatever we do know indubitably or for certain. My schematic casuist uses this piece of "grammar" to attack those who insist that they are never completely certain whether such statements as 'this is a book' are true. If I see a book on my shelf, so the argument goes, and if I make a few tests to convince myself that I am not the victim of a perceptual error or illusion, then I have a perfect reason for believing the proposition. Thus I do not merely believe it; I know it. And since I know it, I know it for certain. Clearly, the argument is a barely veiled *petitio principii.* Clearly, the very difficult philosophical notion of certainty has here under the cover of grammar entered into supposedly ordinary discourse. Clearly, the implicit metaphysics is some sort of realism.

The shortcomings of all this are so grave and so obvious that one must ask why so many clever people have not seen them. Is there, perhaps, a core or central belief which makes all these strange things plausible and is yet at first sight not too implausible in itself? The core of casuism is a confused notion of grammar, derived I think from Wittgenstein's unduly absolute and unduly weakened ideas of form and analyticity. The typical casuist accepts these two notions, form and analyticity, though he does not worry much about them, probably because he thinks that Wittgenstein has done that once and for all. An analytic truth, then, is for him a proposition that is true because of the form it has or, as he also says, by virtue of its meaning. Being linguistic and not factual, it could not possibly be false and is, therefore, beyond controversy. Some even call it truth by definition, a bad slip due to the circumstance that within a language definitions are indeed analytic and, in an obvious sense, beyond controversy. (This is also the source of a line of thought according to which all philosophical propositions are definitions. Philosophical explications are, in a reasonable sense of the term, real definitions; and there is nothing arbitrary about these.) This part of the core stems from Wittgenstein's absolutism. To grasp the other part one merely needs to think of "form" as grammatical form, in some vague sense of grammar or usage which remains completely obscure except that it is always invoked to prevent one from asking philosophical questions. In this way one may come to believe, as Wittgenstein did and the casuists do, that 'everything that is colored is extended' is analytic or, what amounts to the same thing, that to be extended is part of what it "means" to be colored. I do not at all understand this meaning of 'means'.[6] But I understand very well that it can be used to make *everything* a question of grammar or usage. That is patently absurd.

11. *Conventionalism.* Ryle shares the casuists' views on language. Like them, he tenderly probes the idiom; like them, he rejects artificial sign systems. Unlike most of them, he is by now virtually a philosophical behaviorist. But this is not the most important difference. What sets him apart is that he does not shun philosophical propositions. Those he actually propounds may be, and in my opinion are, utterly futile.

---

[6] Historically speaking, I have a hunch. If one accepts this meaning of 'means' then one can convince oneself that all synthetic propositions are really analytic because they are either "implicit definitions" or the deductive consequences of such. This is rationalism of the Hegelian or Deweyan variety. We stand here at the source of some pragmatist undercurrents in recent positivism which are not of the rather trivial scientistic variety.

Yet, the intellectual motives behind them are interesting and genuinely philosophical. Fortunately for all of us, a philosopher's stature is not measured by his beliefs alone. The motives appear most clearly in the papers Ryle wrote before he attained the influence he now has in England. Two stand out.

Ryle is committed to an elementarism even more radical than Wittgenstein's and, equally important, to direct realism. (The Wittgenstein of the *Tractatus* was not very interested in the realism-phenomenalism issue.) The second commitment is admirable in one who is wedded to some sort of philosophical realism, as Ryle always was, probably on common-sense grounds as, say, Reid understood common sense. Such a one sees clearly that the indirect or representative realist of the Lockean or any later variety achieves nothing, merely pushes the difficulty one step back, as it were, since he cannot bridge the gap between the mental object he knows and the physical object that causes it but which he does not know. This, I suggest, is how Ryle came to dislike all mental objects. The dislike is not only the driving motive behind his behaviorism; it also provides the bridge to his elementarism. For the overt ground on which he attacks mental objects, whether they be humble sense data, feelings, percepts, or acts, is that they are all abstract, nonempirical, or Platonic entities (not, we remember, in space and time). They are thus in the same company with simple higher-order characters, with propositions in the classical sense, with golden mountains supposed to exist or subsist merely because they were once thought of, and with any fanciful entity that ever inhabited a philosopher's ontology. Some may think the company mixed and, therefore, the judgment that dooms all its members harsh, not to say rash. I certainly think so. Yet this is, for better or worse, Ryle's brand of elementarism. With it goes, as in Wittgenstein's case, an implicit reliance on the picture metaphor and that strict use of 'naming' which we recognized as its symptom. Probably because he was so sensitive to this cue, Ryle spotted immediately the overcrowded ontology which Carnap now propounds in that curious roundabout way I discussed. At this point Ryle is very consistent. He takes his own medicine, worrying about what any but an atomic sentence could possibly name or, if you please, refer to. The range of his worry is wide indeed. It comprehends not only tautologies but also generalities such as 'everything that is green is extended', moral judgments such as 'killing is evil', and still other kinds of sentences.

The solution we are offered is surprising. I shall take my cue from the rejection of Wittgenstein's doctrine that tautologies are ordinary sentences, peculiar only in that they say nothing. Ryle teaches, more radically, that they are not sentences. This, I submit, is his particular version of the linguistic turn. The implicit notion of sentence is, clearly, the sort of thing that refers to what "exists" or could exist. Of course, Ryle is not so foolish as to reject outright all those suspect kinds of sentences as nonsense. Yet he insists, what amounts practically to the same thing, that they differ from real sentences in two respects. First, they are about language or, rather, about linguistic behavior. Second, they are rules about the use of language and, therefore, like all rules neither true nor false. Furthermore, they are *ex post facto* rules, abstracted from linguistic behavior by one who watches people speak as a coach watches his players, not rules which either explicitly guide the players or justify what they do while on the playing field. This latter emphasis

[75]

has two reasons. First, Ryle wishes to reject the naïve "rationalism" which fancies that, say, deductive inference consists psychologically in the conscious application of a syllogistic rule. Second, he wishes to point out that if such a rule were without further comment offered as a justification of inference one could immediately ask what justifies the rule. As far as they go, the two points are sound. Only, they do not go very far, not beyond exposing once more certain old errors which hardly anybody makes nowadays. Nor does Ryle see that the second argument can be turned against himself. There is indeed nothing in his interpretation of these sentences as *ex post facto* rules of linguistic behavior that would help him to answer a similar question. His interpretation makes the question only more obvious, an answer more urgent. The question is, of course, why just these rules and not others; or would others do as well, say, for instance, those of a three-valued logic.[7] Ryle has no answer; all he tells us is, in effect, "what is being done." This makes his philosophy a form of conventionalism, with the peculiar twist that the convention appealed to or chosen is linguistic custom. There is also, with the modifications required by that twist, the standard casuist unmasking of all classical problems as artifacts of bad grammar.

12. *Conclusion.* Incidentally this essay presents a structural analysis, and in a sense even a historical one, of the several branches of the positivistic movement. Primarily it is an exposition of my own reconstructionism. But I have refrained from either advocating or appraising this position. At least I have tried. In conclusion I shall permit myself a few such remarks, theoretical as well as cultural. Theoretically, I

---

[7] For a detailed analysis of Ryle's logic by one of my students, see N. H. Colburn, "Logic and Professor Ryle," *Philosophy of Science,* 21 (1954).

should like to say that in the principle of acquaintance this philosophy preserves the core of classical empiricism as in the structure of its ideal language it contains the doctrine Russell called logical atomism. Yet it is neither phenomenalism nor realism. It takes awareness seriously and it does not imply ethical naturalism. I hurry to add that I have found all its major pieces ready made. I merely polished their rough edges and fitted them together. If I have added anything at all, it was the effort to bend the philosophies of the act back into the main stream of empiricist thought. This is a contribution that was long overdue, building as it does on the work of Moore and Brentano. Culturally, there is nothing left in this philosophy of the science worship, the implicit materialism, the shallow hedonism, and the frivolous social optimism that have often marred the Continental branch of the movement, though surely not the spirit of Wittgenstein. Nor does it, I think, share the futilitarianism into which the British branch has so unhappily degenerated. Finally, unlike either branch, it is firmly committed to the classical tradition. To use a bad metaphysical word in a good human sense, this is indeed its one commitment that is absolute.

# TWO CORNERSTONES OF EMPIRICISM [1]

QUINE'S RECENT paper, "Two Dogmas of Empiricism," [2] opens with a historical diagnosis. Modern empiricism is said to have been conditioned in large part by two beliefs. The one, worded as I would word it, holds that an epistemologically significant distinction can be made between the two kinds of truth traditionally spoken of as analytic and synthetic. The other is now also known as the linguistic version of phenomenalism. I agree completely with this diagnosis; but I disagree as completely with the burden of Quine's paper. He argues that the two beliefs are ill founded. I shall attempt to show, in this paper, that they are tenable as well as of strategic importance. Naturally, then, I think of them not as two dogmas but, rather, as two cornerstones of philosophical analysis in the empiricist vein. Yet, the disagreement is neither as crass nor as unsubtle as one might infer from my thus opposing, for the sake of emphasis, thesis and counterthesis. With respect to the first issue: Examining some recent attempts at "justifying" the dichotomy in question, Quine finds them circular, question

[1] This paper was read, as part of a discussion with W. V. Quine, at a meeting sponsored by the Institute for the Unity of Science in Boston, Spring 1951. Subsequently, it appeared in *Synthese*, 8 (June, 1953), 435-52. It is here reprinted by permission.
[2] *Philosophical Review*, 60 (1951), 20-43.

begging, or otherwise untenable and inadequate. These criticisms, which make up more than half of the paper, are, in my opinion, most penetrating, admirably lucid, and irrefutable. Also, I share what I believe is their intellectual motive, the rejection of a certain unclear idea of *certainty* that has, from a tangle of historical causes, vexed our philosophical tradition. With respect to the second issue: Whatever we know about the external world is, in varying degrees, subject to doubt. At the one extreme, say, in the case of a novel scientific theory, this is obvious. At the other extreme, I understand and accept the traditional thesis, supported by the traditional arguments, that even a perceptual judgment as simple as 'This is a chair' is not, in principle, beyond doubt. However, this circumstance is counterbalanced by another. In principle we always can and in practice we sometimes do maintain the truth of such judgments in the teeth of what I shall, for brevity's sake, call evidence for their falsehood. I am as impressed as Quine is and as, I take it, most philosophers who think of themselves as empiricists are, with these two pervasive features of our knowledge of the external world. So there is much agreement, negative, as on the first issue, and positive, as on the second. I believe, indeed, that most, if not all disagreements in the empiricist camp have been worn very thin in the discussions of the last decades. We mutually approve of our partial analyses, particularly, alas, of the destructive ones. Nor do we often disagree on the pervasive features of our world that our descriptions of it should portray. What we argue about among ourselves are no longer those analyses and these features but, rather, though sometimes without noticing it, the nature and task of philosophical analysis itself.

This task, as I conceive it, is the solution of the traditional philosophical problems, the simultaneous solution of all these problems, and nothing but the solution of these problems; or, as some put it, the dissolution of the traditional puzzles. There is much in this on which, among empiricists, I need not touch except *sub figura praeteritionis*. For instance, I shall take it for granted that if the second belief, the one Quine calls reductionism, could be maintained, some familiar problems would be solved or, at least, be on their way toward solution. Similarly, I take it for granted that the linguistic version of this thesis marks a further advance in that it keeps us from becoming entangled with ontological assertions of the classical variety. The label, linguistic version of phenomenalism, which I have chosen in order to identify our concerns with those of others, thus turns out to be captious; so we may prefer to speak of the dissolution of puzzles rather than of the solution of problems. What interests me at the moment is that these are *not* the things we argue about among ourselves. Though we may not always know it, our most fundamental disagreements nowadays are about such matters as how detailed and how accurate, in a sense of 'accurate' which is itself in need of clarification, the "linguistic reconstruction" involved in the reductionist thesis must be. This indicates one group of reasons that make me feel that our intellectual situation is very delicate and, in some sense, peculiar. There are two more such groups; to indicate their nature I shall make use of certain cues I planted.

Let me start from the two features of our knowledge of the external world with which, as I put it, Quine and I are equally impressed. There is also another feature of our experience; I shall call it the third. Some things, such as that we have at the moment a chair percept, we know, whenever we do know them, so that it makes absolutely no sense to say that we may doubt them. If I did not sometimes know some such truths, I could not understand what it means to doubt some others. If it were not for them, I could not understand the word 'true'. Nor could I, without understanding this word, understand what it means to say that the truth of some statements is problematic in the sense that, on the one hand, it can always be doubted and, on the other, always be preserved by certain adjustments in a wider context. Quine does not, in his paper, repudiate this third aspect of our experience. But he says very little about it and he also advocates a *rapprochement* with pragmatism. I must say I am puzzled; for the whole intellectual edifice of pragmatism in its dominant instrumentalist form rests on the emphatic rejection of the third feature. As a historical fact this is beyond dispute; controversial is merely whether it is, as I am prepared to maintain, an irreparable shortcoming of that position.

It has appeared that because of the light they shed on each other our three features are really quite inseparable for the purposes of philosophical analysis. This merely illustrates that very intricate and thorough interdependence of all philosophical problems or puzzles that leads me to speak of cornerstones and of strategy. To add one more metaphor, we must beware lest we weave, if weaving it is, a Penelopean garment. More literally, the task is, as I said before, to dissolve simultaneously all puzzles and, as I now add, to account justly for all those pervasive features of our experience that have attracted the philosopher's attention. Many of our disagreements turn, I think, on whether what one has said about a particular issue fits into such a general pattern. This is my second comment about the situation I

[81]

called both delicate and peculiar. Quine's present position leaves the two features both he and I think important serenely secure. Naturally—for are they not his cornerstones? Does not his strategy work from them rather than toward them? Yet I am disturbed by the price he pays and I believe must pay for this. Let us disregard the pitfalls of the material mode and, for the sake of the argument, assume that he does not need to reject the third feature. Even so, I am not willing to say, as he does and I believe must, that the external world is an ontological hypothesis or posit. We may, of course, doubt the truth of 'There are physical objects' in the sense in which a single perceptual judgment is not beyond doubt. In this light, though, all cows are black and we have hardly said anything in particular about that hoary puzzle, the existence of the external world. More important, I don't know what ontological hypotheses are, in a sense that goes beyond the truism I just mentioned, except that we may doubt, as we may doubt so much else, whatever can be said legitimately in the realm of ontology, which is quite a different matter. But surely this will do by way of unsupported assertions. For the moment they may serve as signposts, indicating my strategy as well as my intellectual motives. Later on I shall have to give reasons; and they had better be of the kind which I insist the situation requires.

For my last comment on how we disagree I planted the cue when I spoke of justifying the dichotomy analytic-synthetic. In that sense of the term which has its root in the law and which is the only one I understand, we are not obliged to justify anything, not even, as some still believe, induction. We merely describe the world, for our own peculiar purposes, in our own peculiar way. Justification in the legalistic sense is no more our business than is that other futile and not unrelated quest, the search for some superior kind of certainty. Yet, one part of our task does bear some vague resemblance to that of a man asked to show cause in a court of law. Even there, though, I prefer to speak of *explication* rather than of *justification*. In the case of the dichotomy analytic-synthetic the evidence for a felt difference is as overwhelming as are the arguments in the destructive part of Quine's paper. Thus, caution is in order. Surely, there are some cases where all we can do is to explain how and why our predecessors erred. But whether we can be satisfied with such a negative result is, in each case, a further question, on which one may disagree. This, I submit, is the third kind of disagreement still to be found among us. To my mind, it is better to fail trying than to give up too soon. With respect to analyticity, I believe there are features of our experience that account for what I just called the felt difference. I propose to point at these features, to locate them correctly, as it were, and to state them justly, showing in this manner that it is not all a misunderstanding, a matter of psychology or, as one says in this case, one of degree. To do this sort of thing for a philosophical distinction is what I mean by explicating it and what some may mean when they speak, at their own peril, of justifying it. I say at their own peril, because the main reason the explication of analyticity proved so elusive was that those who sought it also sought for a certainty that is not to be had and for a justification that is not needed.

Much of what follows depends in part and some of it depends wholly on a technic I shall use and which is, therefore, more than a technic. So I must call attention to this phase of my strategy, though I shall be brief since the matter is familiar. I have long sided with those who hold that philosophical analysis proceeds properly through the construction of an ideal language. Quine never explicitly embraced this view, but he is I believe not unsympathetic to it and certainly not as violently opposed to it as some of our British friends, the so-called casuists, and their latter-day offspring, the therapeutic linguists. I may hope, then, that I do not obstruct communication when I speak the only language I feel I can speak, with some expectation of clarity and effectiveness, on issues as fundamental as those that are here at stake.

An ideal language or, as I shall sometimes say, disregarding the problems of a possible plurality, the ideal language has three essential characteristics. First, it is a formalism, that is, a system of signs or, if you please, marks on paper designed without reference to anything else but the shapes and the arrangements of these signs themselves. Second, it becomes, upon interpretation, a picture or reconstruction of ordinary English, that is, of those statements we make or would make, if we had occasion to make them, outside the philosopher's study. Third, we can, by discoursing about it, dissolve the philosophical puzzles. One requirement I urged before, that all philosophical problems be solved simultaneously, as it were, is automatically fulfilled if one adopts this method of philosophizing. The idea is, of course, not to have different formalisms for different problems, but one which is complete in that it is a picture of all ordinary English and adequate in that it allows the discursive solution of all puzzles. When we construct the ideal language, in the first step, and when we interpret it, in the second, we speak ordinary English. This is also true for the third step; for in this discourse, which is the heart of the philosophical enterprise, the statements made in the philosopher's study occur merely in quotes, as it were, as our *explicanda*. This emphasis on ordinary, nonphilosophical English reflects what I owe to G. E. Moore. Whoever thinks that the double role it assigns to ordinary English makes the schema vitiatingly circular hunts for an absolute that is not there; I shall not, because I cannot, argue with him. I turn, instead, to two other arguments that can and must be made. The first may produce agreement where there seemed to be disagreement; the second should at least help us to agree that part of our disagrement is a difference in opinion, not as to what is the case, but as to what philosophers ought to do about it.

That we speak in the ordinary course of events the language I call ordinary English is, of course, a matter of fact or, if you please, of empirical fact or, still more pointedly, merely a matter of fact. Surely, there is nothing certain, in any nonordinary sense of 'certain', about this fact. One may even, if one cares to do so, call it an anthropological fact and go on to assert that my conception of philosophy makes it a branch of anthropology. In a sense this is true; only, it is also trivial. Again we have entered a night in which all cows are black. The philosopher's art is, to me, still the art of distinction. We clarify our thought and, incidentally, the historical puzzles by making all the distinctions that can and, therefore, must be made. To emphasize the "anthropological truism" at the expense of such distinctions is not only unhelpful but definitely harmful. Does Quine really think, I wonder, that all a philosopher can do, when he wishes to characterize the sort of thing Quine does in his *Mathematical Logic*, is to call it a study, albeit a rather abstract one, in the psychology of thought and in the sociology of discovery. If he does not think so, in spite of some

[85]

anthropological *obiter dicta* that crop up strangely in his most recent papers, then I am once more puzzled by the gesture he makes toward pragmatism; for, that pragmatism not only implicitly neglects but explicitly rejects the distinctions involved is, again, a matter of record.[3] Yet there is another side to the story. Just as distinctions must be made correctly, so there is no truism that is not of strategic importance somewhere. The distinction between the two kinds of truth has so far not been made correctly, or, as I had better say, has not been talked about correctly. The anthropological truism has its part in correcting these errors.

Assume, for the sake of the argument, that I shall succeed in what I have undertaken to do presently, namely, to distinguish in the ideal language two kinds of statements, corresponding to the two kinds of truth, analytic and synthetic. Success would consist, first, in explicating, without using them, the traditional formulae such as that "analytical truths are formal, syntactical, or linguistic, while synthetic truths depend on fact." It consists, second, in demonstrating that the distinction thus established does justice to what I called the felt difference and that it is, as I put it, epistemologically significant in that it is crucial for other clarifications such as, for instance, my second cornerstone or, as Quine has it, dogma. If one can thus successfully explicate the old formulae, then one may, if one wishes, continue to speak of factual and of formal truths, at least occasionally, since for some purposes this nomenclature is indeed quite adequate and very suggestive. But if the circumstances require it, as they do on this occasion, then one can add, consistently and without intellectual embarrassment, that the distinction be-

[3] See also M. Brodbeck, "The New Rationalism; Dewey's Theory of Induction," *Journal of Philosophy*, 46 (1949), 781-91.

tween factual and formal truths is itself a matter of fact. Naturally, 'fact' occurs here in two different meanings. The first time it marks the relevant distinction; the second time it is used in the sense in which everything is a fact and in which, therefore, nothing is certain in that indefensible sense of 'certain' in which some advocates of the dichotomy analytic-synthetic think that the truths they call formal or linguistic are certain. I note, for later reference, that I just scored for the first time against that sort of certainty. I turn, next, to the other point about the ideal language that needs arguing.

To his client, the future owner, the architect submits a sketch that helps him visualize the style of the building, the order and arrangement of the rooms, their shape and size. To his workmen the architect gives a large number of blueprints specifying all sorts of detail, down to the dimensions of a lintel and, perhaps, even the grain of a wooden panel. Assuming, for the sake of the argument, that we know otherwise what we mean when we call the ideal language a picture or reconstruction of ordinary English, how accurate and how detailed must this picture be? Is it more like the architect's sketch or more like his blueprints? Quine observes, in his discussion of what he calls the second dogma, not only that Carnap's *Aufbau,* whatever else its weaknesses and strengths, is merely a sketch but also, and more important, that no blueprints in support of the linguistic version of phenomenalism are likely ever to come forth. With this I have no quarrel. Disagreement begins when Quine turns his observation into a criticism of my second cornerstone, arguing as he does that since we cannot really reconstruct physical objects we may as well accept them as ontological posits. To coin a phrase for the convenience of the moment, Quine is a blueprint theorist. I am, emphatically, a sketch theorist. Yet, to repeat, I am as convinced as he is that it is practically impossible to define blueprintwise such words as, say, 'chair' from the kind of inventory of undefined descriptive terms we *Aufbauers* would be willing to accept, say, for instance, a class of predicates referring to qualities of and some spatial and temporal relations among those particulars which it is customary to call sense data. What I maintain not to be impossible, either practically or otherwise, is the reconstruction from such an inventory of such statements as 'a, which was just contiguous with b, is now contiguous with c', where 'a', 'b', and 'c' refer to particulars of the kind just mentioned. If this can be achieved, even if only as one usually says for a two-dimensional visual field and within the specious present, much is achieved. For, as I need not explain, this amounts to an analysis or, at least, to an essential part of the analysis, of the idea of a *continuant* and, therefore, of the ideas of *physical identity* and *substance*. A few more such schematic analyses properly related, explicating such notions as the three just mentioned, constitute what I accept as the reconstruction, complete and adequate for all philosophical purposes, of the idea of a *physical object*. This is what I had in mind when I insisted earlier that the task of philosophical analysis is the solution of the philosophical problems and *nothing but* the solution of these problems. What does not pertain to them is detail that need not and should not appear in the sketch.

The issue of the counterfactuals, which attracts now so much attention, provides as good an illustration as any for what I mean by accuracy in this context. Idiomatically accurate translations of the so-called dispositional terms cannot be constructed from nondispositional terms with the syntactical apparatus of logical atomism. This, I take it, has been settled. But we may still disagree and we do, in fact, disagree among ourselves on whether this forces us to abandon the thesis of logical atomism or whether translations as accurate or, if you prefer it that way, as inaccurate as we can give without abandoning it suffice for the purposes of philosophical analysis. The blueprint theorist has no choice. Ideal language or no ideal language, he must give up logical atomism and commit himself, in Quine's terms, to an ontology crowded not only with physical objects but with potentialities and connections of all kinds and levels, really quite an Aristotelian universe. To defend the other alternative, that of accepting this inaccuracy of the ideal language, is not one of the tasks I have set myself in this paper. It is fortunate, though, that, since I am a sketch theorist, I can choose this alternative. For it will soon appear that my explication of analyticity stands and falls with logical atomism, that is, with the thesis that the syntactical categories of the ideal language are, roughly speaking, connectives, individual and predicate variables, quantifiers and constants corresponding to these variables, and nothing else.

Permit me to conclude this topic with an historical conjecture. The present recrudescence of the blueprint theory of reconstruction and of philosophy in general has, I believe, two main causes. The one is the casuists' excessive concern with ordinary English, with the fine shades of meaning which they so cleverly discern in the spoken word and, generally, with linguistics in a sense that has very little, if any, bearing on the philosophical problems. The futility and the futilitarianism into which this tendency has degenerated are only too manifest. The other cause is the wrong kind of

[89]

concern with and regard for science that prevailed and still prevails among some groups of empiricists. Science often does and eventually always should deliver blueprints, not sketches. Philosophers, however, in this respect as in all others, are not scientists.

I turn now to the explication of analyticity. Very judiciously, I think, particularly for his critical purposes, Quine distinguishes between two kinds of allegedly analytic truth. Supposing "a prior inventory of *logical* particles" such as the connectives, a truth of the first kind "remains true under all reinterpretations of its components other than the logical particles." A truth of the second kind, such as 'No bachelor is married' is supposedly reducible to the first by replacing some terms, such as 'bachelor' by their "definitions," where 'definition' does not necessarily have the meaning of abbreviation in a formalism. Quine's demonstrations that analyticity cannot be grounded in such ideas of definition, synonymy, and interchangeability are surpassingly brilliant and lucid. It is fortunate, then, that I need not deal with that second kind, for it will soon appear that the ideal language contains only definitions in the harmless sense of abbreviation. As I have already shown in part, the "factual" burden "definitions" carry in other conceptions of reconstruction is, by my strategy, placed elsewhere. For another hint about this strategy, one cannot deny epistemological significance to the distinction between analytic and synthetic truths and grant it to that between *logical* and *descriptive signs,* which is at least implicit in Quine's mention of a prior inventory. One motive for my defending the first dichotomy is that unlike Quine I need, in my ontology, the second. Both 'all' and 'green' are in the ideal language; thus both allness and greenness are, in some sense, in the world. Yet there is a "felt difference" between their modes of being there. This difference I explicate by that between logical and descriptive signs. And this, I believe, was also the intent of the old, inadequate formula according to which logical signs and analytical truths are formal or linguistic.

As a philosopher I am not interested in formalisms as such. So I shall henceforth speak only about that formalism which is as likely a candidate as any for the ideal language, namely, the noncontroversial parts of *Principia Mathematica* supplemented by a sufficiency of (descriptive) constants. In this formalism one can with the familiar results distinguish between the two kinds of signs, formally and yet not trivially as, e.g., by enumeration, but structurally, by means of the formation and transformation rules and, in particular, the rules of substitution. (In itself such a formal distinction is, of course, not epistemologically significant; it becomes so only when it can bear the burden imposed on it in philosophical discourse about the formalism.) Quine,[4] I am well aware, does not favor this particular piece of machinery and minimizes it in his variant of the formalism. However, since his preference seems to stem from his ontological views rather than from his philosophy of logic, to whatever extent these two can be kept apart, and since I follow after all good logical doctrine, I do not think it unfair on my part to proceed as I do.

Consider now that rather limited class of truths known as the tautologies of sentential logic. I shall explicate what sets them apart in two steps. *First,* they remain true, *as far*

---

[4] W. V. Quine, "Ontology and Ideology," *Philosophical Studies,* 2 (1951), 11-15; G. Bergmann, "A Note on Ontology," *ibid.,* 1 (December, 1950), 89-92, and also pp. 238-42 of this book.

*as I know and as a matter of fact,* if their descriptive signs are consistently but otherwise arbitrarily replaced by others of the proper syntactical kinds. As far as my campaign against the wrong kind of certainty is concerned, the two qualifications, "as far as I know and as a matter of fact," are of the essence. Here I score for the second time in this campaign. But perhaps one wishing to test my empiricist orthodoxy would now like to ask whether I really agree, then, that one of these substitutions could "conceivably" yield a falsehood. So questioned, I might smile and wonder whether the questioner himself is quite untainted by the heresy known as psychologism. But I would not quibble and I would agree. Yet it remains most remarkable that, having once constructed the ideal language, one can, in fact, recognize the truth of some statements merely by inspecting these statements. This, however, is only half of what must be said; otherwise most any truth could by the proper tricks be made "formal" or "linguistic." I note, then, *second,* that the connectives, which are the only signs that occur nonvacuously in tautologies, have very special properties. They are, in a familiar sense, truth tables; and a sentential compound is a tautology if and only if its truth table exhibits that familiar feature which mathematicians express by saying that the sentential calculus has an adequate matrix representation. Taken together and with what follows, this purely combinatorial, arithmetical schema for the connectives and the vacuous occurrence of all other signs in the tautologies *are* the proper explication of the former being called logical signs and the latter analytic truths.

Not all analytical truths are sentential tautologies. The vacuous occurrence of the descriptive signs is characteristic of all of them. But there are, of course, no truth tables for the so-called functional calculus. Fortunately, their place is taken by the idea of an identical formula. This, too, is a purely combinatorial, arithmetical schema. Originally devised for the lower calculus, it can be extended to the higher types, as Carnap did in *The Logical Syntax of Language.* Everybody familiar with this schema knows that *mutatis mutandis* it does exactly what the truth tables do. This, then, is my explication of analyticity. It has two immediate consequences of strategic import. Applying the technic of identical formulae to the higher types commits one to an extensional ideal language. Since I see no reason to shrink from this commitment, since Quine, too, inclines toward the extensionalist thesis, and since I must limit myself, I shall say no more on this head. Even more fundamentally, I have committed myself to logical atomism. To see this, assume that 'because' in 'I am ill because I smoked too much' corresponds to a primitive sign of the ideal language. If it is a special sign, then my explication of analyticity breaks down because it is not a connective. If it is a substitution instance of a new kind of variable, that is, a syntactical category not known to logical atomism, then I know of no combinatorial schema that does for such variables what the technic of identical formulae does for predicate variables.[5]

I am now ready to turn more exclusively to the problems of the reconstruction. But I should like to show first in an intermediate case the use to which this explication of analyticity can be put. Quine says incidentally that he does not know whether 'Everything green is extended' is analytic.

[5] See also "Logical Atomism, Elementarism, and the Analysis of Value," *Philosophical Studies,* 2 (December, 1951), 85-92, and also pp. 243-54 of this book.

Surely the blur is not due to some blurred notions of synonymy or definition; the idea of defining one of the two descriptive predicates in terms of the other is simply too unreasonable to be taken seriously. So one may, for the sake of the argument, assume that they are both primitive or undefined. From my view, then, it follows immediately that the statement is not analytic. It follows further that whatever tie there is between descriptive characters in such cases, it is not the tie that binds conclusion to premise. Many philosophers would have saved themselves many troubles if they had been able to state this difference justly and clearly instead of lumping it under the notion of entailment. Philosophy, I repeat, is the art of distinction.

In one respect all proponents of an *Aufbau* agree. The undefined descriptive predicates that are, as it were, the basis of the reconstruction are of the kind that has led to the familiar charges of phenomenalism or subjective idealism. Whether this inventory must contain some roots specific to our moral and esthetic experience and to such activities of the Self as knowing and remembering is controversial. Again, the basis needed for the reconstruction of our knowledge of the external world is not controversial, except for some rather technical points which, since they do not concern Quine in his paper, need not concern us in this discussion. So I shall say no more about the basic inventory. The reconstruction itself consists in the designing of definitions for such *definienda* as, say, 'chair'. These are all definitions in the strict and, as I put it before, harmless sense of abbreviation. The procedure is successful, within the limits set by the sketch theory, if and only if (a) we can indicate two classes of statements, A and B, such that the statements of B follow deductively from those of A in conjunction with the definitions;

(b) the statements of both *A* and *B* correspond to empirical laws we believe to be true; (c) all descriptive terms occurring in *A*-statements belong to the basic inventory; (d) a *B*-statement corresponds to an ordinary statement about the external world. All this is familiar. So I shall limit myself to three comments that are relevant to my purpose.

It is worth noticing, *first*, that the ideal language does not and need not contain terms that are names of particular chairs in the sense in which the individual constants (particulars) it does contain or which may be added to it are the names of, say, sense data. In traditional terms this amounts to a refutation of all kinds of substantialism. 'Chair' itself is, of course, a predicate of the reconstruction. What corresponds to *'This is a chair'* of ordinary English is, roughly, a conjunction of *'This* is a chair percept' and a rather complex statement of lawfulness. 'This' thus stands, roughly, for one or several particulars of the ideal language. To put it as I did once before,[6] when I hear the first bars of a certain piece and exclaim 'This is Haydn's Lark', 'this' refers in the reconstruction to these bars, not to the whole quartet. And one sees, upon a little reflection, that this is just as it ought to be. It follows that existential statements such as 'There are chairs' and, similarly, 'There are physical objects' merely assert that there are particulars of a kind I do know. They may be hypothetical in that the particular which, in a manner of speaking, the bound variable represents is not present. But they are not hypothetical in that they assert the existence of kinds I do not know. One may, of course, define kinds one has never seen exemplified, say, centaurs and mermaids, in terms of kinds one knows. Definition does not, in an obvious and

---

[6] "Remarks on Realism," *Philosophy of Science*, 13 (October, 1946), 261-73, and also pp. 153-75 of this book.

familiar sense, involve existence. For the rest I simply do not understand that alleged second meaning of 'hypothesis', the "positing" of a kind unknown. This is why I do not wish to say, as Quine does, that physical objects are hypothetical entities, myths like centaurs and mermaids. And, as I have just shown, one does not need to say it. This unwillingness, caused by that ultimate inability to understand, is probably the main intellectual motive that moves all advocates of philosophy by reconstruction. It certainly is mine.

*Second,* I wish to call attention to a very neat and clear-cut dichotomy within the reconstruction. There are, on the one hand, the definitions and, on the other, the statements that may be truly made in the terms defined. This merely portrays what is familiar from everyday life and from science. Sometimes we ask what a thing *is;* sometimes what *happens* to it under circumstances. Scientists say that they *describe* the initial and the terminal states of a system and, by means of a process formula or law, *explain* how the latter evolves from the former. There is, however, a meaning of 'meaning' that is quite resistant to these distinctions. In this sense, we know the better what 'apple' means the more we know about apples. This meaning is forever open, growing, or, to use a technical term, holistic. Naturally, it cannot be "formalized," either my way or any other. This is the meaning which once Hegel extolled and which now the pragmatists emphasize at the expense of all others. Quine's professed sympathy with pragmatism is quite consistent in this respect. From where I stand this is another irreparable weakness of that position. I do not know how to speak of a process without speaking of what proceeds. The proverb has it that it is easier to ride a tiger than to descend from it. This tiger I wouldn't even know how to mount. In other words, I be-

[96]

lieve that if we want to understand the world we cannot help projecting upon it that dichotomy which is so clear cut in the reconstruction, though, to be sure, in doing this we must be as cautious and as judicious as always when we handle that sharp tool, the ideal language. Yet, I do not deny the importance, let alone the existence, of the holistic meaning of 'meaning'; I believe I can even understand the fascination it has for some. I merely insist that the proper place to study it is the science of psychology. Pragmatists, of course, do not wish to distinguish between science and philosophy and Quine now suggests that we follow suit. At any rate, the ideal language cannot and need not portray holistic meaning. This is another of its inevitable inaccuracies.

*Third,* I am now ready to strike my final blows against the wrong kind of certainty. There are those uncertainties of a general and pervasive nature that arise whenever we speak about the world, and, therefore, when we attempt to project any formalism upon it, or, what amounts to the same thing, upon the ordinary language of common sense and science. These uncertainties I pointed out on earlier occasions. The explication of analyticity is perfectly clear and in this sense certain, in spite of the subtle difficulties that beset the decision whether a sufficiently complicated formula of the ideal language is in fact analytic. These difficulties naturally and quite properly occupy the mathematicians; to introduce them, as some now propose, into the discussion of certainty and analyticity is, I believe, a mistake. Yet, there are some specific uncertainties that spring from the very technic of the reconstruction. We merely draw a sketch and we lose, in drawing it, the holistic meanings. For the solution of the philosophical problems this is an advantage; but when we want to decide whether any given ordinary English state-

[97]

ment is analytic, or more precisely, whether its ideal correlate is, then this becomes a limitation, a source of uncertainty. Only, I think this limitation quite natural and so do not chafe at it. There is the related circumstance, of which our casuist friends make so much, that in ordinary speech we use without defining them words whose ideal correlates would undoubtedly have to be defined. These matters have been talked to shreds; so I shall say no more about them. Yet I find it intriguing to observe that much as they otherwise disagree, there is at least this one point of contact between Quine and the casuist linguists. The patterns into which the relatively few basic ideas group and regroup themselves are indeed full of surprises. To return to the peculiar uncertainties of the reconstruction, there is also the choice of the primitive predicates to be considered. Surely, this choice is a matter of fact; besides, we make it only schematically, sketchwise, not blueprintwise. And what appears to be analytic upon one such choice could, conceivably, be synthetic upon another. But again, this neither puzzles nor upsets me, since the blur comes not from a blurred notion of analyticity but from our ignorance in matters of fact, in a sense in which I can and Quine cannot contrast the factual with the analytic.

Certainty of the wrong kind, our common enemy, is dead. I beg a moment's leave to give it a soldier's burial. More plainly, it will be worth our while to inquire where the reasonable kind of certainty has its place in the reconstruction. I have long insisted that the ideal language contains the act pattern, a direct and not merely behavioristic reconstruction of such sentences as 'I know that . . .', 'I remember that . . .'. This is, of course, quite a story by itself; so I shall merely remark that if one represents in the ideal language the dependent clauses by those particulars which are their names, then the mental verbs become descriptive predicates and the act pattern can, in principle, be reproduced without abandoning either atomism or extensionality. As for the reasonable kind of certainty, to know for certain is, I submit, a species of knowing. Accordingly, the locus of certainty in the reconstruction is the mental verb. I realize that by that special revelation the casuists have received about ordinary English to know simply means to know for certain. Thus they would find it absurd that I might have occasion to say that yesterday I knew for certain what today I know to be false. I think that this is exactly as it should be. To play with a fashionable phrase, this absurdity, or alleged absurdity, is indeed part of the human situation. To accept without analyzing it any other meaning of 'knowing' is to begin where one should end and to prejudge some of the most important issues. We, who do not have to pay this awful price, are yet saved more than one perplexity. We are once and for all rid of that inverted psychologism that makes propositions certain while it is we who are certain about them. We notice, further, that my being certain of something, even if this be an analytic truth, is in the reconstruction expressed by a synthetic sentence. For the mental verbs, we remember, are descriptive predicates. Thus, to be certain of something is a fact among facts, not more certain than some others. We have definitely rid ourselves of all apriorism. Also, we are now in an excellent position to understand why and how our predecessors were misled. It is true enough that when we once know a proposition to be analytic we do, in fact, know this proposition for certain. But, to be sure, this is merely a rather striking fact about analyticity, not part of the explication of this notion. So we see at one glance why the ideas of

[99]

certainty and analyticity must be kept separate as well as why they have, in fact, become enmeshed with each other. There is still another class of truths of which we are, in fact, certain, namely, those propositions about sense data of which I said before that it makes no sense to doubt them. I even believe that the certainty of these propositions is part of the attraction which phenomenalism, linguistic or otherwise, had for some. Russell's *Inquiry* is only the last in a long series of documents one could cite in support of this historical conjecture about intellectual motives. Some sought certainty in logic; some sought it in sense data; but, by some quirk of history and the human mind, they unfortunately all sought some superior kind of certainty.

I agree heartily with everything Quine says about meaning and the so-called meaning criterion. This criterion, whatever it may be, is certainly not part of the ideal language but, rather, part of the philosophical discourse about it. It is something to be explicated, not something to be demonstrated; something to strive toward, not something to start from. Nor must it be treated as a premise or a dogma, though it may turn out to be a cornerstone if found to be adequate and, at the same time, of strategic importance. Freed from the unnecessary and confusing reference to verification, this so-called criterion amounts to a choice of the undefined descriptive predicates of the reconstruction and, at least implicitly, of the syntactical apparatus of the ideal language. In this less garish form, which is its own explication, it is also known as the principle of acquaintance, though there, too, the emphasis was usually on the descriptive rather than on the logical inventory. The choice its proponents indicate by means of it is, I believe, for the most part the one I made. In this sense the criterion embraces my two cornerstones or, as Quine has it, my two dogmas. Only, I am not particularly eager to state them in this manner, for I have long discovered that every opportunity to avoid the term 'meaning' in philosophical discussion is nowadays one more opportunity to keep out of trouble and confusion.

The worst of these tangles—though, really, I find it difficult to choose among them—Quine diagnoses with most elegant succinctness as the identification of meaning and reference. One of its stranger fruits is the following argument that is now being made in favor of some sort of realism: 'Dog' is a meaningful word; hence it must have a referent; but dog percepts are, as everyone agrees, different from dogs; hence they are not the referents of 'dog'; hence there are real dogs. The actual arguments are more elaborate; those who make them prefer to speak of electrons rather than of dogs. But that merely adds to the confusion. Since Quine is as skeptical about all this as I am, I should like to remind him whence and why this Trojan horse has been introduced into the philosophical discussion. If one wishes to study language scientifically and with behavioristic methods, then the definition of "meanings" in terms of reference is indeed not only proper but very clever, and, as far as I can judge, probably inevitable. (In introspective psychology it is a confusion. Titchener knew that and explained it well.) With me this alone goes a long way toward showing how wise it is never to blur the differences between science and philosophy. Quine, however, suggests now that this difference, too, is merely one of degree. The pragmatists, of course, would agree. They, at least, are consistent, believing as they do that the proper approach to the *philosophical* study of meaning, as of anything else, is *anthropological*.

Finally, I should like to comment on Quine's and my conceptions of what both he and I call ontology. There are agreements and there are differences. I shall be brief on both, partly because we have aired some of these matters in an earlier discussion.[7] We agree that the old poser about what there is must be treated syntactically, or, as I would have to say, through the syntax of the ideal language. The most fundamental difference is that Quine wishes to reconstruct the old ontological assertions, or some reasonable equivalent of them, in the ideal language. I merely wish to *explicate* them in that informal discourse *about* the ideal language which is in my scheme of things the last and crowning phase of the philosophical enterprise. For instance, I advocate a phenomenalistic reconstruction only because I know of no other way to dissolve all the old puzzles, not because I wish to say that phenomena or, if you please, sense data are the only things that exist; for I believe that if taken literally the old questions and answers make no sense, or, as one said in the salad days in Vienna, that they are meaningless. I really do believe that. In this sense there is no difference between now and then. The difference is that then I would have let it go at that. Now I feel strongly that we can and must explicate these bad questions and answers and that in doing this we can recover or, perhaps, discover some good questions and answers behind them. To me the most interesting of these good questions and, accordingly, the core of the new ontology is: What are the undefined descriptive constants of the ideal language? One reason Quine does not proceed in this manner, is, perhaps, that he does not take as seriously as I do that positivistic turn which Wittgenstein gave to the empirical philosophy when he proclaimed that certain things cannot be said and which I express by insisting that the

[7] See footnote 4.

proper way to say them is ordinary discourse about the ideal language. But there is still another reason, which is much subtler.

It seems to me that one who says "There is a drugstore around the corner" hardly says anything about existence in the sense in which the old ontologists tried to say something about it. Yet, Quine's reconstruction of ontology fastens on the existential statements of the ideal language and, in particular, on the existential operator and the variable it binds. Now I do not deny that these operators and variables are of some ontological interest. To observe that the ideal language requires such and such inventory of *logical* signs and categories is to point at a feature one may, in a broader sense, well call ontological. Only, since I can distinguish between logical and descriptive signs, I can also distinguish between this broader sense of ontology and that other one, which I think is the central and traditional one and which is best explicated by the quest for the primitive *descriptive* inventory. Incidentally, this recovers the old distinction between existence and subsistence, or, at least, a large part of it. Quine, on the other hand, cannot in principle distinguish between logical and descriptive signs, or, as I had better say, he cannot attribute epistemological significance to the distinction. For, as we have seen, to do this is virtually the same thing as to attribute such significance to analyticity. To put it as one should not, for the sake of making a point, in Quine's world both logical and descriptive signs designate equally, without further distinction. This, I suggest, is why he is so impressed with the idiomatic accident that we sometimes say 'Centaurs exist' instead of 'There are centaurs'; and this is also that second subtler reason for his conception of ontology.

[103]

As for his specific ontological beliefs, if I may again state them as I would, I take him to assert that we must include into the basic inventory certain undefined descriptive predicates, such as the names of kinds of physical objects or 'physical object' itself, though we are not acquainted with any of their exemplifications. This, in turn, leads him to call physical objects myths or ontological hypotheses. That I do not understand this meaning of 'hypothesis', either in ontology or elsewhere, I have said before. Besides, I shun the wrong kind of phenomenalism of which it smacks. I do think that it makes sense to say we are acquainted with physical objects and that we are, in fact, acquainted with them. In the reconstruction, 'physical object' is a predicate defined in terms of what we all agree to be acquainted with; and when I have heard all the tones of a tune and grasped its line, then I have also heard the tune. To repeat, when I insist on what Quine calls reduction, it is not because I do not wish to say or could not say 'There are physical objects', but because I know of no other way to say it intelligibly and of no other path that leads to the simultaneous solution of all philosophical problems. This, I think, also indicates how I would explicate and recover the common-sense core of realism. Quine's present position is not in this sense analytic and untainted by the old ontologies. It hovers uneasily between pragmatism and traditional phenomenalism.

I should like to say, in conclusion, that I believe to have demonstrated at least two of my contentions. I have shown that in one sense the disagreement between Quine and me is as marked as are the differences between the positivist and the pragmatist tempers and between the intellectual and cultural atmospheres in which each thrives. Yet it has also appeared that we agree on virtually all those partial analyses

[104]

that are the secure fruits of the joint labors of recent and contemporary empiricists. We merely differ on how best to talk about them and how to marshall them into a world view, or, if I may say so among empiricists, into a metaphysics.

# TWO TYPES OF LINGUISTIC
## PHILOSOPHY *

### I

OF LATE philosophy has taken a linguistic turn. At least this is true of a large and, by general agreement, significant part of all philosophical activity that went on in the English-speaking countries during the last one or two generations. Also, it is true in a new and characteristic sense beyond the commonplace that many classical philosophers, Hobbes, Locke, Berkeley, and not they alone, knowing both the splendor and the misery of words, taught the distinction between sound and sense, between the sign and what, if anything, it signifies. The causes of this linguistic turn or, if you please, the roots of the movement, as of all major movements of thought, are many, in part diffuse and anonymous as well as very complex. Yet the influence of three men, Moore, Russell, and Wittgenstein, stands out. Virtually all living linguistic philosophers are either directly or indirectly students of at least one of them. From this common origin two distinct types of linguistic philosophy have developed. There is, to be sure, much courtesy between the branches. Both

* *The Review of Metaphysics,* 5 (March, 1952), 417-38. Reprinted by permission.

sides can still talk with each other, as Western liberals can talk with Western conservatives, or as Englishmen and Americans can communicate, in a sense in which they cannot with some others. But there is also much strain and lack of mutual appreciation. Recently one editor even pronounced the great ban against the "other" branch, reading it out of the mother church of "philosophical analysis" and denying its practitioners their place in the succession of the masters.[1] It is difficult to find names for the two branches that are expressive of what is involved as well as acceptable to both or, for that matter, to one. So I shall use two tags that are rather colorless, speaking of the *formalists* on the one side and the *antiformalists* on the other. By way of preliminary identification I shall merely say that the formalists devote themselves to the construction of symbolic systems, so-called artificial languages, while the antiformalists are students of philosophically correct usage, probers and pruners of the language we speak. The formalists sometimes advocate the idea of an ideal language, a formalism to serve as a tool for the sort of reconstruction (*Aufbau*) Carnap attempted in *Der Logische Aufbau der Welt* (1928). The antiformalists were at one time also known as the Cambridge analysts, though now that the movement has spread one had better call it the British school of analysis.

The two books on which this study is based represent the two branches of linguistic philosophy. One an anthology, the other an original work, they differ also in kind. In *Logic and Language* [2] A.G.N. Flew has collected and ably prefaced nine essays by British analysts, the earliest of which, Ryle's

[1] Max Black, ed., *Philosophical Analysis,* Cornell University Press, (Ithaca, N. Y.: 1950), p. 13.
[2] New York: Philosophical Library, 1951.

"Systematically Misleading Expressions," appeared exactly twenty years ago. Nelson Goodman's *The Structure of Appearance* [3] is a new reconstruction; not to recognize its vigor and impressiveness would be most ungracious even if one rejects as radically as I do this particular *Aufbau*. Naturally, I shall say more about Goodman's book than about the essays. Yet I shall begin with the latter and say about Ryle's as much as about all the rest together. To justify this strategy I must put my own cards on the table, indicating where I stand on this controversy or near controversy between formalists and antiformalists. To my mind, then, it is gray against gray, not white against black. Both sides agree, and I agree with them, that there is no experience or, if you please, no experiment that decides what is presumably at issue between phenomenalists and realists. In this important sense, both sides agree, and I agree with them, that all philosophical problems are verbal. But in another equally important sense they are not verbal. This sense both formalists and antiformalists have lost or stand in danger of losing if what they do is no better than what they say they do. Now for my reasons for singling out and starting off with the essay that marks Ryle's sober-eyed and reluctant conversion to the linguistic philosophy. It so happens that he there states very aptly a body of doctrine on which both sides could still agree and from which they in fact branched off at about the time the paper was first published. Also, the doubts and dissatisfactions to which he there confessed contain the starting points of the peculiar dialectics by which both formalists and antiformalists may be driven to extremes. Even better than that, I believe I can make use of these hesitancies to

[3] Cambridge, Mass.: Harvard University Press, 1951.

lend color to my own argument for a middle position which, as one is tempted to say on such occasions, does justice to both sides. That Ryle himself has in the meantime become a hero of the antiformalists is merely a piquant detail and does not deter me.

II

To begin with the common doctrine, consider two statements: 'Satan is not real' and 'Professor Ryle is not a formalist'. If one trusts the *grammatical form* they share, one may be led to ask about reality and the prince of darkness questions which, though they may properly be asked and answered about formalism and the professor, make no sense and have no answers. Grammatical form or, rather, some grammatical forms are thus systematically misleading. This is not to say that the man on the street does not know what he means when he denies reality to the devil. Nor is he misled, for he does not ask the unusual and improper questions. (This is Ryle's acknowledgment of Moore's doctrine of common sense.) It is only philosophers who ask them because, whether they know it or not, they have made it their business to explore the implications of grammar. If they don't know it they end in perplexity, finding problems where there are none. To cure this perplexity all one has to do is to discover the *logical form* of statements. (In the case at hand the discovery was, of course, Russell's.) Then it appears that the improper questions cannot be asked. As far as the alleged problems are concerned, *cadit quæstio*. It follows that philosophy is verbal; bad philosophy in a bad sense, good philosophy in a good sense. *All* good philosophy or *some?* This, twenty years ago, was Ryle's most gnawing doubt. He stayed his answer. Let me for a moment stay mine and turn first to another of his hesitancies.

The spoken word is infinitely subtle, its ambiguities beyond count. How, then, Ryle ponders, can we ever hope to be done and how, if we are, could we know it. In the next breath he reconsiders. Perhaps, "the number of prevalent and obsessing types [of systematically misleading expressions] is fairly small," so that our task has its measure. Here we stand at the branching-off point of the two lines. Some, taking their cue from the after-thought and following *Principia Mathematica,* conceived the idea of a universal schema which, if it were the grammar of our language, would by precluding the improper questions "dissolve" all known philosophical "puzzles" whose number, after all, is "fairly small." These, of course, are the formalists. Sometimes such a schema is called an *ideal language* though it is no more a language that can be spoken than the sketch or even the blueprint of a house can be lived in. This misunderstanding is as obvious as it is persistent. Nor are the formalists themselves quite innocent of it. Many of them are science worshippers; and in science, so-called axiomatization, which is not unlike the construction of a partial artificial language one could speak, is at times both possible and useful. So some formalists behaved as if they wanted to do something of the sort for the whole of English. Even worse, seduced by their scientism, they became slaves of their own creations, playing mathematical games for the sake of the game. Naturally, some of these games turn out to be philosophically irrelevant or even misleading. Against all this British common sense and the British analysts, who were relatively closer to the philosophical tradition, rebelled. There is still another reason for this rebellion. The ideal language rarely provides literal "translations," and often plays fast and hard with usage.[4] And had it not just been discovered that all bad philosophy, the "speculation" which both sides so abhor, stems from liberties one takes with usage? There is, of course, a difference; but this difference the antiformalists do not understand. On another plane, the gentleman's dislike and distrust of everything technical also plays its part. Probably it is no accident that, Russell and Whitehead notwithstanding, the inspiration behind formalism is Continental. Be that as it may, the antiformalists sought salvation in ever greater literalness. So they became what I called them before, probers and pruners of the idiom, casuists ever ready to dissolve puzzles, to purify the usage for a limited purpose, but utterly unwilling to recognize the existence of philosophical problems. Also, just as the other side tends to get lost in irrelevant formalisms, so they spend themselves on puzzles that are often not relevant. Little wonder, then, that Ryle's original sagacious doubt was soon forgotten. For both extremes all philosophy is verbal. I do not believe that this is so. Yet I accept what I called the common doctrine. Let me explain.

Assume there is reason to believe that if the undefined descriptive predicates [5] of a certain formalism are interpreted as the names of such experienced characters as *green, later,* and *toothachy,* the formalism can serve as an ideal language. I do not care at the moment whether this particular assumption is defensible; I merely use it to sketch, by commenting on

---

[4] For this and other problems of reconstruction see W. V. Quine, "Two Dogmas of Empiricism," *Philosophical Review,* 60 (1951) and, in reply, my "Two Cornerstones of Empiricism," *Synthese,* 8 (June, 1953), 435-52, which precedes this article. This paper and the present study are companion pieces, not surprisingly in view of the affinities between Quine's and Goodman's ideas.

[5] 'Undefined descriptive predicate' is here a purely syntactical term. See below.

it, a conception of linguistic philosophy which I, for one, am ready to defend. I shall offer four comments. *First:* If the assumption is justified, then that it is justified is a fact of our world. To grant that much one need not accept Wittgenstein's over-literal picture doctrine about which I am as sceptical as anyone. Also, this fact or alleged fact is of a very special kind. To distinguish such facts from what we ordinarily call by that name is well worthwhile. I call them facts without further qualifications mainly *pour l'amour du geste,* to make the point that not all philosophy is verbal; for philosophers, if they are philosophers, try either to defend or to refute such assumptions. *Second:* Our particular assumption is now also known as the linguistic version of phenomenalism. Though this name is easily misunderstood, it indicates rather aptly the sense in which the classical philosophers, in our case the phenomenalists, dealt not only with puzzles that must be dissolved but also with problems that can, perhaps, be solved. The peculiar facts I mentioned before are at the core of the classical problems. This core we can and must recover or, if you please, explicate. The puzzles and the absurdities that went with them we slough off by means of the linguistic method. For, clearly, it is one thing to assert our assumption and it is quite another thing to say such patent nonsense as that only sense data exist. *Third:* Whether the linguistic method is the only one that avoids nonsense is a further question. The case for an affirmative answer is rather technical. But it certainly seems to be a safe method and not at all as restrictive or iconoclastic as many of its proponents and opponents believe. *Fourth:* In constructing a formalism, in interpreting it, and in thus dissolving the puzzles and recovering the core of the problems, we speak ordinary English in the ordinary way that does not give rise

[112]

to philosophical perplexity. This acknowledges what is sound in antiformalism. That complicated things must be stated without such tools is merely another side of the gentleman's prejudice against anything complicated. That we do construct a symbolism; that we construct it, as one says, syntactically; that we ask whether it could, in principle, serve as ideal language—all this acknowledges what is sound in formalism. This will have to do for a sketch of the conception of philosophy which informs this study. I conclude it by venturing the opinion that though it goes beyond what Ryle said twenty years ago, it contains nothing incompatible with what he then did say in that remarkable essay.

Next to Ryle's in excellence is, in my opinion, Miss Macdonald's essay, "The Philosopher's Use of Analogy," where in her own way she makes very much the same points. Only, the hesitations have disappeared; so the limitations become noticeable. Her paradigm is "substance" and the issue is disposed of, in the familiar way, as devoid of factual import. In one sense of 'object' both subject and predicate of an English sentence refer to objects; in another sense of 'object' this is not always the case. So far, so good. But assume that the ideal language is a subject-predicate schema with a zero level of subjects (particulars). Would this not be one of those peculiar facts I mentioned a moment ago? Would this fact not be the recoverable core of the traditional "problem" which, in this sense, is more than a verbal "puzzle"? Much of what Findlay says in his essay on time is well said; but casuism and the preoccupation with mere therapy, the cure of puzzlement, begin to obtrude. We are told, for instance, that if we wish we may safely say that the past exists as long as we remember that we have, perhaps, created a new usage of 'exist'; for then we shall never be puzzled. Surely, this will not do. Two other essays, one on induction, one on verifiability, exemplify antiformalist futilitarianism at its worst. I, too, happen to believe that there is no problem of induction. Yet, if I may borrow a phrase from an august source, I am not amused when I am told for pages on end that this is so because, if one uses 'reason' as it is ordinarily used in ordinary speech on such occasions, uniformity observed in a fair sample is an excellent reason to expect further uniformity. Again, reconstruction by definition (see footnote 4, above) does not stand finally revealed as a philosopher's folly merely because, though we may today use a term to refer to a certain cluster of traits, another trait of the objects exemplifying this cluster may strike us tomorrow, or because these objects may behave in unexpected ways. Nor is this essay improved by floating fragments of analyses which, though relevant in themselves, are irrelevant to its purported topic, verification. Such philosophical Earwickerism is oppressive. By contrast John Wisdom's piece on gods, which concludes the collection, is rather bracing, the way I find E. M. Forster's novels bracing. Wisdom knows what it is like when the chips are down and we are faced, from within or from without, with evil and destruction. His attempt to say this or, rather, to make it show itself without saying it, in the unusual idiom of philosophical analysis, as Forster in his medium makes it show itself without saying it, is of considerable literary merit. Again I am struck by that correspondence and connection, to which attention is called in the late Lord Keynes' *Two Memoirs*, between Bloomsbury and British analysis, also, alas, in their lesser ranks and their less admirable traits. The shade, the nuance are everything indeed; and they are this by themselves, not because, as the romantics would have it, they give us the run-around by pointing at something else.

[114]

Yet, to be this, they must be the shade and the nuance of something, of a world, of that world both Forster and Wisdom know. Lesser Bloomsbury has split the shade and lost the world. The latter day analysts still cure each other's puzzlements; only, they have nothing left that is worth puzzling about.

### III

Goodman is a philosopher, not a formalist in the extreme and pejorative sense. He outlines a symbolism, interprets it, explains why he thinks it can serve as ideal language, and philosophizes by means of it. There is nothing in this to prevent him from taking his stand on the middle ground I chose between the two extremes. Thus I propose to take him at his best, or what I think is his best, ignoring the flavor of formalism that lingers here and there. But I shall feel freer to do so if I first note some of these flaws. He tends to exalt formal work and even formal detail at the expense of philosophical discourse. As a demand, in principle, for what I called a blueprint rather than a sketch this must be rejected; otherwise, the proper balance is a matter of taste and judgment. What Goodman does is, fortunately, better than what he has to say on this point. And he knows that he himself draws merely a sketch in some respects even sketchier than Carnap's which was his original inspiration. There is a second point on which I prefer his taste to his argument. His reconstruction is in fact phenomenalistic; its descriptive primitives refer to characters exemplified in experience. Yet he disclaims all epistemological preference, insisting that a "realistic" formalism, whose descriptive primitives refer to characters of physical objects, would be equally significant and equally welcome to him. Each is said to solve certain problems, each worthwhile for its own sake. Worthwhile as a chess game is worthwhile, yes; otherwise, no. The only purpose of an ideal language or reconstruction is to solve all philosophical problems, simultaneously as it were, by means of the same formalism, for otherwise we don't know whether we have solved any. I happen to believe that to achieve this goal one must, as Goodman does, proceed phenomenalistically. But again, that is not my point. What I insist on is this criterion of philosophical significance. Partial formalizations can within limits answer some questions; for instance, a realistic "reconstruction," some that arise typically in connection with science. But to anchor any such clarification safely one must eventually plot the partial symbolism against the ideal language. (I speak rather vaguely of plotting in order to avoid technicalities.) A third stricture involves the "constructional" feature the ideal language shares with partial formalizations. In either case one starts from a minimum of syntactical primitives or undefined terms and constructs by means of them definitions or other circumlocutions for a maximum of others. The hope, not usually disappointed, is that the problems which revolve around the English word corresponding to a defined term can be solved by attending to the structure of the definition we have devised or, perhaps, to the fact that it can be devised at all. This minimization and maximization is not a quantitative affair. If, for instance, the answer to a certain question depends on the circumstance that all descriptive primitives refer to the given, then it makes obviously no difference for this question whether the reconstruction contains one such primitive, or a few, or even an indefinitely large number. Again, a familiar issue hinges on whether one can do without primitives that refer to characters. Now, a nominalist would not prove his case even if he succeeded, as we know he can't,

[116]

in defining all other universals in terms of similarity. One universal is as good or, if you feel that way, as bad as many. The significance, if any, of such economy is purely mathematical. Goodman, however, thinks that a reconstruction, to be worthy of the name, must make shift with a very small number of primitives, the smaller the better, and that these primitives should be as simple as we can make them, in a purely mathematical sense of simplicity which he takes pains to explain in a whole chapter. I know of no philosophical problem whose solution depends on such simplicity or such economy. The cues that mislead Goodman, as they misled Carnap, are taken from axiomatization in science. But these flaws do not affect the substance. Goodman, as I said before, is a philosopher. What, then, are the philosophical problems that haunt his dreams?

Goodman is primarily an ontologist; his main concern, in Quine's felicitous phrase, is with what there is. *The Structure of Appearance* is a strike for *nominalism,* a blow against the *existence of classes.* The words are old and familiar; the meanings he gives them are neither. To explain them will take me some time.

To the linguistic philosopher the symbols or, perhaps, certain kinds of symbols of the ideal language indicate what there is. What they name is what *exists.* On this we can all agree, if we do not probe too closely, as the proper method of recovering the core of traditional ontology. Up to now reconstructionists also agreed on two more specific points. We assumed that, relative details apart, the syntax of the ideal language was that of *Principia Mathematica.* And it was at least silently understood that the several signs of a syntactical category should be interpreted as referring to objects that belong, in the traditional sense of "ontological," to the same

[117]

ontological category. Goodman is a radical innovator in both respects. To explain anything radically new is difficult, particularly if the explanation must be brief. I shall try to meet the difficulty in the following manner. First I shall describe, very selectively and most succinctly, what I can so describe since it is more familiar, namely, an ideal language of the *Principia* type and, also, by means of it, my own more specific conception of ontology. This will provide me with the tools for both exposition and criticism of the most salient features of Goodman's system to which I shall, therefore, turn next. Finally, I shall attend to its constructional aspects, the choice of primitives, the definitions proposed, the controversial issues they involve.

*Principia* and related symbolisms distinguish between two kinds of signs, first among their primitives and then, derivatively, among other expressions. Called *logical* and *descriptive* the two kinds are, as everybody knows, exemplified by, say, 'and' and 'green'. As such the distinction is purely syntactical, though even in syntax it is not trivial, as it would be if it were merely a matter of enumeration. But it is also of prime epistemological significance, because of the double burden it is made to bear in philosophical discourse about the interpreted symbolism. For one, there is a clearly felt difference between 'and' and 'green' in that the latter designates something in a sense in which the former does not. One is tempted to say, and it has been said, that while the latter names a feature of the world, the former, not naming anything, is merely a piece of linguistic machinery we need to speak about the world. I think I know as well as the next man that these aphorisms do not stand up under dialectical probing. But then, the task is to explicate such felt differences in a manner that is tenable. That is part of what I mean by solving the classical problems. So we note here a suggestion for a distinction within ontology. Second, the two dichotomies logical-descriptive and *analytic-synthetic* are in syntax inextricably bound up with each other. Untenably but suggestively, analytic and synthetic truths have been called linguistic and factual respectively. What we thought was and I still think is the ideal language allows for an explication of the intended distinction.[6] But one may disagree on whether any such explication offered is tenable as well as satisfactory and yet agree that the distinction itself must be recovered. On this all reconstructionists were up to now agreed. Indeed, they thought the distinction of strategic importance.

The simple clause is analyzed into subject and predicate or, in the case of relations, subjects and (relational) predicate. The respective syntactical schemata, '$\varphi(a)$' and, for a binary relation, '$\rho(a,\beta)$', may be approximately transliterated by 'an entity has (exemplifies) a property' and 'two entities stand in (exemplify) a relation'. But this is not all there is to it. Consider the two sentences 'Henry is green' and 'green is a color', 'Henry' being the proper name of, say, a sense datum. These two sentences are not taken to exemplify the same syntactical schema, '$\varphi(a)$', but two different ones, say, '$f(x)$' and '$F(f)$'. This is, of course, the heart of the classical theory of types. Descriptive terms or, as one also says, descriptive constants divide not just into the two syntactical categories of subject and predicate but into a whole hierarchy, particulars, predicates, predicates of predicates, and so on. The same holds for the corresponding

[6] See my "Logical Atomism, Elementarism, and the Analysis of Value," *Philosophical Studies*, 2 (December, 1951), 85-92, and also pp. 243-54 of this book.

*variables,* 'x', 'f', 'F', etc., which serve the same function as, in idiomatic language, such words as 'thing', 'object', 'individual', 'property'. Variables are technically logical primitives, plausibly enough, if one considers that 'individual' and 'property' do not name anything in the sense in which both 'Henry' and 'green' do. Or, if you please, they refer not to any particular content of the world but, rather, to structural features of it, in the sense in which, vaguely though suggestively, analytical truths are called structural, or syntactical, or linguistic. Together with some logical constants the variables express quantification, 'for all' and 'for some'. Quantification is thus logical, which is again as it ought to be, for allness and someness do not belong to the furniture of the world in the same way as greenness and cathood. The felt difference is, to me, undeniable.

Now for *ontology.* In the broadest sense of fact it is undoubtedly a fact that a certain syntactical machinery is needed to speak about the world. That the ideal language contains certain syntactical categories, for instance, the several types represented by the several kinds of quantifiable variables is thus, in the broadest sense of ontology, an ontological statement. But there is again a clear-cut difference between what this statement expresses and what, if there were such a thing, a list of all descriptive terms needed would express. To speak about the world we certainly need both the syntax and the list. But the accent, as it were, is in the one case on speaking, in the other it is on the world. Only the second question exemplifies, therefore, what I properly mean by ontology and, incidentally, what I believe the classical philosophers meant. The example, however, the demand for a list of all descriptive terms, though the most obvious one, is not a good ontological question. Every philosopher must claim that he can say everything. So there could be no difference on this formulation of the issue between any two ontologies. A phenomenalist, for instance, must maintain that he may use the predicate 'physical object'; what distinguishes him is that he proposes to define it in terms of primitives which refer to quite a different kind of entities. Or, to choose a noncontroversial case, if 'green' and 'square' are among the primitive predicates, then the logical apparatus alone permits us to form the predicate exemplified by what is both green and square. I conclude that, *as to syntax,* the ontological problem is to determine the descriptive primitives. And even this is not a demand for a list but, rather, for the kind of syntactical categories, particulars, predicates, and so on, to which they belong. *As to interpretation,* which we remember takes place in ordinary discourse about the symbolism, the question is what kinds of entities the primitives name.

Two matters sometimes mistaken for ontological or, if you please, *two bad ontological questions* require a moment's attention. The first stems from an insufficient appreciation of the difference between the ideal symbolism and ordinary English. Philosophical statements as to what there is belong to the latter. Mentioned but not used in philosophical discourse, where they belong to our *explicanda,* they have no counterpart in the ideal language. Yet some philosophers believe that while the occurrence of a predicate in the ideal language does not commit us to the "existence of properties," we are so committed if the ideal language contains quantified predicate variables, because in this case we can by means of the "existential" quantifier in the ideal language say 'there is a property such that . . .'. What there is becomes then the question as to what quantified variables, or sometimes even what variables, occur in the ideal language. This makes no sense to me. Who admits a single primitive predicate admits properties among the building stones of his world. But we shall not be surprised to find this conception of ontology accompanied by the rejection of the distinction logical-descriptive. For, if one does not recognize the epistemological significance of this dichotomy, then the variables and the constants of a syntactical category designate equally, as it were.[7] The second bad question confuses ontology and science. There is a sense in which it makes sense to say that all there is are electrons and nuclei, distinguished from each other by relatively few properties and standing in spatio-temporal relations to each other. Twenty-five years ago this was indeed the best scientific information available. All it tells is what the descriptive primitives of an axiomatization of the science of the day may be. Even if it includes behavior science, such an axiomatization is obviously not the ideal language. Nor is it difficult to imagine what may result if the suggestions from these two mistaken conceptions of ontology combine: the idea of an ideal language that contains only particular descriptive constants, the corresponding variables with their quantifiers, a few primitive predicates of the first type, and no other variable. I add that when I speak here and later of such suggestions and of intellectual motives I do not intend to make either biographical or historical assertions. My concern is only with the structural analysis and interdependence of philosophical ideas.

The current meaning of nominalism is that of the British tradition. As to syntax, these nominalists did not, I take it,

_____

[7] See also my "A Note on Ontology," *Philosophical Studies*, 1 (December, 1950), 89-92, and also pp. 238-42 of this book, and, in reply, W. V. Quine, "Ontology and Ideology," *ibid.*, 2 (1951), 11-15.

intend to restrict the logical machinery of variables and quantifiers but, rather, to limit the descriptive primitives to particulars. As it is often put, they construed characters as the classes of individuals exemplifying them. As to interpretation, they made their particulars name sensa, the sort of thing named by the subjects of sense data statements. This is their phenomenalism, which need not detain us. With respect to 'individual', it is customary to call the referents of particulars *individuals,* the variables associated with them *individual variables.* Two intellectual motives for a nominalistic ontology deserve attention. One, subtler and perhaps also more remote, is the desire to avoid predication or, speaking nonsyntactically, exemplification, the puzzle of the One and the Many. As far as it is possible, this purpose is realized by avoiding primitive predicates. The other motive is to deny the "existence" of entities that are *abstract* and not *concrete* in that they are not in space and time or, at least, in time. Non-literally and after a fashion, we all understand what that means. Literally, I do not. Literally, a visual spot is no more *in* space than it is *in* a hue or a tone is *in* a pitch. Sensa exemplify spatial and temporal characters just as they exemplify hues and pitches. What goes for sensa goes *mutatis mutandis* for physical objects and events. This dissolves, and I use the strong term deliberately, the philosophical puzzles relevant for this study among those that revolve around individuality, concreteness, and abstractness. In the sense intended they have no core that needs to be recovered. The confusion they cause is structurally not unrelated to that between ontology and the scientist's search for his building stones. To venture one historical remark, they may even have a common root in the Democritean philosophy.

[123]

Now for the *existence of classes*. 'Class' is not as innocent a word as 'property'. The usual explications such as pointing at apples in a basket won't do, for there we avail ourselves of the shared character of being in the basket. One can, however, in this case, define a predicate of a peculiar kind. Assume, for the sake of the argument, that apples are individuals and that those in my basket, certainly a finite number, are called 'John', 'James', 'Richard', and so on. The predicate is then defined as being identical either with John or with James or with Richard, and so on. Its peculiarity can be stated in two ways. First, it contains no descriptive signs but the names, in particular no descriptive predicate. Second, one can build it by means of the logical apparatus alone whenever one is in possession of the names. Consider, next, that if we so choose we can also mention together, put into a linguistic basket as it were, Napoleon, the moon, and Olaf, my late lamented cat. Yet there is no predicate except such peculiar ones whose extension these three are. For, to be mentioned together is of course not, in a relevant sense, a property of the objects mentioned. This, I believe, is the core of the thesis that classes do not exist. The peculiarity of certain predicates, stated as I just stated it, is its complete explication. Russell's introduction of class signs as so-called incomplete symbols is nothing but a device for defining such "peculiar" predicates in cases where we cannot enumerate their extensions. 'Extension' itself is but another vague word whose explication is implicit in these remarks. Another point is more important. If one believes, as I do, that the ideal language has a certain property known as extensionality,[8]

---

[8] Some peculiarities of its semantic part do not, in my opinion, substantially affect the extensionality of the ideal language. Goodman does not commit himself on this point. But he, too, clearly favors extensionality.

then class and property symbols can be identified with each other, in a certain technical sense which I cannot stop to explain, and so can the corresponding variables. This may become the source of another bad suggestion. One may think that to deny the existence of classes one must exclude all predicate variables from the ideal language.

I am ready to state Goodman's thesis. He limits the logical apparatus of the ideal language to the lower functional calculus without predicate variables and therefore, of course, without predicate quantification. His primitives, besides that of sentential logic, are individual variables with their quantifiers, particulars, and a few predicates of the first type. This gives us immediately two reasons why he is not a nominalist in the current sense of the term. First, he restricts, unlike the nominalists, the logical apparatus. Second, he does not avoid primitive predicates or, if you please, the problem of the One and the Many. Third, we shall presently see that some of his undefined particulars refer to such characters as greenness and hotness. His is thus a purely logical thesis. This is not to say that it is not significant; it is even an ontological thesis, though only in the broader sense. I, for one, do not think that it is tenable. But criticism must wait until I am done with exposition. Olaf is an individual; so is one of his whiskers, one of my memory images of him, any character exemplified in any of these images, and, moving upward as it were, cathood. For the corresponding terms are all particulars. How, then, does he manage to say 'Olaf is a cat'? He introduces a primitive predicate which he transliterates by 'overlapping' and interprets by saying that any two individuals that have a "content" in common, such as two tones exemplifying the same pitch, do overlap. In terms of 'overlapping'

[125]

he defines several such predicates as 'is a part of'. Then he transcribes 'Olaf is a cat' by 'Olaf is a part of cat'.[9]

The possibility, however theoretical, of several ideal languages which are not merely rather obvious transforms of each other must be allowed.[10] On what grounds, then, can one reconstructionist criticize another, reject a symbolism as unsuited for the office of ideal language? There are three kinds of such grounds or reasons. I shall list them in ascending order of cogency and then arrange my criticisms of Goodman in the same order. First, one may hold that the problems the proposed symbolism is designed to solve—with the claim, implicit or explicit, that there is no other way of solving them—are either no problems or can be solved otherwise. Second, one may show that some real problems cannot be dealt with by means of the new symbolism. Arguments of these two kinds question the *adequacy* of the symbolism as a tool of analysis by means of philosophical discourse *about* it. The third kind challenges its *completeness,* pointing out that it cannot serve as ideal language because certain ordinary statements have no counterpart *in* it, are untranslatable, as it were.

Goodman finds the "existence" of anything but "individuals" unintelligible. Syntactically, he cures his puzzlement by admitting into his symbolism only individual variables. When it comes to interpretation he pays the price. We have seen that, if I may speak with some looseness, virtually everything is for him an individual. I have no quarrel with his terminological idiosyncrasy; I merely observe that under the

---

[9] A calculus of individuals was first published by Lesniewski as an axiomatization, without restriction of the logical apparatus, of the part-whole relationship.

[10] See my "Two Criteria for an Ideal Language," *Philosophy of Science,* 16 (1949), 71-74.

circumstances 'individual' means virtually nothing. Moreover, I believe to have shown or at least hinted by what was
said before I even mentioned Goodman's ideas that the
puzzlement caused by abstract [11] entities can be dissolved
and the problems revolving around them solved without that
mutilation of the logical machinery which is the heart of his
peculiar brand of nominalism. *Structurally,* the mistaken belief to the contrary is connected with what I have called
the two bad ontological questions; with the bad suggestion
that may be derived from the puzzle of the existence of
classes; and with the confusions about individuality, concreteness, and abstractness I mentioned among the intellectual motives of what we ordinarily call nominalism. But, to
repeat, I do not presume to write anybody's intellectual
biography. The philosophical discourse by which Goodman
supports his thesis I find unconvincing and often confusing.
It jars me to read that physical objects and classes of such are
events after all. Like 'individual', 'event' is apparently a
good word. Events, I take it, are concrete [11] and intelligible.
I understand only one meaning of 'event'. A physical event,
say, is what happens to or among physical objects and is,
relative to the scale the discourse implies, of rather limited
duration. Any other meaning and, in particular, its significance for philosophical analysis I would have to be
shown.

Goodman explicitly rejects the dichotomies logical-descriptive and analytic-synthetic as devoid of epistemological significance. For him there is nothing there to be explicated. I
disagree. But Goodman's opinion occurs only as an incidental
remark. So it could be that though he himself would not care

[11] I use this term and some others as they are ordinarily used, not
with the special meanings Goodman provides for them.

[127]

to do it, these distinctions and what depends on them could be recovered in his system. I shall show in two cases that this is not so. *First:* The proposed symbolism docs, of course, contain a fragment of logic. With respect to this fragment the distinctions can be made. But if they are made, in the only manner of which I know, then 'overlapping', 'being a part of', and so on, become descriptive predicates. Thus the syntactical distinction between 'Olaf is a cat' and 'Romeo loves Juliet' disappears. Non-syntactically speaking, no difference is left between such relationships as loving and the "relation" between two entities one of which exemplifies the other. Yet the latter is what the scholastics called *secundæ intentionis.* The felt difference is to me undeniable. In the *Principia* language exemplification appears, accordingly, not as a relation but as predication, expressed by such structural devices as juxtaposition. If it is forced into the symbolism itself then it becomes, as one would expect, a defined non-descriptive relation. Besides, Goodman, since he admits primitive predicate symbols, also has exemplification and predication to deal with. Plato was the first, Bradley perhaps not the last who paid the price for neglecting these points. *Second:* Where we speak of the class consisting of the individuals Peter and Paul, Goodman speaks of the individual which is their sum and constructs its name as a descriptive function. But in order to insure the existence of this sum, that is, the availability of the symbol that names it, he must introduce a postulate that turns out to be synthetic, at least within the fragment of logic he admits. Put in the usual manner which, though it is not as precise as one can make it, is very suggestive, that amounts to this. Even if we know the names of all the members of a class, it is still a fact in the narrower sense, not just a feature of the linguistic machinery, that we can speak about the class. The class puzzle or, rather, a sort of converse of it has come home to roost.

The next criticism is, perhaps, the most difficult to answer. Some efforts to the contrary notwithstanding, it seems extremely unlikely that one could ever with a logical apparatus so severely restricted reconstruct those parts of arithmetic which are now based on predicate quantification. The philosophical analyst's duty toward these lovely growths is that of the tree surgeon, not that of the lumberjack. Goodman himself is fully aware of this defect of his symbolism. Yet there is a distinct finitist flavor in what he says about arithmetic, in the sense in which finitism was an issue when Brouwer's ideas first created a stir. The point seems to be that since we are acquainted with but a finite number of individuals, our arithmetic, if we want to be empirical about it, had better be finitistic. I should like to use this opportunity to unburden myself of a remark that has long been on my mind. The reconstruction of arithmetic rests to a considerable extent on the analytic truth Russell called the axiom of infinity. But one may doubt whether there is an infinite number of individuals in the world. Thus the foundations of arithmetic are sometimes thought to be dubious to this extent. All this seems utterly wrongheaded to me. The truths of arithmetic do not depend on whether there is enough chalk in the world to write them down. Nor does one need to be a technical expert in the foundations of mathematics (I certainly am not) to know that if quantified predicate variables are used the critical axiom can be written down within the ideal language with a very moderate amount of chalk. And these variables with their operators, being logical signs, do not designate anything. Thus the dichotomy Goodman rejects once again achieves an important clarification.

[129]

I turn now briefly to the constructional side of the system. The names of sense qualities are among its primitive particulars; the names of the sensa which exemplify these qualities Goodman proposes to construct. He begins by introducing a further primitive relation, togetherness, which turns out to be coexemplification. Two qualities, say, a pitch and a loudness, are together if and only if there is a tone of both this pitch and this loudness. (We meet here another logical relation in descriptive disguise.) The properties with which togetherness is axiomatically endowed circumvent very cleverly certain difficulties that were the downfall of Carnap's *Aufbau*.[12] Even so, Goodman must, in order to achieve his goal, introduce some very peculiar primitives, namely, places in space and time. A sensum then becomes, roughly speaking, the togetherness of what we ordinarily call its qualities with the two qualities of being a certain duration and a certain place, or at a certain place, I hardly know how to put it. Here I can only say what Goodman says about classes, that this is completely unintelligible to me. I am not acquainted with such qualities; so I cannot as an empiricist admit their names among the primitives of the ideal language. Or, as Locke would have said, with such a one I cannot talk. To be in the center of my visual field is no more a character of the spot that happens to be there than its being mentioned by me or, for that matter, its being perceived by me.[13] Goodman might have indicated that in cer-

---

[12] Goodman devotes a whole chapter to a very lucid exposition and critique of Carnap's *Aufbau*. Brilliant as this chapter is, it contains nothing that would surprise any serious student of Carnap or, for that matter, Carnap himself.

[13] Moore's classical critique of *esse est percipi* comes to mind at this point. Empiricists are in danger of committing this sort of error again and again as long as they do not recognize the irreducibility of the act. See my "A Positivistic Metaphysics of Consciousness," *Mind*, 54 (1945), 193-226.

[130]

tain chapters of *An Inquiry into Meaning and Truth* Russell tried very much the same thing with very much the same means.[14] Russell's purpose in doing this was to solve the puzzles and problems of substance and of the solipsistic suggestion of a phenomenalistic reconstruction. These must and can be solved by other means. What he and Goodman would have solved, if their constructions were otherwise admissible, is the puzzle of particularity, which hinges on the occurrence of descriptive primitives which are, as Peirce would have said, purely indexical. But then, the inadmissible qualities they introduce are nothing but indices put up in the world, as it were, in the disguise of characters.

There are further constructions which fill a goodly portion of the book. Their cleverness will, I am sure, delight the formalists. But this is hardly the place to mention them.

It must be clear by now that to my mind, as far as philosophical significance is concerned, Goodman's results are not commensurate with his labors. In this respect *The Structure of Appearance* belongs with the more extreme productions of formalism. But such, alas, is the nature of philosophy that this opinion is not incompatible with the one I expressed at the beginning, that the book is impressive and in many ways admirable. There is a wealth of details some of which strike me as ingenious or even profound. Also, the author has a style of his own and often finds *le mot juste*. What he says is not always clear to me, but it is always clear what he says. These are rare virtues. More important still, he deals earnestly and singlemindedly with fundamental issues and only with fundamental issues. So he addresses himself, like Stendhal, to the happy few.

[14] For criticism see my "Russell on Particulars," *Philosophical Review*, 56 (January, 1947), 59-72, and also pp. 197-214 of this book.

# BODIES, MINDS, AND ACTS *

EACH OF US knows that there are bodies or physical objects. Each of us also knows that there are minds, his own and those of others, each associated with one of those physical objects he calls human bodies, his own and those of others. These two things we all know beyond all reasonable doubt. Philosophers erred, I believe, when they made it their business either to defend or to controvert what everybody thus knows in a commonsensical manner. What sets us apart and sets us our task is this. We also know that if certain crucial pieces of common sense are subjected to dialectical probing, they yield many questions of which common sense never dreams. The task is to answer these questions and to answer them so that the puzzles and perplexities which usually attend them disappear.

The so-called mind-body problem is a whole group of such questions and puzzles concerning the existence and nature of minds, of bodies, and the connections that do or do not obtain between the ones and the others. Descartes was the first who saw them. Or, at least, he was the first to

* This is the opening paper of a symposium on the mind-body problem read at the meeting of the American Philosophical Association at Ann Arbor in May, 1952. The editor of *Philosophy and Phenomenological Research*, where it was originally scheduled to appear, has kindly permitted it to be withdrawn in order to be included in this volume.

group them together, to bring them to the fore, and to state them in a manner that influenced all later thought profoundly. If one says that the mind-body problem has been solved, I shall, therefore, take him to assert that this group of questions and puzzles has been dealt with to his satisfaction by the methods of philosophical analysis. Again, to deny that there is still a mind-body problem may mean just this, namely, that it has been solved. But there are nowadays not a few who, when they say that there is no longer a mind-body problem mean something very different, namely, that those questions and puzzles have become obsolete, as it were, by virtue of extraneous information. We may supposedly dismiss them out of hand, need no longer subject them to philosophical analysis. As one would expect, the extraneous information adduced is scientific, psychological or physiological. Against this I shall affirm that philosophical questions require philosophical answers; that in this sense our problem is not and never will be obsolete; and that those holding the opposite view merely advocate, in a disguised form and without realizing it, a solution which we know is inadequate. Scientism, as always, proves to be an unexamined metaphysics. As to whether an adequate solution has been found, I shall maintain that while our tradition contains many valuable partial analyses, none has been produced during the course of classical philosophy, that is, before the positivistic revolution which took place in this century. Finally, I also believe that an adequate solution now exists. It is high time, then, that I explain what I mean by an adequate solution. To explain this amounts, for me, to stating what I consider the proper method of philosophical analysis. Fortunately, this conception of philosophy is by now not unfamiliar. So I can be very concise.

The proper method of philosophizing consists in the construction of a formalism that has two properties. First, if its undefined signs are taken to stand for certain words of ordinary language, say, of English, then one can by means of it in principle say everything. Second, one can, by discoursing in ordinary English about it, solve all philosophical problems. Such a formalism is called an ideal language. To satisfy ourselves, as well as we may, that any one proposed actually is the ideal language is, of course, an unending task. Instead of rejecting the classical issues, this method frees them, both questions and answers, of that air of absurdity which was the cause of the positivistic revolution and which is due to their flying, or seeming to fly, in the face of common sense. This, by the way, holds also for answers that are probably false, for to be false is not the same as to be absurd in this sense. I shall not in this paper explicitly defend the method; I shall apply it to the problem at hand. So it may, as it should, be judged by its fruits.

Common sense tells us that there are both minds and bodies. Yet some of the classical philosophers did not see how they could consistently hold that anything but minds existed. Others found themselves reduced to the complementary nonsense that only bodies exist. Still others held on to both kinds of existents but met absurdity, and that is as I see it defeat, in trying to account for whatever truck the two have with each other. It will be seen that I just followed the idiom in using the clause 'there are' and the verb 'exist' synonymously. So did the classical philosophers. Thus they did not notice that when they asked themselves whether there are both minds and bodies, they really discussed whether both existed, in a very special meaning of 'exist' which is anything but synonymous with that of 'there are'.

[134]

This, I believe, is the root of their difficulties. I shall now do two things. First I shall distinguish between the two meanings involved. Then, taking two of the classical solutions, I shall show how the distinction helps one to understand what they assert as well as the criticisms that have been directed against them. As for my method of exposition, I shall proceed as if all philosophers had set out deliberately, as, of course, they did not, to specify the ideal language.

Among the signs of this language there are two important divisions. A sign is either *logical* or *descriptive;* and it is either *undefined* or *defined.* 'And' and 'or' are logical; 'green' and 'mermaid' are descriptive; the latter certainly is defined, since there is no way of acquiring its meaning by being acquainted with a mermaid. Both distinctions are needed to understand what is traditionally called ontology. And this we must understand since the heart of our problem, the mind-body problem, is ontological. Ontology searches for an inventory of whatever there is in the world. But logical terms evidently do not name any such thing in the same sense in which descriptive ones do. The descriptive terms are the inventory of what there is or, like mermaids, could be. But in a sense we all agree on what there is or, like mermaids, could be. To interpret ontology as an attempt to construct, in some fashion, a catalogue of all descriptive terms does not, therefore, enable us to understand the disagreements among the classical ontologists. This suggests the following interpretation. When these philosophers asked themselves what existed, they really asked for the entities that were named by their undefined descriptive terms. For how, I wonder, could they otherwise be sane and differ. Some finer distinctions may be drawn. Undefined descriptive terms are either particulars or universals. Some used 'exist' so that, if they spoke our language, they would have to insist that only individuals, that is, what is named by particulars, exist. But I shall make no use of these subtleties. To sum up, what exists, in this special sense of 'exist', is an ontological building stone or simple. Or, as the Wittgenstein of the *Tractatus* with his very restrictive conception of the ideal language might have put it, what thus exists is not stated in the ideal language; it merely shows itself in a catalogue of its undefined descriptive terms.

If this is the key to 'exist', what is the proper reading of 'there are'? How about such statements as 'There are coffee-houses in Paris' or 'There are (no) mermaids', statements everybody makes and which are customarily called existential statements? Their mechanics we have all learned from Russell. 'There are' is a logical phrase and what is asserted is that there is something which may or may not be an individual, of a certain kind, which may or may not be undefined. The gist of the matter, as I see it, is that these statements have no "ontological" significance. They are ordinary nonphilosophical statements of fact. In the nature of things they are often made before we know whether they are true or false; for this reason they are sometimes spoken of as existential hypotheses.

Now we can make at least partial sense out of the classical solutions of our problem. We may, for instance, take a materialist to assert that while there are, of course, both minds and bodies, only bodies exist. The contemporary form of materialism is the philosophical interpretation, or, as I would insist, misinterpretation of the behavioristic conception of psychology. This conception is also of great intrinsic interest for our problem. Psychology is merely a science among sci-

[136]

ences; so surely it cannot answer philosophical questions. But science is a most powerful extension of common sense; so we should pay attention to it. Behaviorism has not convinced me that the materialistic solution is adequate. On the other hand, I know of no better way to convince anybody of how very bad certain bad arguments against materialism are. In other words, I agree with the behavioristic psychologist; I disagree with the philosophical behaviorist. I shall next, in my own way, state the views of the latter. This will also allow me to do justice, very briefly and incidentally, to the claims of the former. For what is clear and, as in this case, not too technical, can always be stated briefly.

Some proponents of philosophical behaviorism call it physicalism. It seems to me we could do nicely without either name; *linguistic materialism* indicates quite accurately what the position involves, for these philosophers abstain as pointedly as anybody from ontological statements in the old style. So they do not say what is absurd. They merely claim that there is an ideal language whose particulars are the names of bodies. This, though I believe it to be false, is at least not absurd. However, it is not quite accurate to say that the physicalists' individuals are physical objects. They are narrow slices of the temporal history of physical objects. I permit myself this simplification in order to dodge the traditional problem of substance, because it does not, as far as I can see, affect my argument.

We may assume that color words such as 'green' are among the undefined descriptive predicates of the ideal language $L$ which the linguistic materialists propose. These are, by the rules of the game, the names of physical colors; the individuals of which they can be predicated are bodies, not such mental things as sensa or percepts. It follows that one cannot simply use this 'green' to say in $L$ that Jones has a green sense datum. Yet this is quite a commonsensical thing to say. People sometimes do see as green objects which they know or later learn are of a different color. This alone establishes sense data as more than philosophical moonshine. So the linguistic materialist ought to be able to speak about them in his ideal language. His solution is to construct in $L$ a defined predicate, 'having-a-green-sense-datum', such that the sentence $M$ obtained by combining it with the name in $L$ of the physical object Jones becomes what is called an adequate reconstruction of 'Jones has a green sense datum'. What holds for this simple English sentence holds, of course, for all others that mention anything mental, be it what we ordinarily call a content, an act, a state, or a quality of a mind. From 'having-a-green-sense-datum', for instance, a not too difficult definitional line leads to two further defined predicates, 'visual-sense-datum' and 'vert' which can, syntactically correctly, be predicated of the same kind of nonindividual entities. Why I have chosen 'vert' instead of 'green' is, I trust, obvious. The upshot of all this is clear. The existence of minds is for the linguistic materialist a problem in definitional reconstruction. The various criticisms of this solution all make use of one or more of three arguments. Two of these I believe to be invalid. The third, which I shall take up last, I believe is valid and refutes the position.

The first argument grants that an adequate definitional reconstruction can, at least in principle, be achieved. Since $L$ then contains not only $M$ but also the counterparts of such existential statements as 'There are sense data' or even 'There are minds', the linguistic materialist can say what common sense says. But, the argument insists, this is merely a verbal trick. The linguistic materialist does not mean what common sense means when it says that Jones has a green sense datum. Calling *P* the expansion of *M* which results from the elimination of all defined terms, I shall try to state the argument more fully. To assert *M* is, by definition, to assert *P*. But *P* asserts merely that Jones displays the behavior that accompanies his having a green sense datum. Let me call *H* the sentence 'If *P* then there is something green'. What common sense means is, according to the argument, asserted by *H; H* being a synthetic statement and the 'green' in its second clause the undefined name of a character exemplified by sense data. If that is, as I believe, the correct explication of the argument, then I have in one instance proved my case. Linguistic materialism is charged, not with denying that there are minds, but with failing to establish that they exist, in that very special sense of 'exist' I have indicated. To this extent the argument is, therefore, without merit. Sometimes it is accompanied by the suggestion that the linguistic materialists add *H* as an "existential hypothesis" to *L*. The linguistic materialists usually reply that *H* is "meaningless." If they mean by this that it is nonsense to say that Jones sometimes has, quite literally, a green sense datum, then they are patently wrong. But they are as patently right when we take them to mean that *L* cannot, by the very rules of their game, contain anything like *H*. The correct objection is, therefore, not against making an existential statement but that *H* cannot be a statement of *L*, since the particulars of *L* name, by agreement, bodies, not sense data. *Epiphenomenalism* is a "solution" of the mind-body problem which officially admits both kinds of particulars or, if you please, individuals. Yet, I believe the logic of their position, aptly indicated by its name, makes the epiphenomenalists the predecessors of those linguistic materialists who injudiciously accept the suggestion of "adding" H to L. The so-called *double-aspect theories*, which some time ago caused some stir in America, follow the same pattern, except that there the emphasis on the physiological correlates of mental states is even stronger than in classical epiphenomenalism. But this merely adds to the farrago. I do not wish to imply, though, that physiologists can ever go wrong when they speak, as it were, epiphenomenalistically. As long as they stick to their field this is merely common sense or, if I may so express myself, scientific common sense. The unforgivable sin consists in taking it philosophically, that is, mistaking it for the answer to the philosophical questions and puzzles it yields under a little dialectical probing.

The second argument attacks the idea of definitional reconstruction. According to the argument, this reconstruction on which the case of the linguistic materialists, such as it is, depends, exists only in their imaginations. It has not with any detail been carried out in fact; it cannot be carried out in principle. The philosophers who make the most of this argument are the various holists and emergentists. To see how weak it is one merely has to consider that everything we know about other minds we know, in fact, from watching the bodies which, as one says, they inhabit. Scientific or psychological behaviorism is, with two qualifications, the view that the reconstruction can in principle be achieved. As to the qualifications, for one, psychologists do not, and, since they are not philosophers, need not worry about the formalization of L. Again, they do not and, not being philosophers, need not assert that L is the ideal language. Scientific behaviorism is not only logically sound; its success as a working hypothesis for psychology is fairly impressive, though perhaps not as dazzling as Watson first expected.

[140]

Long the whipping boy of many philosophers, it recently received support from unexpected quarters. Professor Ryle, in his book, *The Concept of Mind,* bends all his linguistic skill and psychological acuity to the task of a behavioristic reconstruction or, as he probably prefers to call it, analysis of mental terms. One may even wonder whether he is not a linguistic materialist, except, of course, that he makes no use of the ideal language device. What saves him from this horrible fate is that he cannot quite bring himself to deny the existence of sense data. What lures him to the abyss of materialism, linguistic or otherwise, is this. Very often, when we say that somebody is gay or sad, that he knows something, that he hopes or fears something, there is nothing in his mind that answers to these words. All such statements mean, therefore, *in such cases* is either that the person behaves in a certain way or that he is of a certain disposition, that is, would under certain conditions behave in certain ways. I quite agree. Only, I don't think that this is so *in all cases.* One more remark. I think Professor Ryle would be the first to insist that his analysis, for all its relative detail, achieves its goal only in principle. But I also infer from some things he has recently said that he is now rather sceptical about the idea of an ideal language, partly because it is not really a language but merely the schema of one, a reconstruction in principle. Yet, what is meat for the goose is meat for the gander.

The third argument, which I believe is valid, holds that the linguistic materialists' schema cannot serve as ideal language. In order to show that, it is fortunately not necessary to point out all the deficiencies that bar $L$ from this status. It will suffice to discuss the one that falls within the scope of our problem. Assume that somebody called Smith wants to say that he himself, not Jones, has a green sense datum. The only sentence available to him in $L$ for this purpose is $M'$, which he obtains from $M$ by replacing in it the name of Jones' body by that of his own, Smith's. This way of schematizing what is ordinarily expressed by 'I have a green sense datum' and, similarly, the expressions of other experiences of one's self, is thought to be inadequate. I agree. But I also think that the reasons are not always seen clearly or stated correctly. The sound core of the argument is that $M$ and $M'$ are too similar to express adequately the two dissimilar meanings involved; not always clearly seen or stated are the respects in which the two meanings do and do not differ. When I say once that I have a green sense datum and once that Jones does, I mean exactly the same thing, in the sense in which I mean the same thing when I say that two objects, with only one of which I happen to be acquainted, exemplify the same character. In this respect there is no difference between my mind and others and the similarity between $M$ and $M'$ is a virtue rather than a fault. This is why those who, because supposedly there is such a difference, accept $M$ but reject $M'$ make no sense to me. The real difference lies, in a manner of speaking, not in what we know but in how we know it. $L$ ought to be able to express that in Jones' case there is something with which I am not acquainted, of a kind with which I am acquainted if I have ever had a green sense datum. Thus $M$ ought to contain an existential clause where $M'$ does not. In this respect $M$ and $M'$ ought to be, but in fact are not, dissimilar.

I turn next to another of the major classical "solutions." Treating it, too, in its linguistic version in order to avoid absurdity, I should consistently call it linguistic mentalism, or, perhaps, idealism, since it may be taken to establish that while there are, of course, bodies as well as minds, only minds exist, in the very special sense of 'exist' I have indicated. But I shall instead make use of a current phrase and speak of *linguistic phenomenalism*. Eventually I shall reject linguistic phenomenalism in the form in which it is now most frequently held but, again, not because its ideal language has no particulars that name bodies. As before, I shall first state the position, then show where it does well, then where it falls down. Finally, I shall suggest a modification that does yield what I believe is the ideal language. This, of course, I shall not show; I shall merely try to show that it allows for an adequate reconstruction of what common sense knows about minds and bodies. In the course of this I shall have to say something about acts and about the so-called interaction of minds and bodies, which will also give me an opportunity for some observations about the dualistic ones among the classical solutions.

The particulars of the schema $L'$ which the linguistic phenomenalists propose as the ideal language name such things as sense data and elementary feelings and, I note for a later occasion, nothing else; its predicates such as, say, 'green' name characters exemplified by these individuals and, again, nothing else. In a schema of this kind, the existence of bodies becomes a problem in definitional reconstruction. This is, of course, the sort of thing Berkeley first attempted in his own way. Whether it can be done adequately is now again the subject of much debate. I happen to believe that it can, in principle, that is, within limitations compatible with the purposes of an ideal language. But since this thesis is now for the most part attacked and defended on grounds that have nothing to do with the mind-body issue, I shall, for the sake of the argument, assume that

[143]

an adequate reconstruction is possible. My own mind, I shall for the present also assume, offers no difficulties. But how about others? This, I believe, is the area where the position does well. We notice, first, that $L'$ contains the reconstruction $P'$ of the sentence I called $P$, for we can, by assumption, reconstruct statements about physical objects. The important difference is that $L'$ also contains $H'$, the statement corresponding to the existential hypothesis which, as we saw, could not be expressed in $L$. $H'$ reads, of course, 'If $P'$ then there is something green'; 'green' being the undefined name of a sense quality and the individual possessing it, mentioned though not named in $H'$, a sense datum, namely Jones'. All this follows from the rules of the game $L'$. The reconstruction thus reflects adequately the piece of common sense which we express by saying that when Jones displays a certain behavior he has, literally, a sense datum. Furthermore, the two statements expressing in $L'$ that Jones and I each have a green sense datum show the proper similarities and dissimilarities which, we remember, were lacking in $M$ and $M'$. Speaking about my own datum (though, I note for later reference, not saying that I have it) I say in $L'$ 'This is green'; speaking about Jones' I say 'There is something green'. This leads me to two objections that are often raised against linguistic phenomenalism. It can, I believe, dispose of both.

The first of these objections points out that nobody ever has, literally, anybody else's experiences and goes on from there to assert that it is, therefore, meaningless to speak about them. Or, perhaps, it is self-contradictory. The objection is really very confused, so confused that I don't quite know how to put it to its best advantage. The fact from which it starts and which is, indeed, beyond reasonable doubt, can be stated in $L'$. I don't know what else we can be expected to do about it. Furthermore, $H'$ is in $L'$ obviously a synthetic sentence and not either analytic or self-contradictory. This completes the explication of what could reasonably be meant by saying, as some philosophers do, that our never literally sharing experiences is a contingent fact. Finally, $H'$ is certainly meaningful in that it contains no undefined descriptive term naming anything with which I am not myself acquainted. The second objection is over-impressed with another fact. There is no evidence that would refute a class of statements $H''$ obtained by "inverting Jones' spectrum," if I may hint thus briefly at what is after all a very familiar idea. Why, then, the objection goes, not assert $H''$ instead of $H'$? How do we know which of the two, if any, is true? The answer is, very simply, that in a sense we don't. So everything is as it should be.

On bodies linguistic phenomenalism does not do as well. This is not to say that many criticisms that have been directed against it and its classical predecessors on this score may not be disregarded. Properly analyzed, these criticisms merely prove once more that philosophers trying to establish that there are bodies really want to show that they exist, in our special sense of 'exist'. This criterion of adequacy we may safely reject. But there is another objection that cannot be dismissed as lightly. It seems at first sight that $L'$ does not contain two different sentences to express what common sense distinguishes by saying once 'This is green', once 'I see (know) that this is green', or, similarly, 'This is a tree' and 'I believe that (know that, doubt whether) this is a tree'. If this suspicion is justified, then an important piece of common sense cannot be expressed in $L'$; nor can one, by talking about $L'$, deal adequately with the cluster of questions and puzzles that make up the traditional realism-

[145]

idealism problem—two good reasons why $L'$ could not be the ideal language. The point is, of course, G. E. Moore's. Put in this manner it is, I think, still a good point. I turn next to two attempts that have been made to express the two different kinds of meanings by two different kinds of statements in an unmodified $L'$. Neither has, in my opinion, succeeded.

The first attempt takes its cue from so-called analytical introspection. The idea is that if we analyze in this manner what is in our minds when we say 'This is green' and 'I know that this is green' respectively, we shall in the second case find what we find in the first and, in addition, something else. This something else is supposedly all kinds of sensations, mostly kinaesthetic, and feeling tones, the sort of thing for which $L'$ does in principle provide the particulars and undefined predicates to talk about. A sentence $B$ stating this excess finding may, therefore, be formed in $L'$; and, conjoined with 'This is green' to '(This is green) and $B$' taken as the expression of the second of the two meanings involved. Similarly in other cases. The logic is beyond reproach. The trouble is that my introspection yields no such thing; nor does, I am convinced, anybody else's. We could, therefore, not know what the terms in $B$ mean and would no longer understand $L'$. The requirement which this introduces, that we must be acquainted with what the undefined descriptive terms of the ideal language name, is, by the way, not an a priori principle of "empiricism," whatever that means; though I believe it is the most reasonable explication of that much overworked word, empiricism. The fewer such labels, except as something to be explicated by our method, the better. I simply find, then, that a schema that does not fulfill the requirement raises more questions than one can answer

[146]

by means of it. So it cannot be the ideal language. The second attempt is, as it were, the behavioristic version of the first. $L'$ being stronger than $L$ in that all statements about physical objects can be reconstructed in it, one can in $L'$ form the two presumably different statements $P'$ and $P_1'$ which correspond to the behavioristic accounts of Jones' once seeing something and once knowing that he sees it. Since such accounts contain descriptions of what Jones actually says or under certain conditions would say in these circumstances, they should indeed be different. In this manner the difference between the two meanings can, therefore, in Jones' case as well as in my own, be expressed in $L'$. But we have learned from the examination of linguistic materialism that this is not sufficient. So this attempt, too, fails.

The modification of $L'$ which I shall propose aims at an adequate expression of the sentences that contain such verbs as 'knowing' or, if you please, at an ideal language that can adequately speak of what the tradition knows as mental acts. To introduce this proposal properly, some preparation is necessary.

So far I seem to have taken it for granted that there are minds, provided only that there are sense data and other equally minute mental things. Many think that this is as uncautious as it would be for a geologist who has discovered one little bone to take it for granted that he can from it reconstruct the whole animal. Some philosophers, Brentano and probably G. E. Moore among them, even hold that this bone does not belong to that animal. For they do not consider sense data mental objects. Be that as it may, most champions of mind conceive it as a continuant, called Self, that stands with other things, be they its contents or physical objects or propositions or what not, in the peculiar nexus

[147]

of the act. Anything so complex probably cannot be named by the particulars of a schema that could serve as ideal language. Yet I shall again, as once before, dodge the problem of substance; for I don't think the simplification affects my argument. Even the difficulties of the dualistic solutions of our problem can, I believe, be explained by assuming that the Selves of which the philosophers who advocated them spoke can be named by particulars of the ideal languages which, according to my expository fiction, they proposed. The heart of the matter is that selflike and bodylike particulars cannot side by side live in the same linguistic universe without begetting absurdity. (They do, of course, after a fashion, in ordinary English; and this is one of the reasons why it can get us into philosophical trouble.) If they do, there are two possibilities. Either there are, as seems more than plausible, or there are not some fundamental transactions, named by undefined descriptive terms, into which Selves and bodies sometimes enter with each other. Assuming there are none, one is eventually led up the tree of absurdity by being forced to accept some version of a world split between appearance and a reality we could never know. If, on the other hand, there are such transactions, then their occurrence should make a causal difference to what happens in the world in a manner in which, according to the common-sense core of epiphenomenalism, there is no such difference. This, I am sure I need not further explain, is the predicament of interaction. It is equally obvious that the two monistic solutions escape at least this sort of perplexity. But there is still another difficulty with which the proponents of the second alternative or, to call them by their traditional name, the presentative realists, must cope. They must try to answer such absurd questions as where in physical space the oblong data which a square surface sometimes presents to minds are located. These quibbles, no matter how ingenious they may be in themselves, leave me with a stale taste. It appears, then, that while we may need acts, we cannot countenance agents in the sense of the traditional solutions.

To judge by my own experience, Hume was right when he reported that his inward gaze encountered no such thing as a Self or knower. Yet, I am convinced that he denied too much, for, unlike him, I do sometimes encounter knowings and, similarly, the other propositional attitudes, as the acts are now also called. But, I repeat, I find things known without finding anything that knows them, just as I find green things without finding anything that greens them. The inference from knowings to knowers is one of the illusions produced by ordinary grammar. So we need not, like those to whom it seemed inescapable, close our eyes to the act because we cannot brook an agent. At least one of the propositional attitudes—I shall call it knowing—I cannot further analyze introspectively. *L''*, the ideal language I propose, contains in addition to the undefined terms of *L'* at least one more to name this introspective simple. Again, I should like to make it clear that in this I follow no principle, unexamined or unacknowledged, that compels me to introduce into the ideal schema an undefined term for every character which I cannot decompose introspectively. I simply find that, as we saw, talking in and about *L''* one can handle the existence of physical objects adequately while this cannot be done with *L'*. On the other hand, it may well be that a schema that does not contain at least one undefined term for each of the various kinds of introspective simples cannot be used to solve all philosophical problems. I believe, for

[149]

instance, that the tangle of questions and puzzles known as ethics cannot be put straight without at least one undefined term naming a specific character that is also introspectively simple. But with this further addition, of which naturally I shall say no more in this paper, the descriptive inventory of the ideal language is, in my opinion, complete.

It is not enough to say that 'knowing' is added to $L'$ and let it go at that. The new term must be given syntactical status. Is it a nonrelational predicate, a relation, or perhaps, something else? It may have been noticed that not once in this paper have I spoken of the "relations" between minds and bodies. The purpose of the circumlocutions by means of which I achieved this feat was not merely to avoid suggesting a knower. There is a further peculiarity. The classical philosophers who were aware of it set the acts apart by saying that they and they alone "intend their contents" or that the latter "intentionally inexist" in the former. In ordinary grammar the peculiarity shows itself in the appearance of dependent clauses. 'Knowing green' may always be the name of a dispositional property. 'Knowing (it is known) *that* this is green', a sentence I shall henceforth call $K$, refers sometimes neither to behavior nor to anything mental other than what is literally expressed by $K$ itself. But to transfer $K$ directly to $L''$, is to introduce not only a new undefined term but also a new syntactical category. To see that, consider that its other undefined terms are all either particulars or predicates, nonrelational or relational. And a predicate combined with a sentence yields gibberish such as, in the nonrelational case, 'Red (that) this is green'. It does not, as 'knowing' in ordinary grammar, yield another sentence. Once more, there is no a priori reason why one should not thus enrich the syntax of the ideal language. Only, the consequences of this step may be expected to be rather momentous. One of them falls within the scope of our problem; so I shall examine it. The sentence 'This is green', which I shall henceforth call $G$, is contained in $K$ in the same sense in which it is contained in 'This is green and that is red'. This explicates what the classical philosophers meant when they considered knowing something a complex fact, that is, a fact that contains at least one other fact as an ingredient. The perplexities to which this view leads in the cases of memory, of other knowledge of the past, and of imagination are notorious. I know of no way out of them. To transfer $K$ directly into $L''$ is to take the linguistic side of this road to absurdity. The only way out is to construe 'knowing' in $L''$ as a nonrelational predicate and the name of what is known as a particular. This is, specifically, my proposal. I shall not go into any details here. But I think I should take up the one objection that has some color and is of a philosophical nature. It claims that we are already by the rules of our game committed to a name of what $K$ asserts to be known and that this name is $G$, which is a sentence, not a particular. Let it be granted for the sake of the argument that sentences are, in some broad sense of the term, names. Even so, a sentence is not the name of the awareness which, as it occurs, it expresses or represents. What it names, if it names anything, is the content of this awareness. What must occur in $K$ is the name of the awareness it mentions. $G$ represents this awareness, but it is not its name.

One more remark in conclusion. Selves play a rather conspicuous role in common sense, as the personal pronouns do in the language we speak. Having got rid of 'I' where it makes trouble, I may, therefore, be expected to put it back where it doesn't. My answer is in substance the same Locke

[151]

gave. I should say that even in a schematic reconstruction, which is all we need and can hope for, the expression for 'I' is very complex, just as the expressions for such phrases as 'this stone' and 'that tree', which serve us as proper names of physical objects, are very complex. The former must indeed be more complex than the latter, since it contains not only references to the physical object that is my body but also further ones, to bodily sensations, to feelings, and, crucially, to acts of knowing and remembering. The case of the other personal pronouns is analogous. I should think that most of what needs to be said on these matters can safely be left to the scientists. Some of it, though, may prove of philosophical interest. The task is, fortunately, unending.

# REMARKS ON REALISM *

POSITIVISTS and phenomenalists of all sorts maintain, and long have maintained, some variant of the following thesis concerning the existence of physical objects: Such statements as 'There is (exists) now a wall behind my back' are synonymous with a class of statements of which the following is representative 'If I shall turn my head (have certain kinaesthetic experiences), then I shall also have the visual experience called 'seeing a wall'.' This amounts to proposing what many of us call a philosophical analysis of 'exist' or, more precisely, of one meaning of 'exist'; for the thesis implies that this verb, in the sense in which we use it when we say 'This wall exists', is dispensable in the sense of being definable. Realists, who oppose the thesis, hold that 'exist', in the sense mentioned, is what I would call an undefined descriptive predicate; and then they go on to recommend that instead of defining existence in terms of what we (shall) see, we had better say that we shall, if we turn, see a wall because there is a wall (and because we have put ourselves in a position to perceive it). Thus one could say, perhaps, that the realists wish to convert the positivistic position; instead of founding existence upon experience, they want to found experience

* *Philosophy of Science,* 13 (October, 1946), 261-73. Reprinted by permission.

(among other things) upon existence. To be sure, this is but a bare and crudely formulated schema of an issue that has been argued for a long time. Also, contemporary analysts for the most part do not discuss the issue directly; they give their attention to preliminary and, therefore, more fundamental questions. Like experienced chess players, who know to which characteristic situations in the middle game certain openings will eventually lead, we try to convince each other of the excellence of our respective openings. There is, in particular, one fundamental or opening move that is now widely discussed and which, I believe, most of us examine with a view to the position in which we shall find ourselves—in the middle game—with respect to the realism issue. I refer to the clarification of the relations between meaning and verification [1] or, to put it the way positivists do, to the formulation of an adequate meaning criterion. Let me indicate the connection between these questions and the crude schema I have given for the realism issue. According to current garden varieties of positivism, a statement is (empirically) meaningful if it is verifiable by (future) experience. 'There is a wall behind my back' is, in this view, meaningful because it is synonymous with a class of statements each of which is verifiable by future experience. More pointedly, the familiar common-sense statements about the existence of physical objects are considered as *meaningful because they are verifiable*. This has again the subjectivistic ring realists dislike so much; so they may again be inclined to convert the positivistic position, if only tentatively and because they feel that a piece of realistic common sense would thus be preserved. But to make the conversion is to say that 'There

[1] 'Verification' is used in its generic sense which includes falsification and, if you please, also confirmation and its opposite.

is a wall behind my back' is *verifiable because it is meaningful.*

One of the conclusions of the following analysis may be expressed by saying, as the realists do, that the familiar statements about the existence of external objects are verifiable because they are meaningful—and I shall arrive at this conclusion within the framework of my own positivistic position. But perhaps I had better explain why I believe such a "verbal" concession to be important when it occurs in the context of what is, after all, a positivistic position, and also what in my opinion constitutes a positivistic position on the realism issue. To begin with the second question, a positivist will (1) embrace the thesis that has been stated in the opening sentence of this paper, and he will (2) distinguish two meanings of 'exist'. The first meaning is that in which the term occurs in 'This wall exists (This is a real wall)'; this meaning we have, in (1), analyzed and thus, in a well-known sense, rejected. In its second meaning the term occurs in descriptions, that is, in the phrase 'There is (exists) a such-and-such', which we symbolize by combining the prefix '*E*' with a bound variable. This phrase, thus symbolized, belongs to the logical or nondescriptive skeleton of our language; its use is, therefore, by no means prejudicial to one's position on the realism issue while, on the other hand, failure to distinguish between the two meanings of 'exist' confuses that issue beyond repair. One of the pecularities of the situation is that positivists who neglect the distinction are virtually forced to accept the patently absurd meanings of the ambiguous formula *esse est percipi.* All this I discuss elsewhere,[2] as *one* partial clarification of the realism issue; in the present

---

[2] "Sense Data, Linguistic Conventions, and Existence," *Philosophy of Science,* 14 (April, 1947), 152-63, and also following this article.

paper I propose to analyze, as *another* partial clarification, another group of interrelated questions. But I have still to explain why I have, in this introductory statement, singled out a result which some will be inclined to regard as a mere verbalism, and a trifling one at that, namely, that we should say, and as positivists may say, that certain statements are verifiable because they are meaningful, rather than to say that they are meaningful because they are verifiable.

The point has something to do with my views on the nature and function of philosophical analysis. Whether or not philosophical analysis is, as many believe, definitional reconstruction is not at the moment my concern, though I think that as such sweeping formulae go, this one is rather suggestive. But while we may not know exactly what reconstruction is, there is, to my mind, no uncertainty about what it is that we wish to reconstruct. Philosophical analysis tries to reconstruct ordinary common sense and nothing but ordinary common sense. In arriving at this opinion I have been greatly influenced by G. E. Moore; so I shall, as a means of explicating it, indicate where I disagree with what I take to be his views on the matter. (1) I wish to circumscribe common sense so narrowly that all philosophical statements, no matter how inchoate or naive, remain excluded. 'This is a real wall' is, according to this view, a common-sense statement; 'Walls are real' is a border case, to say the least. (2) I would insist that while the reconstruction of common sense is our goal, our analysis (or reconstruction—that amounts to the same thing) need not and, as a rule, will not itself be commonsensical. (3) Reconstruction is, in a certain sense, purely linguistic. This means two things to me and I shall, in order to explain them, use the case at hand. (a) In reconstructing such words as 'real', 'meaningful', 'verifiable'—terms that belong only in *some* of their usages to the language of common sense—we must not be expected to vindicate their metaphysical meanings, that is, to reconstruct sentences in which they occur and which, though they belong to our philosophical tradition, do not belong to the language of common sense. (b) We shall be the more successful the more closely we reproduce, in talking about our reconstructed language, the verbal patterns of our common usage in all those cases where this usage does lie within, or very close to, the limits of common sense. In this sense, I agree with the realists, the schema 'verifiable because meaningful' does preserve a piece of "realistic" common sense, which the converse seems to abandon. And in this sense, I feel, it is incumbent upon positivism, as upon any other serious metaphysical position, to preserve the common-sense cores of all other positions.

## I

The meaning criterion I propose has two parts. To be meaningful, a statement is, *first*, required to have a certain form. It must be what logicians call a well-formed sentence according to the (syntactical) rules of that logic which, as we have overwhelming reasons to believe, is in fact the logic of the language that we all speak about the world, or—to put it even more cautiously—which would become the logic of our language, if that language could be perfected in the direction perfection has been sought during the past decades of analytical labor. This logic is a subject-predicate schema with an unramified type rule, and it contains the ordinary connectives ('and', 'or', etc.) as well as operators and variables ('all', 'some'); it is, in brief, the logic of the noncontroversial parts of *Principia Mathematica*. This part of the criterion has the familiar consequence that the existential schema, 'There is a such-and-such', and the various schemata for universal statements, such as 'Every so-and-so is a such-and-such' are all well formed, while 'This exists (Ea)' and 'green exists (Ef₁)' are not.[3] The *second* part of the criterion is what I have elsewhere [2] called a Principle of Acquaintance (abbreviated: PA). I shall state it for a sense data language, that is, for a language whose particulars (proper names) refer to the sort of momentary givennesses many philosophers call sense data and whose undefined predicates (of the first type) designate qualities of and relations between sense data. Stated for this language, the PA requires (1) that a particular is to occur in a statement only if its referent is immediately apprehended—in perception, memory, or imagination—by the speaker; and (2) that an undefined predicate is to occur in a statement only if at least one exemplification of it is known to the speaker. Thus, if 'green' and 'square' are, by assumption, two undefined predicates with which the speaker is acquainted while he has never seen a green square, then the two propositions 'There are green squares' and 'All squares are green' are both meaningful for him, though he is, for obvious reasons, not likely to entertain the latter. The customary example is 'There are centaurs', or something like that, rather than 'There are green squares'. But I do not yet want to mention physical objects. So much for the proposed version of the meaning criterion. It restores, quite generally and not just for certain statements about physical objects, an important piece of common sense, for it allows us to say unambiguously that when a proposition is meaningful, it is so by virtue of what we know when we entertain it. Now for some comments and explanations.

---

[3] Symbols with subscripts, such as 'f₁', stand for constant predicates; 'f' is always a variable.

1. To see clearly what the PA implies for existential statements, we observe that in order to make legitimately the statement '$(\mathrm{Ex})f_1(x)$' we must know at least one instance of its predicate, say '$f_1(a)$'. Note, furthermore, that the schema 'If this is a such-and-such then there is a such-and-such', in symbols

$$f_1(a) \supset (\mathrm{Ex})f_1(x),$$

belongs to the tautologies of our language. To say the same thing differently, '$f_1(a)$' implies '$(\mathrm{Ex})f_1(x)$'. An existential statement with an undefined (nonrelational) predicate is thus, according to the criterion, a statement of a very peculiar kind. It is either meaningless or it is not informative, in the sense that it does not assert anything that we cannot deduce from what we must know to be in a position to make it. In other words, if it is meaningful then it is necessarily true. But let us now look at the case of undefined relations. If an undefined relation is to occur, the PA requires again that we know at least one exemplification of it, say, '$r_1(a, b)$'. If we know this, then we can meaningfully make either of the following two statements

$$(\mathrm{Ex})r_1(x,d), \qquad (\mathrm{Ey})r_1(c, y).$$

*Both these statements are informative,* in the sense that neither is implied by '$r_1(a, b)$', which implies merely the three statements

$$(\mathrm{Ey})r_1(a, y), \qquad (\mathrm{Ex})r_1(x, b), \qquad (\mathrm{Ex, y})r_1(x, y).$$

Finally, as has been seen in the case of the green squares, existential statements that contain defined predicates may be informative, in the sense in which I have used 'informative', irrespective of the relational or qualitative nature of these

[159]

predicates. But, of course, defined predicates are meaningful if and only if none but meaningful undefined predicates occur in their (well-formed) definitions.

2. To illustrate the case of undefined relations, assume 'earlier than' to be an undefined relation, known to us, as one usually says, from the specious present. Then I can, when hearing a certain kind of noise, meaningfully and informatively say 'This is a noise and there was a lightning flash that preceded it'; and I can say this, meaningfully and informatively, *whether or not the lightning flash lies in the specious present and whether or not I remember it.*[4] The example is important in itself, for presently it will be seen that one of my results rests on the assumption that some spatial and temporal relations are among the undefined predicates of the language that we speak about the external world. This is, by the testimony of my experience, indubitably so. To those who deny it I can only say, as Locke would, that I cannot communicate with them, just as I cannot talk with a blind man about color.

3. If all the predicates that occur in a universal statement are meaningful according to the PA, then the statement itself is meaningful according to the first part of the criterion. Thus the statement 'A noise (i.e., an instance of a certain quality) is always preceded by a lightning flash (i.e., an instance of a certain other quality)' is meaningful provided that we are acquainted with the two qualities that are, for the sake of illustration, assumed to be undefined. But from this universal statement (empirical law) in conjunction with the statement 'This is a noise' the statement 'There was a lightning flash

[4] In symbols, 'n(a).E(x)[l(x).p(x,a)]', where 'a' is the name of the particular noise, 'p' stands for 'precedes' and 'l' and 'n' for the (undefined) predicates 'lightning flash' and 'noise'. The example makes it clear that the 'is' in 'there is' is timeless; in particular it does not mean 'there will be'.

that preceded this noise' can be inferred, quite independently of whether or not the referent of the inferred statement lies in the specious present, in the future, or in the past, and whether or not, in case it happens to lie in the past, it is being remembered.

The case of the past deserves attention, since its correct description disposes of the familiar contention that positivism implies what some call solipsism of the present. The particulars of the language that is here considered do not refer to physical objects. But it is worth noting that if they did, we would already be at the end of this analysis. For then it would follow from what has been said that we can say and, in the light of the criterion, must say (1) that statements about the past, such as 'Caesar crossed the Rubicon' are meaningful in their own right quite independently of verifiability or verification and (2) that we infer them, whenever we do not remember them or do not accept them on authority, from what we know now. (3) We verify them as we verify most other statements, namely, indirectly, by inferring from them, in conjunction with empirical laws, statements that describe what we can immediately apprehend. Or, as I had better say, we verify them if and when we apprehend what these latter statements speak about. All this restores another important piece of "realistic" common sense, which is, I believe, the kernel of the traditional arguments for the reality or existence of the past.

That we can not now or in the future apprehend what I shall for the moment permit myself to call the past particular is thus shown to be what I believe it to be, namely, a matter of contingent fact, a consequence of the axiomatics of time, as it were. And since time, that is, the temporal relations, is *in* our world, this factual feature is extraneous to the analysis

[161]

of the realism issue and of meaning. This, at any rate, is what I mean by calling contingent what one would otherwise hardly think of calling so. For contingency is, in the last analysis, a matter of levels or, as one also says, a relative notion. But let me make one more remark about this question of the past. Perhaps it has been noticed that I was very careful not to prejudge the analysis of memory. I am, in fact, inclined to believe that memory is a direct and irreducible source of knowledge about the past in exactly the same sense in which perception may be said to be such a source for knowledge of the present.[5] But on the other hand I would say this. The question whether we could, without memory, be sure that the world has not been created at this moment is, to my mind, not a good question. I am afraid it is one of those questions that do, in a sense, justify the temperamental use of 'meaningless' in which my positivistic friends so often indulge. Furthermore, I see no reason to believe that we cannot, in one sense, know everything about the past that could be known about it if it were present, by inferring it from what we know now. The point is that, if we know it by memory, we do *not*, in principle, know *more*, but we know whatever we know *differently*, since we know it through an additional source. Nor should it be overlooked that knowledge derived either from our own memory or, inductively, from that of others, if it jibes with other knowledge, provides additional evidence for the truth of statements about the past. If this is all that is meant by those who cite the fact of memory in their arguments for the "reality" or "existence"

[5] The analysis of memory is part of the reconstruction of those levels of our language which refer primarily, not to the "external world," but to the activities of the "Self." That is why memory does not need to be discussed, for its own sake, in the present context. See also "A Positivistic Metaphysics of Consciousness," *Mind*, 54 (1945), 193-226.

of the "past," then I have no quarrel with them. I would insist, though, that their way of speaking, far from constituting an analysis, is itself rather badly in need of analysis.

Physical objects are not particulars, not, at least, according to the view here taken or, as I had better say, not in a sense data language; and because of the many clarifications it yields reconstruction of the sense data language has long been among the classical problems of analysis. In this language physical objects are patterns, and what I have said about the past particular does, therefore, not apply to them directly. On the other hand, the reader may easily convince himself that the analysis of ordinary statements about the past, such as 'Caesar crossed the Rubicon' does not offer any new problems if what I have said in this section is taken in conjunction with what I shall say in the next. So I shall not return to the question.

## II

A lightning flash followed by a thunder clap exemplifies a *pattern* of which, as I have insisted, the temporal succession forms a part. Simultaneous sounding of the c-major tonic triad in the middle octave exemplifies another pattern, and it is worth noticing that in this case, too, the simultaneity of the three tones is part of the pattern, for if they are sounded in succession, say, for instance, in ascending order of their pitches, then they constitute quite obviously a different pattern. It is in this sense of pattern that physical objects are (as Berkeley first pointed out) spatio-temporal patterns of undefined qualities and (as we have to add) relations. If this is so, then we must turn to the analysis of *existential statements about patterns*, that is, as we shall see, to the analysis of the form '$(Ef)$ . . . .' and its cognates. For so far, it will be

[163]

noticed, I have dealt only with existential statements about particulars, that is, with statements that contain the clause '(Ex)'. But before turning to this task, I wish to correct a slight inaccuracy in what I have just said, and I also wish to make a few preliminary remarks.

1. Let 'c', 'e', 'g' signify the pitches of the chord mentioned and let 's' stand for the relation of simultaneity. Then one can define the predicate 'triad (tr)' as follows:

$$tr(x, y, z) = c(x) \cdot e(y) \cdot g(z) \cdot s(x, y) \cdot s(y, z) \cdot s(x, z).^{6}$$

The pattern is, in this simple instance, a triadic relation of the first type. Generally it can be said that a pattern is a relational predicate. From logic we remember that the definition is of the kind that is called *in use* and that in such definitions the variables that occur in the definiendum do not carry any implication of existence in *any* sense of the term. But let us also remember that in such definitions *the definiens may contain operators that bind different variables,* that is, variables which, as definitions are usually written, occur only on the right side.

Assume now that we say, upon hearing it, 'This is the c-major triad'. Upon analysis this turns out not to be an existential statement at all, for it reads 'tr($a_1$, $a_2$, $a_3$)', where '$a_1$', '$a_2$', '$a_3$' are the names of the three particulars that we hear. Assume, next, that we hear the opening strains of the Eroica and say 'This is the Eroica', by which we mean that the orchestra has actually started and will continue the performance of this symphony. Suppose, for simplicity's sake, that what I have called the opening strains was a pattern of four particulars, $b_1$, $b_2$, $b_3$, $b_4$, and let '$f_1(b_1, b_2, b_3, b_4)$' de-

---

[6] 's(x,z)' may be omitted if the transitivity of 's' is assumed.

scribe this pattern in the same way in which '$tr(a_1, a_2, a_3)$' described our triad. The predicate 'Eroica', as it occurs in the sentence under consideration is then not '$f_1$' but a different predicate. For the definiens of this predicate, call it '$f_2$', contains a large number of existential statements about all the tones that follow the opening strains in the Eroica. Thus if we say, 'This is the Eroica', we do not mean '$f_1(b_1, \cdots, b_4)$' but, rather, '$f_2(b_1, \cdots, b_4)$' or, perhaps phenomenologically more nearly correct, '$f_1(b_1, \cdots, b_4) \cdot f_2(b_1, \cdots, b_4)$'. Clearly, either of these two statements is a paradigma of the Berkeleyan analysis of such statements as 'This is a wall', while what we mean, or ought to mean, when we speak in philosophy of the reconstruction of physical objects is the definition of '$f_2$'. To put it loosely, a physical object is a pattern that is never fully apprehended. In this respect, 'This is a wall' is more similar to the statement 'This is a noise and there was a lightning flash that preceded it' than it is to '$tr(a_1, a_2, a_3)$'. This is the inaccuracy of my preliminary statement that I wanted to correct.

2. As a pattern, a physical object is much more complex than a symphony, so complex indeed that nobody can, other than *in principle,* write out its sense data score. This state of affairs is the starting point of a well-known line of criticism. Positivists are told that before presenting their views in principle they had better get on with the business of actually reconstructing the physical object; and, more often than not, the advice is accompanied by the prediction that any serious attempt at actual reconstruction will soon show it to be impossible of achievement. This prediction is usually based on certain opinions about time, change, and substance; for most of these critics hold that time, change, and substance have categorial status in a sense in which their positivistic op-

[165]

ponents do not believe this to be the case. Now I am at the moment not concerned with explicitly arguing against such opinions. I merely wish to draw attention to the fact that the reasons that are given for them are themselves always stated in principle only. And what is meat for the goose is meat for the gander. I, for one, believe that philosophical analysis is always clarification in principle only. Thus, the proper way to go about the reconstruction of physical objects is not to reconstruct one but, rather, to clarify schematically the problems that would arise in any actual reconstruction. But to do this is to do the *sort* of thing that I am trying to do, no matter how inadequately or mistakenly, in this paper. Having said this, I feel I should also say that some positivists take the challenge to reconstruct the physical object in all details more seriously than it deserves to be taken. Probably this failure of nerve is at least in part caused by the wrong kind of preoccupation with science. But then, are the scientists able to compute the number of leaves the next storm will shake from the tree in front of my window, or, for that matter, do they even strive for this foolish and futile sort of perfection?

Somebody may grant all this and ask how much, in principle, ought to be included in the definition of a physical object. Ought we, for instance, to include all or some of its effects on other physical objects, not to mention other percipients. Instead of answering the question, I would rather say that it is not a very important and, in one sense, not even a good question. How much we include in the definitions of physical objects and how much we put into empirical laws about them is, in a sense, a matter of convention.[7] And, of

---

[7] This is, in principle, the point of fn. 6.

course, the more we have put into the definition, the less certain we can be that there are physical objects. Historically, since the notion of substance is a hypostatization of that of physical object, philosophers' proposals as to what to include were often guided by their respective ideas concerning the essential characteristics or nature of substance. If one's aim is to reconstruct the common-sense notion of physical object as it refers to walls, chairs, and tables, then one will include a good measure of spatial and temporal coherence, persistence, and continuity, and, besides the obvious "sensory qualities," not much else. This, at any rate, is what I mean by physical object.

III

1. Since physical objects are patterns, and patterns, as I have used the term, are defined relational predicates, it *appears* that existential statements about physical objects contain such clauses as '(Ef)'. Let us see. Assume that I have heard all the tones of the musical scale and also all sorts of sequences of them while I have, perchance, never heard the simple chord which I have defined for the sake of illustration. 'There are triads' (or 'There is a triad') is then for me a meaningful and informative existential statement. But it reads '$(Ex, y, z)tr(x, y, z)$' and is thus an existential statement about particulars, not about patterns. *In this respect* ordinary existential statements about physical objects are exactly like 'There is something green'; the only difference seems to be that they may be informative while the latter statement, as has been seen, is not. However, one must not overlook the possibility that the critical clause, '(Ef)', occurs in the definiens of a pattern as complex as 'chair' or 'wall'. Before

considering this possibility I wish to show why the ordinary existential statements are *always* informative.

What I have in mind when I speak of ordinary existential statements about physical objects are statements that we make in the ordinary course of events. They all go beyond the immediately apprehended and are of the sort for which positivism, according to its critics, cannot account. 'There is a wall behind my back' is one example; 'There is a dog outside (now)', said when I hear a bark while sitting in my room; 'There was a man walking here (in the past)', similarly inferred from a footprint in the sand, are others. To see that such statements are always informative, one merely has to remember that physical objects are spatial and temporal patterns and stand in spatial and temporal relations to each other. In asserting one of these statements one asserts, therefore, the existence of particulars not immediately apprehended that stand to particulars immediately apprehended in undefined relations. That such statements are always informative has been seen in the first section. To give a simplified paradigma, if 'a' is the name of what I see to the extreme left of my visual field, then 'There is something to the left of a' is informative since it cannot be deduced from what is immediately apprehended or from what I must know to make it meaningful, though it may of course be possible to deduce it if empirical laws are added as further premises. To perceive the immediately apprehended as a physical object amounts to the adding of such premises. In terms of the Eroica illustration, '$f_2(b_1, \cdots, b_4)$' is inferred from '$f_1(b_1, \cdots, b_4)$' and the law '$f_1(x_1, \cdots, x_4) \supset f_2(x_1, \cdots, x_4)$'. This, however, as I implied before, is not a phenomenological account of what happens when we recognize the opening strains of the Eroica.

[168]

2. Existential statements concerning predicates [8] occur explicitly in ordinary speech. Take the case that someone is looking for some object of use and tries to match it in color with another object before him without being able to name the color for which he is looking. Such a person may say, meaningfully and informatively, 'There is a color that matches this'. Call the color of the object before him '$f_1$', and assume, for simplicity's sake, that 'matching (M)' is a known and definite relation of the second type. Then the English statement transcribes into an expression that contains the critical clause, namely, '(Ef) Color(f) · M(f, $f_1$)'.[9] At this point there may be some doubt whether, in view of the PA, the "correct" transcription is not '(Ex, f) f(x) · Color (f) · M(f, $f_1$)'. As I understand it, the situation is this. The two statements, while they are formally different from each other, are both meaningful and informative, and there is not much point in choosing one of them as the correct transcription. In particular, what one might wish to safeguard by insisting that only the second one is correct, is already safeguarded by the PA itself.

Since positivistic meaning criteria are often held to be unduly restrictive, let me use this form to point out how encompassing the one I have proposed really is. Assume '$f_3$' to be the name of the highest pitch I or, for that matter, anybody can hear—if we are to trust what the scientists tell us about these things. Then the statement 'There is a pitch higher than $f_3$' has the form of the color matching statement and is, ac-

---

[8] At this point it comes to mind that the axiom of choice, which belongs to the logical skeleton of our language, is essentially a statement of this form.

[9] Notice that this and everything that follows is completely independent of the question of elementarism, that is, the question whether or not any reconstruction of our language must contain some undefined predicates of the higher types.

cording to the criterion, meaningful as long as I am, from other instances, acquainted with the referents of 'pitch' and 'higher-in-pitch'. This, I submit, is perfectly commonsensical, for I can with a partially colorblind man talk about colors beyond his acquaintance in a sense in which I cannot talk with a blind man about color. Also, I suspect that the current criteria would in such a case either arrive at the wrong answer or bog down in a tortuous and pseudoscientific discussion of what is meant by 'verifiable in principle'.

I turn to the one question that is still before us, namely, whether bound predicate variables occur in the definientia of physical objects. Now if one wishes to reconstruct the common-sense notions, then one will have to see to it that such statements as 'This wall has a rear side and this rear side has *some* color' become deducible from 'This is a wall'. This makes it necessary that the definiens of 'wall' contain, among others, the clause 'there is something which has some property which is a color'; in symbols, '$(Ex, f)f(x) \cdot Color(f)$'. So we see that the definitions of physical objects do contain existentially bound predicate variables. In the example I have chosen the existential phrase refers, in fact, to an *undefined* predicate that we cannot name. As far as I can see, this is the only case in which such reference occurs ineliminably in the definiens of a physical object. For whenever the reference is to an instance of some member of a class of *defined* properties, then we can also define this class and replace the original reference by one to an exemplification of it. This leads to the last point I wish to make. While I have so far not distinguished between statements such as 'There is a dog outside' and 'There are centaurs' on the one hand and the most general statement, 'There are physical objects', on the other, I have, in fact, always dealt with statements of the first kind. Now I wish to point out that the last mentioned statement, 'There are physical objects', does not require special treatment. It is, in particular, not of the form '$(Ex, f)f(x) \cdot F_1(f)$'; in words, 'There are instances $(x)$ of certain patterns $(f)$ which are the patterns of physical objects $(F_1)$'. All one needs to do is to exclude from the definition of the pattern itself everything that is not considered characteristic of physical objects in general.

The whole section may be summed up by saying that existential statements about physical objects, including the most general ones, are really existential statements about particulars and undefined predicates. This is a very unprecise way of speaking, but after I have tried to say what it means more precisely, such summing up is, perhaps, suggestive.

IV

1. It seems that I have come to the end of my argument. For either I am greatly mistaken or I have, in the course of a positivistic analysis, recovered several important pieces of "realistic" common sense concerning the existence—past, present, or future—of physical objects. In conclusion I shall indicate how the last result, the one I just summed up so inaccurately, may be used to restore another important piece of common sense that lies in the general area of the so-called mind-body problem. This, however, is more by way of an appendix; so I shall try to be brief rather than explicit.

Positivists, if they know what they are about, are all behaviorists. By this I mean that they believe—and must believe if they wish to be consistent—that in principle it is possible to analyze the ordinary statements we make about *other* peoples' minds in terms of the behavior of their bodies—including such complex and subtle behavior as speech considered as physical event. Thus, if I say 'Mr. X has a mind' or 'A mind or self, namely, Mr. X's, is connected with his body' I make, according to this view, statements about a very complex pattern exemplified by particulars that belong, in an obvious sense, to the physical object that I call the body of Mr. X. Probably one should not say that such an analysis is a matter of mere common sense; I certainly shall not say it after I have so vigorously insisted on a very narrow circumscription of common sense. So I shall merely observe that, if stated in this manner, the thesis does not have the non-sensical implications that belong to the stereotype often referred to as behaviorism. Be that as it may, it is not my intent to defend directly the commonsensicality of the behavioristic thesis, not even in the form in which I just stated it. My purpose is, rather, to show how one of its *apparent* consequences, which I, too, consider as highly offensive to common sense, can be made to disappear. Let me explain.

Suppose somebody proposes the following argument: "I grant that without being philosophically inconsistent, you may say, as ordinary people do, that physical objects exist (are real) and that, in particular, Mr. X's body exists. But now you make a further claim, namely, that you can, as you put it, reconstruct such statements as 'Mr. X has a mind' or 'Mr. X's consciousness exists'. By this, I take it, you mean that Mr. X's mind is what you call a pattern and that, though this pattern is different from the one which you say is Mr. X's body, you still find it exemplified. And this, according to your positivistic friends, is all you mean by saying that Mr. X has a mind. I shall grant you this, too, though merely for the sake of argument. I shall go even further and assume that our scientists have constructed what some of your friends call a psycho-physiological dictionary, so that they may know the state of somebody's consciousness either from what he says or from the goings-on in his central nervous system. In other words, I assume that what you assert to be possible in principle is what at present it is not, namely, an actual scientific fact. What I wish to ask is whether, in view of this fact, you would be willing to say that Mr. X's mind *is* his brain. Truly, I do not see how you can avoid saying it."

Yet I would say no such thing, since saying it is, in my opinion, tantamount to taking a metaphysical position I do not wish to take. I refer, of course, to the various double aspect and identity theories of mind. In answering the further question, how I could avoid arriving at such views in the course of my analysis, I shall once more use a musical illustration. Assume that somebody amuses himself by trying to locate the tunes of some other pieces in the score of the Eroica. As long as he is ready to pick very small phrases or even individual notes from the parts given to the various instruments, he is certain to be successful in some cases. Suppose that he has thus "found" our national anthem. Would we then have to say that the Eroica *is* our national anthem, or even that the latter *is a part* of the former? Is it not more reasonable to say, instead, that whenever the Eroica is performed, there is objectively, among the manifold of patterns exemplified, also that of our national anthem, though we may not be aware of it subjectively? In the case of the mind-melody in the body-symphony I do not suggest, of course, that we are not subjectively aware of the former, though we may not be aware of the particulars and relations that constitute it just as we are, in perceiving it, not aware of those that constitute a physical object. In some other respects the analogy is more adequate. For instance, just as we may say that each performance of the symphony is also a performance

[173]

of the anthem, we may say that whenever there is a living human body there is also a mind connected with it. The only difference is that in this case the patterns are such that there is nothing artificial or far-fetched about saying it. Furthermore, the behavioristic thesis, as I understand it, asserts that the ordinary statements about minds are to be analyzed in terms of the ordinary behavior of inviolate human organisms. This and only this pattern is what the behaviorist may call "mind." The central nervous system is a different pattern, exemplified by different particulars, none of which is apprehended in the ordinary course of events. This pattern is that of a physical object, and its name is "nervous system," not "mind."

This should suffice to indicate how another important piece of realistic common sense may be recovered. In fact, the statements under consideration express the common sense core of what is known as a dualistic position. For, if existential statements are analyzed as I have analyzed them, and as I believe they must be analyzed, then one can and must say this: Minds are one kind of thing; physical objects and human bodies in particular are another. But there are minds in exactly the same sense in which there are bodies, and they are connected in the manner common sense believes them to be connected.

Some may accept this analysis and yet feel that it does not do what I claim it does, namely, reconstruct realistic common sense within a positivistic frame of reference. These critics would have to argue that the realistic thesis is hidden somewhere in my unexamined presuppositions. The presupposition most likely to be singled out for this role is that our language contains variables and operators, that it is what one could call an all-some-language. This, it may be argued, is a fact and, moreover, a fact of the kind that to assume it is to assume realism. Here is what I would answer. I grant that this character of our language is, in *some* sense, factual. Contingency, as I have said before, is after all a matter of levels. Yet I insist that this so-called fact is of exactly the same kind as the "fact" that 'it rains or it does not rain' is a tautology or that the syllogism is valid. It is, if I may so express myself, a syntactical fact or, to use an older term, *secundae intentionis*. It is not *this* kind of fact philosophers have claimed to make explicit by their various formulations of the realistic thesis. But then, someone may be of the opinion that whenever they insisted that there was *something* to be made explicit, realists were groping for an expression of this very fact. Such a critic may say that in this rather remote and unhistorical sense I am a realist. With this I would agree for, as far as I can see, no argument is left.

# SENSE DATA, LINGUISTIC CONVENTIONS, AND EXISTENCE *

THE FOLLOWING remarks have been stimulated by Mr. A. J. Ayer's recent essay "The Terminology of Sense Data." [1] In this paper Mr. Ayer restates several of the points he has made in his book *The Foundations of Empirical Knowledge.* The context of his argument is that of the traditional distinction between two kinds of things, sense data, percepts, phenomenal or direct givennesses on the one hand and so-called physical objects on the other. In *this* context, Mr. Ayer's argument is, to my mind, very admirable; so I do not intend to comment on it. In some *other* contexts, some of his formulations may, I fear, give rise to misunderstandings; these, naturally, are the points on which I wish to comment. But before specifying them, I had better make sure that we are talking about the same thing by briefly restating several of Mr. Ayer's points. With some of these, if I understand them correctly, I find myself in agreement; the merit of some others I shall presently examine.

As long as it is a matter of general principle, of the pattern of our analysis rather than of its specific content, I feel that

* *Philosophy of Science,* 14 (April, 1947), 152-63. Reprinted by permission.
[1] *Mind,* 54 (1945), 289-312.

[176]

Mr. Ayer is justified when he warns us not to confuse what he calls empirical fact with what one might call matters of linguistic convention. Mr. Ayer himself, in his last essay, does not use the phrase linguistic convention. But, if I am to judge from the larger context of his writings, it is a phrase he might use or to whose use he might at least not object when it is employed to refer to the kind of thing he suggests when he says that we *make* 'x is directly apprehended' entail 'x has whatever characteristics it appears to have' as well as 'x exists'. If I understand him correctly, this procedure of producing entailment is analogous to that followed in so-called definitions in use. Presently I shall give some reasons why I take him to propose that 'x is directly perceived' be considered as the definiens of 'x exists', or, at least, as something closely comparable—I am here not striving for the precision of the mathematical logician. If this proposal is accepted, then it is also correct to say that the statement 'x is directly apprehended but does not exist' becomes self-contradictory. This is what Mr. Ayer himself says in his last paper.

Next I take Mr. Ayer to mean that to make these linguistic arrangements and to discuss, in the manner in which he discusses it, the use of a language thus arranged is the thing we must do and the one thing we can do in order to make our fellow philosophers understand what the sort of thing we are talking about is; for this sort of thing (namely, sense data) is not quite of the commonsensical kind and our reference to it is, therefore, subject to the peculiar hazards of philosophical discourse. I should like to add that this sort of thing being there and being what it is, is not itself a matter of linguistic convention. Mr. Ayer, I am confident, would not dissent, though he might feel that what I wish to emphasize is a trifle on the obvious side and that he has made the matter

[177]

plain anyway. It is indeed obvious to me and, I believe, to most students who are in general agreement with Mr. Ayer's analysis. But then, too many unnecessary difficulties have been created by careless or, at least, carelessly worded claims positivists have made for the miracles one can work by reducing philosophical problems to matters of linguistic convention. That is why I feel that it pays to be very explicit.

In the first section of this note I shall make some comments of my own on the terminology of sense data. The second section contains some general remarks on the matter of linguistic conventions. In the third and last section I shall criticize the proposed linguistic convention to the effect that, whenever 'a' is the name of a sense datum, 'a exists' and 'a is directly apprehended' be made to entail each other.

I

Perhaps it has been noticed that I have used the expressions 'sense datum', 'percept', and 'phenomenal givenness' as roughly synonymous. They do all refer to objects of one sort, in the sense in which what ordinary usage means by 'physical object' is a thing of another sort. For certain of his purposes, I see, therefore, no harm in Mr. Ayer's practice of using 'sense datum' as a generic term. The most likely candidate for such use, though, in the sense that its choice minimizes the danger of misunderstandings, is, I believe, 'phenomenal givenness' or 'direct givenness'. Having made this choice, one can say—and one is, in saying it, in fair agreement with psychological language—that ordinarily a large class of our givennesses consists of percepts (of physical objects), while under appropriate circumstances we also have or, at least, in some sense approach givennesses of the kind called sense data. If one adopts, as I shall, this more specific and, I think, quite common usage of 'sense datum', then 'this is an apple' does not describe a sense datum but a percept, while such statements as 'this is green' or 'this is to the right of that' do describe sense data, provided that 'this' and 'that' designate phenomenal objects of that simplest kind known as the *particulars of a sense data analysis*. I shall not explain the italicized phrase, not because it does not need explanation, but because I assume most philosophers to be familiar with the pertinent meanings of 'particular' and 'sense data analysis'. In this sense of 'particular', the 'this' in 'this is an apple', though it refers to a phenomenal object, does not refer to a particular. It is, in that respect, different from a 'this' that occurs in a sense data statement. Accordingly, Mr. Ayer would probably say—and I think one may very well say it, at least in a preliminary manner—that the grammatical rules for the different 'this' can be expected to differ from each other. Also, the difference may make a difference, and actually does make a difference, in the analysis of the ambiguous phrase 'this exists'. But of existence I intend to speak later; for the moment I merely wish to explain and, to some extent, justify my own terminology.

By a *sense data language*, then, I shall not mean what one might call a *percept language* but, rather, a language whose names refer to the particulars of a sense data analysis and whose undefined predicates and relations are such terms as 'green', 'hot', 'later', and 'louder'. Correspondingly, 'chair' and 'apple' may be undefined predicates of a percept language, but not of a sense data language. Upon such usage the term *sense data analysis* becomes ambiguous. It may signify an attempt, or the result of one, to indicate classes of statements that contain no names and undefined predicates other than

[179]

those of a sense data language, so that these classes are, in some complicated sense, equivalent to such perceptual statements as 'this is an apple'. Or it may signify the indication of classes, either of sense data statements or of perceptual statements, equivalent to such statements as 'this is an apple', when the latter is taken to refer, not to a percept, but to a physical object. The second meaning is, quite obviously, Mr. Ayer's. That explains why he chooses his terminology the way he does and why he finds it adequate for his purpose.

This purpose—I need hardly mention and, certainly, need not explain it—is to produce, in a refined form, the traditional positivistic analysis of such common-sense statements as that physical objects are real and exist independently of their being perceived. *If one is a positivist,* then one will accept this analysis as a clarification of the grammar of reality and existence. If one is a cautious positivist, then one will accept it for what it is worth, namely, as *one* partial clarification of this particular piece of grammar. Let me explain the two qualifications I just made. The one, indicated by the italicized protasis, concerns the acceptance of a general pattern of analysis; the other insists on the *partial* character of the clarification achieved. The first registers an opinion for which I shall give some reasons in the next section; namely, that the sense data controversy is not, or at least not entirely, a matter of linguistic convention in any good and important sense of the term. The second has something to do with that *other* partial clarification of the grammar of existence that started with Russell's analysis of descriptions and the introduction of the symbol '*E*'. With this meaning of the idiomatic 'exist' I shall presently concern myself. At the moment I wish to show, in a general way, what is gained by the distinction I

[180]

have urged. In order to avoid verbiage, I shall speak of the first and the second partial clarification of the grammar of 'exist', referring to them in the order in which they have been mentioned. To repeat, the first clarification deals with the sentence 'this (physical object) exists'; the second with the sentence 'there is (exists) a such-and-such'.[2]

The ambiguity I pointed out in the meaning of 'sense data analysis' is in many ways rather unimportant. For—to speak loosely but, I hope, suggestively—the problems and difficulties of the three analyses that lead from physical objects to percepts, from percepts to sense data, and from physical objects to sense data are, by and large, the same; also, the third is, as it were, the sum of the first two. What is important is that the issues that lead to the second partial clarification arise in all three analyses. They must, therefore, be met even in the realm of the phenomena, quite independently of the question of physical objects. The particular issue that leads to the first clarification arises only in connection with physical objects, that is, in the first and third analyses. Thus one can accept the second clarification without being committed to the first. Such "fractionation" of a problem constitutes, in an obvious sense, progress in the direction away from dogmatism. But this is not all. A positivist will notice that the two clarifications agree with each other and form, together with some other materials, the total pattern of his analysis of reality and existence. Such supplementation is excellent intrinsic evidence for the soundness of an approach. But to

---

[2] In the customary symbolic notation, '$(Ex)f_1(x)$'. I wish to draw attention to the fact that I have not attempted in this note to analyze philosophically the corresponding sentence '$(Ef)F_1(f)$' or the sentence '$(Ex,f)f(x) \cdot F_1(f)$'. Concerning these matters see my essay "Remarks on Realism," *Philosophy of Science,* 13 (October, 1946), 261-73, and also preceding this article.

obtain it, the fractionation must, of course, have been made and not lost sight of; for how could one otherwise know that certain things are two things and not one.

## II

'Convention' connotes arbitrariness and choice; 'linguistic convention' connotes, accordingly, arbitrariness and choice in matters of language. That we speak English and not French, that we use 'green' and not 'red' to designate a certain color is a matter of choice in a trivial sense with which I shall not further concern myself. In a nontrivial sense, there are, I believe, two possible kinds of choices that ought to be distinguished from each other, namely, first, the choice *of* a language and, second, choices *within* a language once chosen. Now I am prepared to maintain that the "choice" of a language is not in any good and simple sense a matter of convention. In order to explain what I have in mind, I shall briefly discuss what some seem to believe are the alternatives of such a choice. Without particular concern for reference and use, logicians design certain formal patterns they call languages. *Some* of these patterns are, in a familiar sense, abstracts, idealizations, or reconstructions of our ordinary language or of some part of it. They contain a certain distinguished class of sentences, called tautologies or analytic sentences; there are also, closely connected with this notion, the notions of entailment and contradiction. In other words, each of these patterns has a *logic*. There are, furthermore, in those symbolic patterns which are *not* idealizations of our language, classes of sentences that have, within their respective "logics," structural properties analogous to those of the tautologies of our language. These sentences may be called the tautologies of their respective patterns or logics. What this means is that logicians have succeeded in generalizing, *in the mathematical sense of the term,* the notions of tautology and entailment. So-called *n*-valued languages or logics illustrate what I have in mind. What I wish to guard against is this. Some people seem to believe, or speak as if they believed, that we are at liberty to choose among the various symbolic patterns the one we wish to use when we speak about our world, or more specifically, that we choose the class of sentences which we wish to make our tautologies—in a *not* purely formal meaning of 'tautology'. This, I believe, is not so; we have, details apart, no choice in the matter. The point, though amenable to much indirect clarification, is so fundamental that no direct argument can be offered to support it. However that may be, at present I am merely concerned to clarify our ideas on linguistic conventions. There is only one more thing I wish to say about logic as such before leaving this topic for some future occasion. In "choosing" our logic we determine not only the class of the tautologies and the relation of entailment but also, and even more fundamentally, the occurring logical particles and sentential forms, such as 'there is (exists) a such-and-such'.

The "choice" of one's logic, then, is one thing I take to be considered, erroneously, a matter of linguistic convention; let me now turn to another such thing. There, too, it is, I believe, erroneous to speak of *linguistic* convention, though this time the error is of a different kind. Many analysts who call themselves empiricists or positivists of some sort wish to choose or, as one should rather say, wish to *use* their language in accordance with the following two rules or principles. (1) A name (of a particular) is to occur in a statement only if the particular named is known to the speaker. Inaccurate as this formulation is, I shall, instead of trying to improve it, content myself with indicating what it means in the case of a sense data language. If such a language is used in accordance with the rule, the occurrence of a proper name indicates that the particular named is immediately apprehended by the speaker. The apprehension, however, need not be of the kind called sensing; the particular may as well present itself in memory or in imagination. This rule I shall call the *Principle of Proper Names.* (2) An undefined predicate is to occur in a statement only if an exemplification of it is known to the speaker. Since this is the rule Stace [3] has recently identified as the *Principle of Observable Kinds,* I shall assume that the reader will understand it without further comment. Applying a familiar term, one may refer to these two rules concerning the two kinds of objects (particulars and universals) with which we are acquainted, as the two cases of a *Principle of Acquaintance.* This principle, together with the "choice" of that logic for which certain parts of the *Principia Mathematica* still provide the most adequate schema, is, I believe, a more nearly correct form of what is sometimes called an *empiricist meaning criterion,* that is, the kind of thing Mr. Ayer speaks about in his first book, *Language, Truth, and Logic.* In other words, for a statement to be accepted as empirically meaningful by Mr. Ayer or, for that matter, by myself, it must exhibit a certain logical structure and must be used according to the Principle of Acquaintance. I have called this form of the so-called meaning criterion more nearly correct because it avoids the customary appeal to verification with its proleptic reference to time and, in particular, to the future. What this appeal tries to express

---

[3] "Positivism," *Mind,* 53 (1944), 215-37. See also my essay, "Undefined Descriptive Predicates," *Philosophy and Phenomenological Research,* 8 (1947), 55-82.

is, to my mind, more adequately expressed by the Principle of Acquaintance. Now it can, perhaps, be said that the acceptance of the Principle of Acquaintance or any other such rule is, in some sense, subject to choice. But the way I put the whole matter should make it clear that what one here chooses is a cornerstone of one's metaphysics, not the kind of thing anyone could reasonably call a way of speaking or a linguistic convention.

There are genuine choices within a language. In a language constructed and used according to the meaning criterion there is, for instance, the obvious choice of the particulars which we actually name among those we could name in agreement with the Principle of Proper Names. Next and more important, there are definitions. Concerning the latter, I shall take two things for granted; namely, first, that we can, in a language that contains the necessary logical apparatus, make definitions and, second, that all definitions are tautologies (analytic sentences). What terms we actually define depends, objectively, on the nature of the facts we wish to describe; subjectively, it is determined by convenience. The American people have recently accepted 'Nisei' as meaning, by definition, 'American-born person of Japanese ancestry', while 'Lisei' ('American-born person of Lithuanian ancestry') has, for obvious reasons, not been received into our language. What I have just called a matter of fact and convenience may, if looked at in a certain abstractive manner, very well be considered as a matter of choice. Nor is the whole thing as trivial as it appears at first sight. Consider, for instance, the well-known analysis of the statement that one thing cannot be at two places at the same time, which Mr. Ayer has proposed in his first book. If I understand him correctly, Mr. Ayer asserts the statement 'one physical object

[185]

THE METAPHYSICS OF LOGICAL POSITIVISM

cannot, at the same moment in physical time, be at two different places in physical space' to be a tautology. This, he believes, is so because, upon analysis, the statement appears to be entailed by the definitions of 'physical object', 'physical time', and 'physical space' in a sense data language; and because a statement entailed by one or several tautologies is itself a tautology. Now I agree with Mr. Ayer that some statements turn out, quite surprisingly, to be tautologies if they are analyzed in this manner; that the statement he investigates is of the kind on which such analysis ought to be tried; and that, for these reasons, definitional reconstruction is an important tool of philosophical analysis.[4] Yet I disagree with Mr. Ayer's opinion that the statement considered is actually a tautology. Closer analysis would, I believe, reveal that this statement is not a consequence of the three definitions, or groups of definitions, Mr. Ayer mentions, but, rather, that it is a consequence of these definitions *and* of certain generalized nonanalytic statements (empirical laws) about those phenomenal relations among sense data which we call spatial and temporal such as, for instance, that 'later' is transitive, asymmetrical, and irreflexive. Thus, these laws express the factual core of the statement under consideration.

It is interesting to speculate on the causes of what I take to be Mr. Ayer's error on this particular point. One contributing cause, or so I believe, is a certain customary looseness in the use of 'grammatical' which assimilates this term, erroneously, to 'analytic'. We have come to speak, in what is otherwise a very attractive simile, of the grammar of colors; on a

---

[4] Several writers recently expressed the opinion that the use of definitions as a tool of philosophical analysis leads to certain difficulties to which they refer as the paradox of analysis. These issues I had to neglect in the present discussion, but I have taken them up in the paper mentioned in the preceding footnote.

[186]

different level of complexity, we say at times that 'I feel your pain', if taken literally, makes no sense according to the grammar of the personal pronouns. All this, I submit, can be very misleading. Some fundamental empirical laws have indeed been frozen into what grammarians, but not logicians, call the grammar of our ordinary language. Only in this sense—a purely philological sense, as it were—are certain non-tautological generalities on a par with tautologies. In a positivistic metaphysics there is all the difference in the world between 'everything is either red or not red' and 'nothing is (at the same time) red and green'. The use of 'grammatical', which I have criticized, blurs the distinction; the vagueness it encourages is part of the fog that beclouds this whole area of linguistic or grammatical convention. It will be noticed that when I speak, in the preceding section and elsewhere in this note, of the grammar of existence, 'grammar' is used in its stricter, logical (syntactical) sense.

One more and, to my mind, particularly unfortunate confusion can be traced back to the same sources. Let me explain. Watching how people actually use a language that is not formal, we often do not know whether a certain statement they make is the definition, or part of the definition, of one of the terms that occur in it. In order to find out one must, following a well-known line of thought, observe how the users of the language behave. If observation reveals that there is no possible state of affairs that they would accept as negative evidence, then the statement is to be construed as a definitional tautology. In displaying or not displaying this kind of behavior users exert what one might call an implicit choice. As far as it goes, this is perfectly correct; yet it is the starting point of what I like to call a verbal bridge, that is, of a more or less implicit fallacious argument. Here are

[187]

the successive links of the bridge. One, definitions are a matter of choice. Two, definitions are tautologies. Three, tautologies, *including the nondefinitional ones,* are a matter of choice or linguistic convention. Put this way, the fallacy is obvious. Also, it should be clear that the proposed observational test is a matter of anthropology; and the philosophy of logic begins where anthropology leaves off. To believe, as some contemporary British analysts apparently do, that to articulate clearly the "logic" of such observational tests is all we can do about the philosophy of logic constitutes but another variant of either psychologism or scientism. Perhaps one could call it a casuistic or a common-sense variant. But to have recognized a position in the philosophy of logic as either psychologistic or scientistic is, I take it, tantamount to having refuted it.

Whenever rules about the choice or for the use of a language are discussed, one question of fundamental importance suggests itself. The question, or perhaps I had better say the objection—for it seems to throw serious doubt on the significance of this whole business of rules—is the following. In what language does one state the rules concerning the choice or use of one's language? One possible answer is that the statement of these rules must be considered as merely "informal." In other words, these rules are not properly part of the language or, rather, not part of a proper language, that is, of a language that satisfies certain requirements set up "informally" by the philosophers who propose this answer. What I dislike about their solution is that it is dogmatic in refusing to proceed with analysis where I believe further analysis is possible. Also, it excludes itself, at least in a certain sense, from further consideration. An alternative answer maintains that the rules are them-

[188]

selves part of the language whose structure and use they regulate. Some who believe that such self-reference leads to insurmountable difficulties and yet dislike the first alternative have devised a third kind of answer. They maintain that our language is, in a certain sense, not one language but a hierarchy of sublanguages. Upon this view, our two rules or, rather, what corresponds to them in a more exact formulation, would belong to a sublanguage that is called the pragmatic metalanguage of the sublanguage in which we speak about sense data. In stating such rules we do, therefore, not proceed *pre*scriptively but, rather, we clarify *de*scriptively or, if you prefer, we reconstruct the grammar of such descriptive terms as 'perceiving' and 'knowing'. But I notice that in using 'grammar' the way I just did I have slipped into the usage I criticized a moment ago. 'Axiomatics', instead of 'grammar', is the better term; for the clarification obtained is strictly comparable to the one we achieve in, say, an axiomatic reconstruction of geometry. Though it has undoubtedly many difficulties of its own, this view is, to my mind, the most promising of the three. To mention one advantage, the Principle of Acquaintance itself becomes part of a descriptive reconstruction of our language, not a dogmatic basis of it. Nor is it, upon this view, analytic and, therefore, less easily mistaken for a "linguistic convention." Thus we approach, in our own manner, Husserl's admirable ideal of philosophy as a descriptive discipline.[5]

[5] I now (1953) consider this formulation inadequate. I still believe that the act verbs must be represented in the ideal language. But I prefer not to speak of its various layers as sub- or metalanguages. This terminology is rather misleading. One thing it blurs is that the whole construction is carried out in ordinary English, yet without any reference to prospective interpretation. There is nothing "dogmatic" about that. Furthermore, the Principle of Acquaintance is a "principle" only in the sense that if one can construct an ideal language conforming to it, then certain philosophical positions can be clarified. This clarification occurs, of course, in ordinary English.

[189]

### III

Unqualified rejection of an undefined predicate of existence is one of the cornerstones of all positivistic philosophizing. Or, perhaps, I had better say that positivists will always attempt to achieve the reconstruction of our language without introducing an undefined verb 'exist'. This formulation agrees better with my desire to minimize the dogmatic and to maximize the descriptive aspect of philosophical analysis. For one proceeds, in an obvious sense, descriptively when one tries to reconstruct the language that we actually speak about our world; and one is not, in the ordinary sense, dogmatic when one points at the clarifications that a certain kind of reconstruction, *if successful throughout,* would produce. A positivist who wishes to be as explicit and as undogmatic as he can possibly be on this particular issue of existence would, therefore, have to say this: "I am committed to a reconstruction (or analysis, that amounts to the same thing) without an undefined predicate of existence because such an analysis, if otherwise successful, eliminates certain difficulties which, if I am to judge from the historical arguments among realists and idealists, cannot be eliminated otherwise. In this sense, and only in this sense, did I speak of a cornerstone of my metaphysics."

It will be well to state clearly how this commitment relates to what I have called the two partial clarifications. The first, it will be remembered, is an analysis of statements that refer to physical objects, such as 'this chair exists (this is a real chair)'. To believe that some such statements do not yield to further analysis is to admit 'exist' as an undefined predicate. In order to avoid this alternative, positivists accept the first clarification, which maintains that any such statement may be replaced by a class of statements of either a sense data or a percept language, none of which contains a predicate of existence, though they may contain, and do in fact contain, the phrase 'there is (exists) a such-and-such'. For in this latter phrase, which is the starting point of the second clarification, 'exists' is not a predicate at all, either defined or undefined, but an inseparable part of the so-called existential operator, which is a logical or nondescriptive symbol of its own kind. Nor is this operator indispensable, for, according to a familiar tautology, 'there is a such-and-such' means the same as 'not-(everything is not a such-and-such)'. Thus, whatever difficuties may be discovered in this meaning and use of existence must already inhere in the meaning and use of 'not' and 'all'. I mention this because certain passages in Russell's recent *Inquiry* sound as if he believed that an empiricist cannot very well account for negative and for universal statements. I, for one, am entirely out of sympathy with such a conception of empiricism; probably I do not even understand Russell's Parmenidean scruples. Or is the supposed difficulty, perhaps, but another result of the failure to keep meaning and use sufficiently distinct from truth and verification? If so, then the error is the same as the one I have pointed out in the current formulation of the meaning criterion. On the other hand, if one accepts the all-some-not machinery of our logic, then one can, in a sense data language, speak, without naming them, of things which, if one could name them, that is, *if they were present*, would be sense data. At least, such an empiricism is not that straw man of an in-front-of-my-nose

[191]

philosophy which some critics still insist on fighting. Yet, I repeat, the somethings whose existence we thus assert, which we describe, which we include in our all-statements "are" sense data. I realize, of course, that formulations such as this are the starting point of the traditional dialectic. It may start from the 'are', which I have just quoted for emphasis; or it may start from the clause 'if they were present' (or, still more unfortunately, 'if they existed'), which I used a moment ago. *In our ordinary language,* I am convinced, *the magic circle of this dialectic cannot be broken;* earlier or later one will be caught in the snares of whatever one says. The decisive clarification lies in the fact that *the whole mechanism of variables and operators* through which we predicate of nonpresent or—if they will have it this way— nonexistent sense data *belongs,* in the reconstruction, *to the logical, nondescriptive skeleton of our language.* Variables (and operators occur only in connection with variables) do not refer to anything, in the sense in which names and constant predicates do refer to something. The ontological issue has, therefore, no direct connection with the analysis of the phrase 'there is a such-and-such'. The implicit belief in such a connection, probably caused by the error of not distinguishing sharply between the proper areas of the two partial clarifications, is, to my mind, as vexing as any of the illusions that beset the ontological problem. Apparently it has led to what is one of Russell's most curious—and, at the same time, most widely known—opinions, namely, that we know sense data by acquaintance and physical objects, *otherwise in the same manner,* by description. If one could, properly speaking, say that variables refer to anything, one could express this opinion by saying that the 'x' of a sense data language refers sometimes to sense data and sometimes to

[192]

physical objects. This is patently absurd. Russell's [6] persistent tendency to connect his theory of descriptions, whether definite or indefinite, with the realism issue is, to my mind, one of the main reasons that his epistemological analyses are so much less admirable than his logical achievements. This, however, is merely by the way. I turn now to Mr. Ayer's views on existence.

In which sense and to what purpose does Mr. Ayer wish to say that something that is a sense datum exists? That he does wish to say it is quite obvious from his proposal that, if 'a' is the name of a sense datum, 'a exists' and 'a is directly apprehended' be considered as entailing each other. Assuming, as I shall, that the language with which we deal is a sense data language, I shall not need to insert every time the clause 'if 'a' is the name of a sense datum'; the names of a sense data language cannot refer to anything else. But what, I repeat, is Mr. Ayer's meaning of 'exist'? As long as we concern ourselves, as he does, with sense data (or percepts), the meaning of existence that is pertinent to the first clarification cannot be involved. As for the second meaning, it has been seen that we can speak of the existence of things not directly apprehended; in fact, just when we wish to speak of such things the phrase 'there is a such-and-such' proves to be most useful. Under the circumstances it is difficult to be sure what Mr. Ayer has in mind. Yet I shall venture an opinion. I believe that *what he wishes to express is the rule which I have called the Principle of Proper Names.* That his formula does, after a fashion, imply what this rule states seems to me fairly obvious. So I shall proceed to

---

[6] See, for an early statement, "Knowledge by Acquaintance and Knowledge by Description," *Proceedings of the Aristotelian Society,* 11 (1911), 108-28 (particularly p. 114).

explain why I believe that there is nothing else that it could plausibly express.

I have at least two reasons for the opinion that Mr. Ayer does not believe 'exist' is an undefined predicate. As I have said before, it is extremely unlikely that anyone who holds positivistic views also holds this belief; and Mr. Ayer's frame of reference is, by and large, positivistic. This is my first reason. Second, if 'exist' were an undefined predicate (and if 'directly apprehended' is taken to be undefined), then the sentence 'something exists if and only if it is directly apprehended' would be strictly comparable to the sentence 'something is hot if and only if it is green' and could, therefore, not be a tautology. Or, rather, to consider it a tautology one would have to hold that tautologies can be produced by linguistic or grammatical convention, in a sense in which we have seen that this is not the case. Now I am not at all sure that Mr. Ayer would agree with everything I have said about grammar and linguistic conventions in the preceding section. On the other hand, I have not found in his latest exposition anything that would indicate that he has at this point fallen into this particular error. I conclude, therefore, that he proposes 'something exists if and only if it is directly apprehended'—or, as I had better say now 'something exists means something is directly apprehended'—as a definition of 'exist'. This, it will be remembered, is what I said he meant at the beginning of this paper; but there I did not give any reasons. Formally, there is still the possibility that he intended to define direct apprehension in terms of existence. This, however, is hardly reasonable; besides, 'exist' would then again have to be construed as an undefined predicate.

Mr. Ayer's definition, or so I am prepared to maintain, is both useless and very confusing. As was seen in the discussion of his thing-time-space illustration, the unraveling of long and rather complex chains of definitions may lead to genuine clarifications. Definitions as simple as the one proposed cannot yield any such clarifications; all they provide are synonyms, in the ordinary philological sense of the term. 'To be apprehended directly' or, as I shall permit myself to say at this point, 'percipi' is thus offered as a synonym of 'esse'. Now we have seen that the two important clarifications of 'esse' do not have the slightest tendency to reveal it as a synonym of 'percipi'. If it is to be of any significance at all, Mr. Ayer's proposal implies therefore, first, that there is a *third* meaning of 'esse' which philosophers have struggled to clarify, and, second, that with this meaning 'esse' turns out to be a synonym of 'percipi'. These two assertions are patently and irremediably false. The reasons I would adduce for their being false are those stated in G. E. Moore's "Refutation of Idealism." But then, someone might ask, why not simply introduce 'esse' as a defined verb synonymous with 'percipi', thus salvaging Berkeley's formula by "linguistic convention"? Doing this certainly does not mean that one *must* confuse what are now the three partial clarifications of existence. If the matter is put that way, then no argument is left, except that some may feel that the third "clarification" does not clarify anything and is futile at best. Moreover, I cannot help feeling that, far from trying to resuscitate Berkeley's formula, we should take particular care to reconstruct our language so that it cannot even be stated. For as long as we shall retain it, its idealistic overtones will, I fear, continue to befuddle us—even if we do not, like the Hegelian idealists and the pragmatists, disregard the phenomenal objectivity of the given, or, like most of Berkeley's positivistic followers, deny the phenomenal givenness of the cognitive act.

[195]

Let me conclude by saying that I do not believe Mr. Ayer actually holds any of the opinions which I have criticized so harshly. As I have said before, I think that his "esse est percipi" was offered as a formulation of the Principle of Proper Names. I believe to have shown that this formulation has little to recommend itself.

# RUSSELL ON PARTICULARS *

THE FOLLOWING remarks have been stimulated by an argument Russell developed through three chapters (VI-VIII) of his recently published *Inquiry into Meaning and Truth*.[1] In this part of the book he examines the possibility of an analysis of the kind commonly known as a sense data analysis, without, however, referring to particulars, that is, in terms of universals only. Indicating the lines that he thinks such an analysis would have to follow, he arrives, tentatively, at the conclusion that it could be carried out successfully. Presently I shall criticize Russell's proposals, and I shall also be critical of the reasons he gives for the importance of this kind of analysis. To restate the last point, I believe, contrary to Russell's opinion, that a "particular-free" analysis would not tend to throw any light on those philosophical puzzles—if puzzles they are—which he thinks it would solve. I shall also contend that such an analysis is, in fact, impossible, though I agree with Russell that, for reasons different from his, its possibility would be philosophically rather significant. In the first section I shall, in my own manner, formulate the problem and what I take to

* *The Philosophical Review*, 56 (January, 1947), 59-72. Reprinted by permission.

[1] Bertrand Russell, *Inquiry into Meaning and Truth* (New York: W. W. Norton, 1940).

[197]

be its significance. In the second section I shall present what I believe is a proof of the impossibility of a particular-free analysis. In the third section I shall briefly state my criticism of what Russell does and of his reasons for doing it.

I

By a sense data analysis I mean an attempt to describe all percepts, though not necessarily all contents of consciousness, by means of a language whose simplest or basic sentences are of the kind exemplified by 'this is green' or 'this is later than that', where the descriptive universals 'green' and 'later' have their ordinary (phenomenal) meanings, and where the referents of 'this' and 'that' are objects of the sort many philosophers call simple momentary givennesses or sense data. The referents of 'this' and 'that', thus used, are often called *Particulars*. Since 'particular' has also a purely linguistic meaning I shall, in the present note, capitalize the term whenever it occurs in its nonlinguistic sense. As far as the notion of a sense data analysis is concerned, there is the further proviso that the descriptive universals that can be properly predicated about particulars are the only undefined universals needed. In other words, a sense data analysis always undertakes to define such descriptive predicates as 'stone' and 'tree', that is, the universals predicated of physical objects. For the most part, though not always, there is also the explicit claim that predicates such as 'color', occurring in 'green is a color', that is, quite literally, all predicates of higher type, can be thus eliminated. Important and controversial as all this is, for the purpose at hand we can let it go. For, if the referents of the basic sentences of an ordinary sense data language can be described in a particular-free manner, then it follows that whatever can be said or, if you please, reconstructed in an ordinary sense data language can also be said or reconstructed in a language of that special kind. And whether or not this is so is, following Russell, the one question I have undertaken to examine. But in order to state precisely what is meant by 'particular-free', one must first consider the linguistic meaning of 'particular' and distinguish it carefully from that of 'Particular'.

As far as I know no philosopher has ever proposed the use of a language that is not of the subject-predicate form in the ordinary linguistic sense [2] of subject and predicate, a sense common to Indo-Germanic grammar and the formal languages of the kind developed in *Principia Mathematica*. In these languages expressions that can occur both as subjects and as predicates are, in a purely linguistic sense of the term, called universals. The universal 'green', for instance, occurs as subject in 'green is a color', as predicate in 'this is green'. Expressions that occur as subjects, but not as predicates (and which are not, in Russell's sense, descriptions) are called *particulars*. Whenever I write 'particular' with a lower-case initial, it ought to be understood in this grammatical sense. Now I am ready to state Russell's problem. He does not suggest that we abandon the subject-predicate schema. Thus the analysis he proposes is not particular-free; nor is it, if I understand him correctly, Particular-free. The point is this. In an ordinary sense data analysis the referents of the particulars are the Particulars. What Russell suggests is an analysis in which the referents of the particulars are Universals, or, more precisely, the referents of those universals that occur in the basic sentences

---

[2] It should be noticed, though, that 'predicate', as here used, includes relations.

of an ordinary sense data language. It will be noticed that I have now extended the device of upper- and lower-case initials to "universal." Also, it will be seen that "particular-free" is really not a good name for the kind of analysis Russell proposes; yet I shall, for want of a better term, continue to use it occasionally. If, then, in such an analysis the referents of the particulars are to be Universals, one might ask whether, conversely, the Particulars are to be designated by universals. This would indeed be so. But I feel that before attending to these matters I should state the advantage which, in the opinion of some philosophers, might be gained from a particular-free analysis.

The awkwardnesses in which particularity involves us are many. There is, first, a difficulty concerning the psychological or, as I would rather say, the *phenomenological* status of Particulars. As it is usually put, the point is that the content of even the simplest awareness is never one or, in the relational case, several *quid,* but always, whether property or relation, a *quale,* that is, a Universal. Against such views one could defend the unqualitied Particular by pointing out its indispensability in fixing the location of the qualities. But those who are skeptical of Particulars might insist that such location is itself a matter of relational structure and that the pertinent spatial and temporal relations, themselves Universals, are, upon correct analysis, found to obtain among qualities. At this point some would, perhaps, speak more cautiously of exemplified qualities; as far as I can see, this caution neither adds to nor detracts from the argument.[3] If, then, one is on such grounds skeptical of Particulars, one

---

[3] The reason for my belief that such caution or qualification is irrelevant can be stated in a very ancient terminology: exemplification (predication) is a relation *secundae intentionis.*

may incline toward the opinion that the particulars of an ordinary sense data analysis are, in a manner of speaking, artifacts of language. And there is, of course, no better way of proving this contention than to construct a usable and adequate language whose ground layer of particulars refers not to Particulars but to Universals. The case of these skeptics would be further strengthened if what comes, within the new language, closest to being the proper name of a Particular should turn out to be a construction, in the sense in which whatever can be obtained by the method of extensive abstraction is sometimes called a construction. However, I do not mean to recommend such vague and, to my mind, dangerous usage of 'construction'. Outside of mathematics, extensive abstraction consists simply in the definition of descriptive universals from undefined ones; the referents that exemplify such terms are, of course, not in any reasonable sense constructed. To say the same thing differently, the distinction between defined and undefined descriptive predicates, fundamental as I believe it to be, does not imply the kind of discrimination, either phenomenological or ontological, that is connoted by a certain usage of 'construction'.[4] Yet an analysis in which the names of the Particulars, or what comes closest to them, turn out to be defined predicates would, I believe, realize and, at the same time, clarify a further tenet of those who do, on the grounds now considered, object to Particulars.

There is, second, another cluster of awkwardnesses tied up, not with the phenomenological status of the Particulars but, rather, with the *linguistic* or, if one wishes to speak

[4] For a fuller discussion of these issues see my essay on "Undefined Descriptive Predicates," *Philosophy and Phenomenological Research*, 8 (1947), 55-82.

loosely, with the logical status of the particulars. So it is natural enough that these difficulties have lately come in for a good deal of attention on the part of logical positivists. It seems, though, that a good case can be made by historians who trace the issue back to Hegel, to the idealistic tradition in general and, perhaps, even to the Eleatics. I have reference to the argument about proper names; and 'proper name' is, within an ordinary sense data analysis, a synonym for 'particular'. Readers of Russell's *Inquiry* will remember that he uses at one place the expository device of calling Particulars by such names as 'John' and 'Henry', thus replacing the idiomatic 'this is green' by 'Henry is green'. More formally one writes, instead of 'John' and 'Henry', letters such as '*a*' and '*b*'. This brings us face to face with the difficulty that '*a*' and 'Henry' do not connote anything in the sense in which 'green' and all other descriptive universals do connote an identifiable character. 'This' and 'here', as Hegel already knew, designate everything and, therefore, nothing. To put it the way Peirce did, proper names are indexical, and not presentative signs. So far the argument has run parallel, though in a different vein, to the one I have called phenomenological. Peirce's formulation leads on to a further difficulty, the one that makes us prefer '*a*' or 'Henry' to 'this' and similar spoken gestures. Uneasiness about these gestures as such is one of the philosophical motives behind the recent insistence on the so-called metalinguistic approach and its impressive technical development. Quite untechnically speaking, the idea is that spoken gestures represent, informally or idiomatically, the semantical tie and transcend, by the same token, the language which they thus relate to its referents. So they cannot, according to this view,

[202]

occur in formal or philosophically correct language. The 'a' and 'b' we are forced to use for proper names in formal languages have indeed the virtue of making it clear that an index taken out of its context does not indicate anything. Nor are these signs either presentative, like all names of Universals, or structural in the sense in which the connectives and the copula are structural, nonreferential, or logical. They constitute, besides the structural and the presentative signs, a third class by itself, representing, properly according to one view, the category of particularity or, improperly according to another, what does not really belong in the language itself. If one is of the latter opinion, what is more natural than to ask whether one could not build an adequate language in which all nonstructural signs are fully and unambiguously presentative, that is, a language whose particulars are on a par with its universals in that they all refer to identifiable characters or Universals? Thus one is again led to the particular-free language Russell wishes to design.

These, I feel, are two groups of *good* reasons for being interested in the problem of a particular-free analysis. Its possibility would, as it were, definitely settle the points I have mentioned; or, perhaps, I had better say it would settle them as definitely as one could ever hope to settle any philosophical issue. This, however, does not mean that the actual impossibility of a particular-free analysis indicates the unsoundness of the views which such analysis, if possible, would conclusively establish. Its impossibility merely shows that particularity is indeed a fundamental or categorial feature of our world. The mistaken belief that this state of affairs is irreconcilable with a positivistic metaphysics has something to do with the *bad* reasons that led Russell to investigate the problem. But of these matters I propose to speak later.

II

A particular-free language cannot even adequately describe perceptual fields so simple that they can be described by basic sentences of an ordinary sense data language. In order to prove this, I shall show that the usual statements which are needed to describe such a field, that is, statements whose particulars refer to Particulars, cannot be adequately reconstructed within a language whose particulars refer to the Universals that present themselves in these fields. If one shows this, one has, I take it, also shown that our world as it is, or, for that matter, any world in this one categorial aspect like ours, cannot be so described. Specifically, I shall consider, within the specious present, a series of qualitied points. A linear arrangement of patches of different shapes, colors (hues), and brilliancies exemplifies a perceptual field of the kind I have in mind. It will be noticed that, like Hume's atoms, my points are really extended. This is merely a simplifying assumption and must not be taken to indicate agreement with Hume's views on continuity, divisibility, and infinity. Agreement or disagreement with Hume on these matters is equally irrelevant. For, if one could in a particular-free manner describe a world, spatially and temporally discontinuous but otherwise like ours, then one should also be able so to describe our own continuous universe. The same holds true for the number of undefined descriptive characters, that is, in the illustration I have chosen, the number of, by assumption, unanalyzable shapes, hues, and brilliancies. For again, particularity is not in any

[204]

manner connected with the number of undefined descriptive characters, whether this number be finite, denumerable, or that of the continuum. But before making any assumption concerning this number I had better explain more carefully the formal aspect of what one would have to do if one were to carry out Russell's program.

The particulars of the language from which one starts form a class, $a$. Its members—let us call them '$a_1$', '$a_2$', '$a_3$', and so on—refer by assumption to such Universals as green, blue, round, square, bright. The undefined descriptive universals of the language are of three kinds. Either they are (1) spatial or (2) of the kind exemplified by 'this green is brighter than that red', where 'this' and 'that' do, of course, not refer to particular instances of these colors, which are Particulars, but to particular shades of them, which are Universals. Or they are (3) nonrelational predicates such as 'color', 'shape', and 'brilliancy'. As far as I can see, the predicates of the second kind are not at all relevant for the problem at hand, and I shall not, therefore, mention them further. The predicates of the third kind I shall neglect for the moment but shall return to them presently. So there are only the spatial relations left. Of these there are, under our simplifying assumptions, but two; one of coincidence, call it '$S$', and one of order, call it '$P$'. '$a_1 S a_2$' reads '$a_1$ coincides with $a_2$'; '$a_1 P a_2$' reads '$a_1$ precedes $a_2$'. The statement '$a_1 S a_2$' will be true if the field of which it is predicated contains at least one point that exemplifies both Universals mentioned. S is, accordingly, symmetrical and reflexive, but not transitive. To fix the ideas, let us further assume '$a_1 P a_2$' to mean that $a_1$ is to the left of $a_2$. This statement will thus be true whenever it is made about a field that contains at least two points so that the left one has the character $a_1$ while the right one has the character $a_2$. Though the points themselves are serially ordered, it is easily understood that $P$ does not have the properties of asymmetry, irreflexivity, and transitivity which are characteristic of serial order. For in a field in which at least two points have the same character $a_1$, one has '$a_1Pa_1$'; in a three-point field of the type $a_1a_2a_1$ (say, green-blue-green) one has '$a_2Pa_1$' and '$a_1Pa_2$', but not, as one would if $P$ were transitive, '$a_2Pa_2$'.

To describe in our peculiar language a field of the kind considered is to state or know all the instances of the relations $S$ and $P$ that obtain in it. For this, as far as spatial arrangement is concerned, is all there is to be known, or, if you please, all that can be said in such a language. To ask whether our ordinary language and everything we can actually say or know in it about these fields can be reconstructed in a particular-free manner amounts, therefore, to proposing the following *bundling problem*. Assume that a given class $a$ is the field of two given relations, the first of which, $S$, is symmetrical and reflexive, while no condition restricts the generality of the second, $P$. Do such $a$, $S$, and $P$, if known or given, uniquely determine a *series* $a_1$, $a_2$, $a_3$, $\cdots$ of subclasses of $a$, which may have members in common and which satisfy the following three conditions? (1) There is a subclass to which both $a_1$ and $a_2$ belong, if and only if $a_1Sa_2$. (2) There are at least two subclasses, $a_1$ and $a_2$, so that $a_1$ is a member of $a_1$ and $a_2$ a member of $a_2$, and so that $a_1$ precedes $a_2$ in the serial order of the subclasses, if and only if $a_1Pa_2$. (3) If the relation $P$ holds between one element of a subclass $a_1$, and one element of a subclass $a_2$, then it holds also, in the same order, between any two elements of these two classes. Intuitively speaking, the bundles or subclasses are of course our points; they are classes or predicates of our peculiar

[206]

particulars; and the question is whether these predicates can be defined—by extensive abstraction, as one says—in terms of the two known relations. For these to be known or given means, as far as the formal aspect of the matter is concerned, that, in the case of $S$, a set of pairs of elements of $a$, and, in the case of $P$, a set of such ordered pairs are known or given in exactly the same sense in which the data of a mathematical problem are said to be known or given.[5] What it means for $S$ and $P$ to be given phenomenologically is a different matter, and one that does not concern us here. Also, it is virtually obvious that the bundling problem has, in the general case, either no solution or more than one; only under special conditions will the solution be unique. Yet an explicit argument is a little long-winded; so I shall present it in three steps.

1. In agreement with what has been said before, I shall assume that the class $a$ of identifiable characters is finite. The class of all bundles or points that are different from each other in the sense that they do not exemplify the same characters is, therefore, also finite. So are, in this case, the sets of pairs and ordered pairs that determine $S$ and $P$ respectively. There is, however, no limit to the number of points in fields completely characterized by a finite $a$, $S$, and $P$. This can be used to demonstrate the inadequacy of our language. Assume that, for a finite $a$, $S$, and $P$, the series $a_1, a_2, \cdots, a_k$ constitutes one solution of the bundling problem, and assume, furthermore, that $P$ consists of all the ordered pairs that one can form from the elements of $a$. It is easy to see that for such a $P$ the series $a_1, a_2, \cdots, a_k$, $a_1, a_2, \cdots, a_k$ and, generally, those obtained by repeating the original series of $k$ points any number of times are also

5 It is not required that the two members of a pair are different.

solutions. I shall, as a next step, show that there are solutions of bundling problems with this particular $P$.

2. Consider the case of five characters, $a$, $b$, $c$, $d$, $e$; and make both $S$ and $P$ consist of all possible pairs. Form the ten possible triples of characters; write them in lexicographical order, $abc$, $abd$, $\cdots$, $cde$ and call them, in this order, $\alpha_1$, $\alpha_2$, $\cdots$, $\alpha_{10}$. Everybody can, with a little patience, see for himself that the series $\alpha_1$, $\alpha_3$, $\alpha_4$, $\alpha_5$, $\alpha_9$ is a solution of this particular bundling problem. But so is the series $\alpha_1$, $\alpha_3$, $\alpha_4$, $\alpha_5$, $\alpha_7$, $\alpha_9$, the series $\alpha_1$, $\alpha_3$, $\alpha_4$, $\alpha_5$, $\alpha_9$, $\alpha_7$, and others. Though it is not difficult to formulate a general rule, it is hardly worth while to do so. At any rate, one sees that the ambiguity is even more radical than we have already been led to expect by the possibility of iteration. All this means, of course, that *there are fields which differ in number, order, and kind of points, and among which we could not discriminate by means of our peculiar language.* So this language is, in an obvious and obviously pertinent sense of the term, inadequate. Yet there is one objection to this conclusion which is, I believe, worth considering.

3. Some might agree with me that such relatively contingent features as continuity and the number of characteristics have nothing to do with the much deeper-lying categorial feature of particularity, but might, at the same time, feel that there are other features, of comparable depth, which I have neglected and which, if included in its assumptions, would so modify the bundling problem as to make it yield, at least within reasonable range, unique solutions. It so happens that there is, indeed, one feature that one could not unnaturally connect with particularity and which also lies—in the opinion of many, though not in my own—sufficiently deep to justify the expectation that its

introduction might make a difference. I am thinking of the fact that the same monochromatic patch or point cannot exemplify two different colors; that it cannot, generally speaking, bear two undefined characters of the same "dimension." Recognizing these dimensions means, within our particular-free language, to introduce the third kind of universals, such as 'color' and 'shape', which I have mentioned at the beginning of the section. To introduce them formally and so to introduce the critical feature amounts to (1) dividing the class $\alpha$ into mutually exclusive subclass $\beta_i$, and (2) postulating that the relation S does not obtain between any two different members of a $\beta$-class. But even under this additional assumption very simple bundling problems have no adequate solution. Consider the case of two $\beta$-classes, each of which has two members. One may think of two shapes $(a_1, a_2)$ and two colors $(b_1, b_2)$. Choose now S and P so that they consist of all the pairs that are possible under the additional assumption and you will find that $a_1b_2$, $a_2b_1$, $a_2b_2$, $a_1b_1$ and $a_1b_2$, $a_2b_1$, $a_1b_1$, $a_2b_2$ are two series of points (not to be confused with pairs, though each of them happens to bundle two characters!) which satisfy the conditions of this particular bundling problem. That means, of course, that we could not, in our peculiar language, discriminate between two fields that contain the same four points, all different from each other, in different orders. Again, the result could be generalized; but again, it is hardly worth the trouble to do so. For we have already, and as far as I can see conclusively, proved the inadequacy of a particular-free language.

III

It will, perhaps, be best to begin the discussion of Russell's argument with a broad and interpretative outline that reveals what I have permitted myself to call the bad reasons for his interest in a particular-free analysis. So I shall do this first; afterwards and in conclusion, I shall gather some detailed comments and criticisms.

1. Everybody who is but superficially acquainted with Russell's philosophical career knows that the problem of ontological realism has never ceased to occupy and, I dare say, to vex him. It is almost as if he were torn between what he would probably call phenomenological subjectivism or empirical idealism on the one hand and the charms of a realistic sanction for what we all accept, in a common-sense manner, as the teachings of physics and physiology on the other. According to these teachings one might say, in a slight paraphrase of certain passages in the *Inquiry,* that whenever I have a cat-percept, then there also *is* a cat—at least as a rule, and we are not concerned here with the exceptions. For Russell the realist, such being there of a cat is a piece of empirical *impersonal* knowledge; Russell the phenomenalist insists that "what we directly know when we say [in a perceptual judgment] 'this is a cat' is a state of ourselves." [6] There is nothing new in all this, neither within Russell's work nor otherwise. New and, in a certain sense, interesting is the way by which the Russell of the *Inquiry* proposes to escape the classical dilemma. His point of attack is the 'this' in the perceptual judgment 'this is a cat' or, for that matter, in the basic sentence 'this is green'. He first spends some time in pointing out the mutual substitutability

[6] *Inquiry,* p. 142.

[210]

of 'this' and such expressions as 'I-now'. The oversimplified and, in my opinion, outright mistaken conception of the Self and the perceptual act which probably underlies this part of the argument is not now my concern. The point is that for Russell the indexical signs, or *egocentric particulars* as he calls them, are the carriers of the subjectivity, in the full classical sense of "subjectivity." Also, Russell thinks— and this has something to do with what I have called linguistic reasons for the interest in our problem—that all particulars are in a sense like 'this' and thus infected by the same subjectivity. If, therefore, indexical particulars could be eliminated from our perceptual judgments, then, he feels, "there can be empirical impersonal knowledge, and two men who believe (say) that hydrogen is the lightest element *may* be both believing the same proposition." [7] In case there should be any doubt left that the realism issue is behind all this, let me add that we read, in the same paragraph, "that it is the ideal of science to dispense with egocentric particulars." Here, then, is the main motive and key to the understanding of Russell's proposal to do away with indexical particulars.

There is also, as a subsidiary motive, the antisubstantialist argument. If one regards 'this is red' as a subject-predicate proposition, then one finds, according to Russell, "that 'this' becomes a substance, an unknowable something in which properties inhere, but which, nevertheless, is not identical with the sum of its properties." [8] Historically, that is, in view of the role particularity has played in the Aristotelian tradition, the connection is quite understandable and *prima facie* plausible. Also, it is understandable that an "empirical"

[7] *Ibid.*, p. 157.
[8] *Ibid.*, p. 120.

realist wants to dissociate himself from substantialist views. Structurally, however, Russell's antisubstantialist argument against the Particulars is merely the ontological version, as it were, of what I have called, in an earlier section, the phenomenological reasons for uneasiness about Particulars. This has something to do with my considering Russell's two motives, both the antisubjectivist and the antisubstantialist, bad reasons. And the time has indeed come where I must state my grounds for this rejection. I must say, then, with due respect to Russell, that these grounds are, at the present stage of the analytical enterprise, obvious. Another way of saying the same thing is that they are implicit in the *purely phenomenological way in which the whole issue of particularity and particular-free analysis can be treated* and in which I have actually treated it in this note. The possibility of a particular-free analysis is, indeed, an issue within phenomenology and, as positivists would expect, amenable to linguistic elucidation. But if the issue is one *within* the given, then the result of such elucidation, whatever it may be, cannot possibly bear on questions which concern the status of the given and are thus, in a sense, *about* it. Russell's solution of the classical dilemma, startling at first, is, therefore, purely verbal; and *verbal*, I am afraid, is not what modern analysts mean by *linguistic*.

2. The outstanding characteristic of Russell's specific proposal for the construction of a particular-free language is the introduction of spatial coordinates as nonrelational Universals. His exposition of the idea suffers from an abrupt and unnecessary substitution of "physical" for phenomenological material. But if allowance is made for this complication, the thing amounts to this. To lie on a certain distinguished curve in the visual field is, according to Russell,

a nonrelational Universal (quality) exemplified by all the points or patches on such a curve. If this were so, then one could indeed, instead of speaking of a certain point being red, refer to the bundle consisting of redness and the (spatial) qualities characteristic of the coordinate-curves at whose intersection the point mentioned lies. Here several comments come to mind.

To begin with a purely historical observation, one wonders whether Russell realizes that his proposal revives the doctrine of *local signs*, which has played such an important part in the nineteenth-century discussion of space perception. The term is Lotze's, but the one who most articulately insisted that there are qualities of the kind Russell introduces and, also, that they are intrinsically and irreducibly spatial was Helmholtz's vigorous opponent, Emil Hering. Second, as far as the actual phenomenological givenness of such characters is concerned, there is no other argument than that to which the great British tradition eventually resorts in such cases: go and see whether you find it in yourself! I don't; but perhaps that is merely because I am, and not just on phenomenological grounds, convinced of the essentially relational nature of space. There is, third, another point that disturbs Russell and which, if I understand him at all, comes down to this. Either one assumes that no two different points exemplify the same coordinate-qualities or the device does not do what it is supposed to do, namely, to use Russell's language, guarantee the nonidentity of discernibles. But if one does make this assumption then one faces what is, for Russell, a further difficulty. That no two points have the same coordinate-qualities is a piece of generalized knowledge, that is, according to a line of thought that goes through the whole of the *Inquiry*, knowledge that is not certain and, perhaps, not even empirical. Yet this particular piece of knowledge is of the kind Russell would prefer to consider as certain; just as he prefers an analysis in which what he conceives to be the identity of indiscernibles becomes analytic. To clear up these difficulties, which are, I believe, more apparent than real, one would have to analyze our ideas of certainty and identity; I do not propose to take up either in this note. It should be noticed, though, that I was, in the second section, able to discuss the impossibility of discriminating, within our peculiar language, among fields that contain the same bundle once, twice, or any number of times *without* ever bringing up the philosophical issues connected with the notion of identity.[9] And I have, in doing this, also taken account of spatial relations and not, like Russell, arbitrarily restricted myself to the intrinsic properties of the points, that is, to the qualities in the bundles. The last remark leads to my fourth and last point. I wish to call attention to the extraordinary manner in which Russell neglects the relational aspects of space and proposes to construct it, in a fashion that reminds one of Hume, Hartley, and James Mill, out of qualities conceived in the analogy of sensations. Certainly this does not go well with the incipient holism that is so noticeable at many places throughout the *Inquiry*. But then, such reluctance to do justice to the fundamental importance of relational Universals is, I am afraid, not peculiar to Russell; rather, it is characteristic of both the materialistic and empiricist traditions. This, however, is a large subject, one that I have taken up elsewhere.[10]

[9] The injection of the identity issue is thus but another unnecessary complication of the argument. Also, Russell's conception of identity is inadequate, really a fusion between three different notions. Concerning these matters, see my "Notes on Identity," *Philosophy of Science*, 10 (1943), 163-66; 11 (1944), 123-24.

[10] See note 4.

# PROFESSOR AYER'S ANALYSIS
# OF KNOWING *

IN HIS inaugural lecture [1] Professor A. J. Ayer makes an excellent case for certain opinions that agree closely with some I tried to defend some time ago.[2] In this paper I shall, naturally enough, deal with what I believe is the one major point of disagreement. To pursue this concern properly, it will be necessary to mark off first, at least in a cursory fashion, the area of agreement. I begin, therefore, by stating in my own words and at my own risk three philosophical propositions which, if I understand him correctly, Professor Ayer supports in his inaugural lecture. But I want to make it clear that when I say that an analyst like Professor Ayer defends a philosophical proposition, I mean that he proposes a certain kind of analysis for a group of ordinary or common-sense propositions and that the philosophical propositions are a suggestive or, perhaps, only a conventional label for the clarification that is the hoped-for result of the analysis itself. Here, then, are the three propositions. (1) We do in a common-sense way understand what is meant by speaking of a thought, of its expression, and of its object; yet this threefold

* Analysis, 9 (June, 1949), 98-106. Reprinted by permission.
[1] Thinking and Meaning (London: H. K. Lewis and Co., 1947).
[2] "A Positivistic Metaphysics of Consciousness," Mind, 54 (1945), 193-226.

distinction must not be used uncautiously in certain contexts of analysis. (2) One of the meanings of 'true', which happens to be the one that has caused most trouble to philosophers, involves a relation among symbols rather than a relation between symbols and what they denote. (3) There are, properly speaking, no mental acts. Since the second and the third proposition are stated in technical language, I shall add one explanatory sentence for each of them. The meaning of (2) may also be expressed by saying, as Professor Ayer does, that the problem of truth is semantical, where 'semantical' carries the connotation of 'formal' as opposed to 'factual'. Proposition (3) enjoins us not to construe such sentences as 'I see now something green' or 'I doubt whether it will rain today' by analogy to such sentences as 'John drives the car' or 'This is to the left of that'.

The objection I wish to raise concerns the part of Professor Ayer's analysis for which the third proposition serves as a label. To state my point before arguing it, I believe Professor Ayer denies more than needs to be denied in order to make sure that there are, properly speaking, no mental acts. Also, he denies more than one can safely deny; his asceticism falsifies what one may, with some latitude, call his introspective account of those mental states to which we all, when we are not philosophizing, refer by saying that we know, or doubt, or believe, or entertain a proposition. Accordingly, I shall *first* show that Professor Ayer's analysis of knowing implies certain assertions about what *I* experience whenever I know something. By the testimony of my experience these assertions are false. *Second*, I shall explain how, in my opinion, this factual error vitiates Professor Ayer's philosophical analysis.

[216]

Following Professor Ayer's example I shall use '*p*' not as a variable but as an abbreviation for such sentences as 'This is green'. Keeping this in mind, one can say that the following two statements summarize his analysis of the sentence 'A knows that *p*'. (1) The sentence speaks about certain dispositional properties of A. (2) While these dispositional properties may not be the only thing involved, the sentence does not refer to a specific state of mind of A; this for the very good reason that there is no such state. It is true, though, that Professor Ayer mentions in passing the possibility of certain "feelings" of A being involved in the meaning of the sentence. To this I shall attend presently. As for the main point, I have not the slightest doubt that we do on *some* occasions use the critical sentence so that Professor Ayer's analysis of it would be correct. Sometimes we even use the sentence '*I* know that *p*' so that his account would be adequate. Imagine, for instance, that while I drive a car along a road so familiar that I need not pay attention to it, an officious companion points out to me that there is a turn ahead, to which I reply 'Yes, I know'. An experimental psychologist may even use the sentence 'This rat knows that *p*' with a very elaborate meaning that is closely related to what Professor Ayer proposes as the proper analysis, on *all* occasions, of 'A knows that *p*'. Such an analysis in dispositional terms I shall henceforth call a *behavioristic* analysis.

Assume that A has, as one usually says, a green datum and that he is aware of it in the sense that he would, if asked, immediately say 'This is green'. Some describe this state of affairs by saying that he has the datum and thinks the thought of its being green. But we are warned against the uncautious use of such phrases by the first of the three philosophical propositions I stated at the outset. Be that as it may, it is evident to me that a behavioristic analysis of A's having, in this sense, a datum is possible. But I also believe that there is, *over and above the dispositions mentioned* in such an analysis, another thing, namely A's *mental state*, to which I shall refer as a state with the *text* 'This is green'. Thus, when I speak of a mental state with the text '*p*', I do not just refer to the words, as types, that are used to assert what '*p*' asserts. Nor do I merely speak of the occurrence of a set of tokens of this type; A would produce such tokens in certain other mental states, with very complicated texts, when, as one usually says, he is lying. A behavioristic analysis, on the other hand, mentions many things, among them tokens that occurred or would occur under certain conditions, but it never mentions mental states. In this sense a behavioristic analysis is not an adequate analysis "of" a mental state. As for Professor Ayer's analysis of knowing, my contention is that where he does not simply present us with behavioristic accounts and actually mentions mental states, he denies the existence of certain states that do occur in *some* of the cases in which we say that we know something. But I see that before continuing I must eliminate a possible source of confusion.

I happen to believe that there are, in some sense, mental states numerically different from my own, yet it is not necessary to complicate the present discussion by introducing into it the puzzles connected with the belief in the existence of other minds. Whatever the solution of those puzzles is, I do know at least that *I* do have mental states and that my "having" them is a fact different from—though, of course, not causally unrelated to—the facts mentioned in a behavioristic analysis of my having them. I know, furthermore, that sometimes I do have states with the text 'I know that $p$' and that these are different from certain "corresponding" states, which I sometimes also have, the text of which is '$p$'. So I shall not in the rest of this paper speak further about A's states but only about my own. Nor shall I make any pretense of trying to explain *directly* what these states are. To do this would be like trying to explain color to a blind man. But since I believe that my readers are not, in fact, blind, that is, that they are sometimes aware of their being aware of something, I shall add two *indirect* clarifications.

*First*, a warning against reading too much into the expression 'corresponding state' is in order. As used in the preceding paragraph, it refers merely to a relation among the texts of states, not to any relational or other state or part of such. *Second*, since 'knowing' is sometimes so used that one can only know what is the case, I think I should say that this is not the meaning in which I use it and to which I wish to direct attention. This latter meaning is, perhaps, more adequately rendered by the cumbersome phrase 'being immediately aware of'. Nor is 'awareness', as I use it, a generic term, of which 'doubting', 'remembering', 'believing', 'willing', and so on, are instances. Presently I shall propose to analyze states with such texts not as different kinds of awareness (generically) but, rather, as awareness (specifically) of different kinds of content. If 'knowing' is so used, then I may know what is false in the obvious sense that I may be immediately aware of a datum which, upon further information, I shall judge to have been illusory. An analysis that proceeds along more or less familiar lines shows that such falsehood is a very complex affair, as remote from the basic semantical

[219]

meanings of 'false' and 'true' as certain ordinary meanings of 'knowing' are from that of 'being immediately aware of'. It should be clear by now that it is my intention to keep out the former in order to clarify the latter. Professor Ayer, as I see it, allows his interest in the behavioristic analysis of the former to seduce him into overlooking the latter.

What I have said so far can be summarized in terms familiar to all students of the history of philosophy by saying that I do, *in some sense,* assert what Professor Ayer denies, namely, the existence of mental acts. Though there are several reasons why so many philosophers committed themselves to this denial, one thing, I believe, can be said about all of them. These philosophers did not see *in what sense* they could admit the existence of acts without at the same time committing themselves to other opinions, on related issues, which they were unwilling to accept. To speak, as I do, about states with texts '*p*' and 'I know that *p*', *without* assuming that these states themselves are related as their texts may or may not be related is, I believe, *one such sense—* the only one in which, if the traditional label is to be used, I am prepared to maintain the existence of acts.[3] One of the related issues, that of Self, in a sense in which many of us are not ready to admit that the term denotes anything, I shall here sidetrack by substituting such phrases as '*p* is known' or 'It is known that *p*' for 'I know that *p*'. This makes 'knowing' a one-term predicate rather than a relation; thus one need not look for the second term, or, to use again traditional language, for the subject of the act.

[3] Why and how this avoids commitments, I, too, am determined to avoid, I tried to show in "A Positivistic Metaphysics of Consciousness." But it is not necessary to have read that paper in order to understand what follows in this.

II

Volition is, perhaps, the one act that has received more attention than any other on the part of both philosophers and psychologists. So I shall relate my next comments to the text '*p* is willed'. As is well known, the psychologists of the nineteenth century who followed Wundt and the Associationists rather than Brentano, Ward, and Stout, all analyzed states with this text according to the following schema: They were considered as "complex" states "compounded" of partial states, one of these partial states being one with the text '*p*', the others consisting of, say, muscular sensations and feelings. The rather technical sense 'feeling' had in these schemas I shall not explore beyond noticing that there are no grounds whatsoever, except that of everything being what it is, on which a feeling datum, thus understood, could be intrinsically distinguished from a sense datum so-called. The radical changes that took place in the science of psychology since this doctrine—I shall call it the classical doctrine—was first advanced, did not make it easier for a just appraisal of it to prevail. Too many things tended to become mixed up with it, foremost among them the status of introspection as a method of the science of psychology. Two things, I believe, must be carefully distinguished. First, it still seems that the classical doctrine was a sound, though *mis*stated anticipation of physiological fact. I, for one, believe, that a behavioristic *re*statement of it will eventually be vindicated. Second, the classical doctrine is not, and never was, the result of genuine introspection, it is merely a speculative extrapolation from introspection, attempted by such men as James Mill, Bain, and Wundt under the pressure of their preoccupations with the nature of knowledge in general and of the science of psychology in particular. But I see that I have again reached the point where one must beware of explaining color to the blind. So I shall once more fall back on indirect elucidation and turn to a question that is of a rather peculiar kind. For though it is a question that was once thought to be of great philosophical import, it does not disappear, as we have come to expect, after having been subjected to proper analysis. There still remains a question; only, the answer to it is no longer important. I refer to the question as to the number and kinds of irreducible acts, in the sense in which all classical psychologists, whether they followed Wundt or Brentano, spoke of the number of discriminable hues and pitches.

As far as the science of psychology is concerned, this question has been submerged by the functionalist-behaviorist revolution. Yet, my position being what it is, it seems that I must face it again. I would say, then, that I can do with one and only one act. Or, to drop the traditional term, I incline to the belief that (states with) such texts a '*p* is willed', '*p* is doubted', '*p* is remembered', can be all analyzed into (states that have) texts of the form '. . . is known'. To give a schematic illustration, I propose to analyze '*p* is willed' into 'it is known that *p* and it is known that *q*', where '*q*' is the text of those muscular and feeling states that occur as partial states in the classical analysis. With this notation the classical analysis itself would, of course, be represented by '*p* and *q*'. It is this latter pattern which, I take it, Professor Ayer has in mind when he briefly mentions the "feelings" that may be involved in some cases of knowing. But then, it seems that I rejected the classical analysis because it is merely speculative and not, as has been claimed for it, a true introspective

[222]

account. If this is so, why should not my schema be rejected on the same ground?

Let us first agree to call 'undefined descriptive terms' predicates that are, in a familiar respect, comparable to 'green', 'middle c', and 'later than'. With this in mind, here is what I would say. I do believe that the analysis I suggest can be carried out without introducing any undefined descriptive predicates that do not denote characters actually exemplified in some of my mental states. But I do not claim that I can introspectively analyze, say, a volitional state of mine in accordance with the proposed schema; or, to speak loosely, I find that some of my acts are simple, thus making 'knowing', in some sense, an undefined descriptive predicate. This should absolve me from the classical error of mistaking my analysis for what it is not. But if that is granted, I am at once up against other questions and difficulties. If it is not introspective, in what sense is my analysis an analysis at all? What is it expected to achieve and what, in particular, are the criteria of its success? Also, if neither Professor Ayer's analysis nor mine is introspective, why should mine be preferred to his? On what grounds can I maintain, as I am indeed prepared to maintain, that only the one I propose is correct? Assuming that I have made no other blunders, do I not mistake for a real difference what is merely the difference between alternative formulations? Obviously, I must answer all these questions. With that I shall have done.

Take all statements of the form '*p* is ...' or '... that *p*', where the dots represent one of the terms under consideration, 'known', 'willed', 'believed', and so on. Call the class of these statements the act pattern. I explain next what I mean by saying that a certain manner of analyzing the act pattern is successful. Consider, for instance, the manner I have pro-

posed. Upon this particular analysis, '*p* is willed' tautolog-
ically implies '*p* is known'. Since I cannot, in fact, will any
thing without being aware of this thing—different meanings
of 'willing' are either behavioristic or in some other sense
derivative—the analysis is, with respect to this particular consequence of it, adequate. An analysis is successful if it is, in
this sense, adequate with respect to all its tautological implications, including such implications of factual truths, after
these truths have been stated in terms of the analysis. A
successful analysis is thus what some call a successful reconstruction or axiomatization, at least schematically or in broad
outlines, of (a part of) common-sense or ordinary language.
Assume, next, that there are several successful analyses of
the act pattern. Obviously, it is not a good question to ask
which of them is, upon this criterion, the correct one. All one
could ask is which of them, if any, is the most comprehensive,
one analysis being called more comprehensive than the other
if the class of the tautological implications of the latter is
a proper subclass of the class of tautological implications of
the former. If there are two or more successful analyses of
equal comprehension, to ask which of them is right is like asking which of the several known axiomatizations of Euclidean
geometry is correct. Nor are there any obvious reasons why
in this case one of the two equally comprehensive analyses
(assuming that there are exactly two) should not be built
with one basic verb, say, 'knowing', while the other starts
with two such verbs, say, 'knowing' and 'remembering'.
Whether or not this is actually so is, as it were, a mathematical problem. All this goes to show in what sense the old question as to the number of basic acts is not a factual question.
But there are, of course, the facts of analytical introspection
in the classical sense of trying to isolate a minimum class of

elements or building stones. These facts, however, most of us no longer consider as very important either for philosophical analysis or scientific psychology.

It is not necessary to pursue further this line of thought; I can already make the point I wish to make. In calling Professor Ayer's analysis incorrect I do not mean to express a preference among several equally comprehensive analyses of the act pattern; nor do I merely mean to assert that my analysis is more comprehensive than his. The point is, rather, that Professor Ayer's behavioristic "analysis" of knowing, willing, and so on (not of 'knowing', 'willing', and so on), is not at all an analysis of the act pattern in the sense in which I have offered one. For I propose what some call a linguistic clarification of the texts of some mental states; he gives a causal account—from without, as it were—of their occurrence. To say the same thing differently, if philosophical analysis is, as I believe it to be, linguistic analysis, it must analyze language from the standpoint of the speaker, not from that of the behavior scientist who observes him.[4] And it seems to me that no matter how mistaken I may otherwise be, I am at least doing philosophical analysis in this sense. Professor Ayer is not. This, at any rate, is what I have in mind when I call his analysis incorrect.

Some readers may agree with this criticism of Professor Ayer's opinions, and yet wonder on what grounds to choose between my proposal and what I have called the classical doctrine, provided that the dubious claim of being the result of introspection is no longer made for the latter. To clarify this point, I would admit that the choice does not concern a matter of fact. But then I would hurry to add two more re-

[4] See also my note "Philosophical and Psychological Pragmatics," *Philosophy of Science*, 14 (1947), 271-73.

marks. First, I believe I have shown that my analysis, if it is at all possible, clarifies the hoary puzzle of the act. Second, I would say that such an analysis of the act forms an indispensable part of the dissolution of other philosophical puzzles. But to pursue the latter point leads to questions which I have taken up elsewhere and which are not directly connected with Professor Ayer's analysis of knowing. The sole purpose of the next paragraph is to guard against misunderstandings that could arise from what has been said in this paper.

First, I wish to repeat that in *some* cases in which we say, in the ordinary course of events, that somebody knows something, mental states which Professor Ayer mentions when he does not talk about speech or about other overt behavior do indeed occur in the knower. Second, what I have offered here is merely the bare outline of an analysis. In speaking about willing, for instance, I have done nothing to illuminate the difference between states with such texts as 'thinking of taking a walk', 'wanting to take a walk', 'deciding to take a walk'. But, then, this was not my purpose in this paper; I merely wanted to call attention to the possibility of what I have called a successful analysis of this sort of texts in terms of awareness ('known that . . .') and, of course, a great variety of dependent clauses ('. . . $p$'). This also indicates how I would meet the objection that the very example I have chosen reveals the absurdity of my position, since what is willed is obviously not a proposition. After all, I did not say either that the text 'This is green' *is*, literally speaking, the state or, if you please, the datum to which it belongs. The desire to make that clear was one of the motives that led me to speak of states and their texts, which, I fear, some will think is a rather clumsy terminology. One might say, for in-

[226]

stance, that if 'text', as I use it, means anything at all, it refers to the description of a mental state. So why not simply speak of states and their descriptions? What I try to avoid, in avoiding 'description', are the connotations the term has in the philosophical phrase 'phenomenological description'. For it has been seen that in a successful reconstruction the texts of *some* states could be quite dissimilar to the strings of words elicited from a subject that has them and is asked to describe them, no matter whether the introspection proceeds phenomenologically (à la Brentano and Husserl) or analytically (à la Wundt and Titchener). This was my second motive in choosing my terms as I did. Thirdly, as I have hinted before, I do not wish to prejudge, or to appear to prejudge, the issues behind the first philosophical proposition stated in the opening paragraph. The heavy-footed terminology I have chosen does, I believe, help to avoid this appearance.

# ON NONPERCEPTUAL INTUITION *

THE PHRASE "nonperceptual intuition" has been borrowed from Broad,[1] who uses it when he discusses problems that are, I believe, closely related to the issue I wish to raise. Thus, in choosing it for the title of this note, I hope to provide a hint about the general context of my remarks. However, I shall state my problem quite independently.

Consider the statement

(1)          Everything that is green is extended,

which I shall, in the symbolism of *Principia Mathematica*, transcribe by

(2)                    $(x)[gr(x) \supset ext(x)]$.

Some philosophers feel that (2) is not an adequate transcription of what (1) says, or, at least, of what we could say upon being acquainted with a single particular that is both green and extended. One possible argument in support of this objection rests on two premises.

(a) The following two classes of statements are the only ones that express *certain* truths. (a1) Analytical statements,

* *Philosophy and Phenomenological Research*, 10 (December, 1949), 263-64. Reprinted by permission.

1 C. D. Broad, *Examination of McTaggart's Philosophy* (Cambridge: Cambridge University Press, 1933), Vol. I, pp. 51-53.

that is, substitution instances of such forms as 'p v ~ p' and '(x)[f(x) ⊃ f(x)]', in which, to use Quine's suggestive phrase, the names of particulars and of characters (properties and relations) occur only vacuously. (a2) Statements molecularly compounded of statements that contain only the names of particulars and of simple characters, such as 'gr(a)' and 'color(gr)', provided that we are acquainted with what they express. I assume here, for the sake of illustration, that 'gr', 'ext', 'color', are simple or, as one also says, undefined predicates.

(b) Nonanalytical statements containing universal operators in a nonvacuous manner, such as (2), do not express certain truths.

If these premises are accepted, the argument may be stated in this manner:

(c) Since (1) is, in fact, certain, (2) is not an adequate translation of (1). It seems to me that some philosophers who accept (a) and (b), argue (c) and also believe that

(d) every significant statement can be transcribed into a *Principia*-like symbolism,

propose what amounts to transcribing (1) by

(3)                           C(gr, ext),

where 'C' stands for a simple, relational character of the second type. 'C' may then be retranslated by such phrases as 'essentially connected' or 'necessarily coinherent'; it is, of course, the peculiar nature of this character, with which we are supposedly acquainted, that led to the use of the phrase "nonperceptual intuition."

I am now ready to state the only point I wish to make in this note. *Upon assumptions* (a), (b), *and* (d) *transcription of* (1) *by* (3) *leads to the same difficulty which, in the view*

[229]

*of its proponents, argues against the transcription of* (1) *by* (2). Before showing why this is so, I shall mention what the proposal does achieve. First, (3) is of the form (a2) and, therefore, according to this view "certain." Second, the objection that while we are now acquainted with a state of affairs veridically expressed by (3), we may conceivably, at some other time, be acquainted with the referent of the negation of (3) can be dismissed as irrelevant. For a sagacious proponent of (3) merely insists that what would happen in this case is of the same kind as what would happen if one and the same particular were found to be both green and not green. And this sameness he establishes by pointing out that the two pairs 'gr(a)', '∼gr(a)' and 'C(gr, ext)', '∼C(gr, ext)' are essentially of the same form and, of course, both logical contradictions.

For any two predicates, '$f_1$' and '$g_1$', '$(x)[f_1(x) \supset g_1(x)]$' does, of course, not imply '$C(f_1, g_1)$'. But it seems to me that, conversely, if 'C' really means what it is intended to mean, the second of these two expressions must in all cases imply the first. In terms of the illustration, the proponents of (3) must be able to maintain consistently the certainty of

(4)         $C(\text{gr}, \text{ext}) \supset (x)[\text{gr}(x) \supset \text{ext}(x)]$.

Thus, they would have to show that (4) belongs to one of the two classes (a1) and (a2). But (4) does not belong to (a1), since it is quite easy to find three predicates of appropriate types which, if put for 'C', 'gr', 'ext' in (4), yield a sentence that is not even contingently true. Nor can (4) belong to (a2), since it contains nonvacuously the generality (2). This, in particular, is what I had in mind when I said that the supposed difficulty reappears. I infer, tentatively, that intuitionistic philosophers, if they want to be consistent, cannot be

[230]

satisfied with introducing certain "nonperceptual" simples. They must, or so at least it seems, reject the current criterion of analytic truth.

An argument of the same kind could be constructed for a simple term of causation. The only difference is that, as I have shown elsewhere,[2] the simple term is not, properly speaking, a predicate but, without being a connective, a connector of sentences. And the introduction of such a syntactical category is, of course, in itself a major change in logic.

[2] Pp. 40 ff. of "Frequencies, Probabilities, and Positivism," *Philosophy and Phenomenological Research,* 6 (1945), 26-44.

# CONDITIONS FOR AN EXTENSIONAL ELEMENTARISTIC LANGUAGE *

1. The expressive possibilities of extensional languages have been studied by philosophical analysts for some time. Since the question I propose to discuss is part of this larger issue, I shall begin by restating a familiar syntactical definition of extensionality. A symbolic language S is called extensional if formal equivalence between any two of its predicates implies the equivalence of any two expressions, the second of which is obtained from the first by replacing all or some occurrences of one of the two predicates by the other. Taking nonrelational predicates of the first type one has: If S is extensional, then

$$(1) \qquad f(x) \equiv_x g(x) \cdot \supset \cdots f \cdots \equiv \cdots g \cdots$$

is a theorem (tautology). The dot patterns with 'f' and 'g' are used to represent the two expressions.

2. Consider now the problem of constructing a symbolic language $S_1$ that is adequate for speaking about a certain area, say, for instance, a fragment of the world of tones as we know it with respect to pitch and loudness. To explain what is meant by 'adequate', I shall say that $S_1$ is required to contain (the equivalents of) such statements as 'This is a

* *Analysis*, 8 (January, 1948), 44-47. Reprinted by permission.

middle c', 'This is higher in pitch than that', 'Middle c is a pitch, not a loudness'; and, also, such statements as 'This (quality) is a loudness'. The occurrence of 'quality' in the sentence last mentioned is due to the scarcity of idiomatic terms for the qualities within the dimension of loudness; 'soft is a loudness' would be an idiomatic equivalent, though admittedly a poor one, of what $S_1$ is supposed to contain. But it is not supposed to contain (the equivalent of) such difficult terms as 'quality' whose status in a symbolic language is a major problem in itself, except in such clauses as '(f) ...f...' and '(Ef) ...f...', which are customarily transscribed by 'for all qualities so that ...' and 'there is a quality so that ...'.

It seems natural to attempt the construction of $S_1$ by adding to the (logical) formalism of the functional calculus a class (not series!) of undefined nonrelational predicates for pitch ('$p_1$', '$p_2$', ...), another such class for loudness ('$l_1$', '$l_2$', ...), two undefined relational predicates ('ld', 'hg') corresponding to 'louder' and 'higher-in-pitch' and, finally, two more predicates, 'P' and 'L', for 'pitch' and 'loudness'. A number of particulars ('a', 'b', ...) must also be made available. Such formulae as '$p_1(a)$', 'ld(a, b)', 'P($p_1$).∼L($p_1$)' will then represent such statements as 'This is a middle c', 'This is louder than that', 'Middle c is a pitch, not a loudness'. From this it will be seen that in $S_1$ all the undefined predicates, *except* 'P' and 'L', are of the first type. 'P' and 'L' are of the second type.

3. I am ready to state the question with which this paper is concerned. But before stating it, I wish to make it clear that I do not, in this paper, intend to contribute arguments in support of either an affirmative or a negative answer. I merely propose to show how the answer to *this* question

depends on the answers to two *other* questions. And now for the question itself. *Is it possible to define, within S₁, two second-type predicates 'P̄' and 'L̄' so that (a) their definientia contain only the undefined predicates of the first type, and (b) 'P̄' and 'L̄' can be proved to be formally equivalent to 'P' and 'L' from premises that correspond to true (factual) statements about tones and themselves contain no other undefined predicates than those of the first type?* The statement of the transitivity of 'louder', 'ld(x, y) · ld(y, z) ⊃ₓᵧᵤ ld(x, z)' may serve to exemplify the form of the expressions admitted as definientia by (a) and as premises by (b). It will be seen that they belong to S₂, where S₂ is the *lower* functional calculus, supplemented by some descriptive terms and, if needed, by quantification with respect to its predicate variables. The definitions mentioned in (a) will, of course, be definitions in use. The affirmative answer to the question I have asked may be called the thesis of *elementarism* or, more precisely, elementarism with respect to the area which S₁ is required to describe adequately. If the qualification concerning the scope of S₁ is tentatively omitted, the choice of the name 'elementarism' will, I believe, seem reasonable. For, if it is thus generalized, the thesis asserts—somewhat vaguely but, I presume, intelligibly—that in a symbolic language that is "adequate for all purposes" definitions that fulfill conditions corresponding to (a) and (b) can be devised for all undefined predicates of all types but the first.

Some may agree that a certain symbolic language, such as S₁, is "adequate" for a certain area and, also, that the thesis of elementarism holds for it, and yet may refuse to admit that the symbolism (S₂) obtained by omitting (from S₁) the undefined predicates of the higher types is "adequate" in the same sense. The probable reason for this refusal is twofold. First, the defined predicates of the higher types, such as '$\overline{P}$' and '$\overline{L}$', are merely formally equivalent to the undefined predicates, such as 'P' and 'L', which they are supposed to "replace." Second, these formal equivalences are the consequences of factual statements, namely, the statements referred to as premises in (b). The question, or questions, this criticism raises is a *further* question, and one that I do not propose to discuss in this paper.[1] To understand better the sort of thing the thesis of elementarism, as here defined, does assert, it may be helpful to recall one of the possible meanings of the ambiguous term 'nominalism'. This latter term may be taken to mean that in an adequate language with a logic like (or very similar to) that of the functional calculus all undefined predicates, including those of the first type, can be "replaced by defined terms." Thus construed, the thesis of nominalism is, I take it, patently absurd. But I am, in this paper, not talking about nominalism; I mentioned it only because I wish to elucidate what the sort of thing I am talking about is. To minimize vagueness and to avoid certain complications, I shall limit myself to $S_1$ and shall not consider the thesis of elementarism in general. The limitation is, perhaps, not as radical as it may appear at first sight, for it seems plausible, to say the least, that if the thesis of elementarism holds in general, it will also hold for $S_1$.

4. Assume that, *as is actually not the case,* all the tones and only the tones of a certain pitch $p_1$ have a certain loudness $l_1$. The formula '$p_1(x) \equiv_x l_1(x)$' of $S_1$ would then be

---

[1] For a discussion of some of these questions see "Undefined Descriptive Predicates," *Philosophy and Phenomenological Research,* 8 (1947), 55-82, where I have also proposed actual definitions of '$\overline{P}$' and '$\overline{L}$'. These definitions contain a syntactical identity; the question of extensionality was thus left open.

true (correspond to a true statement). Therefore, if $S_1$ is an extensional language, the formulae 'P($p_1$)' and 'P($l_1$)' are, according to (1), either both true or both false, and the same holds for the pair 'L($p_1$)', 'L($l_1$)'. But we know that, in fact, 'P($p_1$)' and 'L($l_1$)' are both true and that 'P($l_1$)' and 'L($p_1$)' are both false. It follows that, if in $S_1$ two undefined predicates of the first type are, in fact, formally equivalent, then $S_1$ cannot be both extensional and adequate, in the sense in which I have used the term 'adequate'. This, I believe, is the point of a very succinct remark by Quine.[2]

5. The lower functional calculus is known to be extensional and so is, therefore, $S_2$. Any defined predicate, '$\overline{P}$' or '$\overline{L}$', that could be devised in $S_1$ according to (a) and (b) would, therefore, be possessed either by both or by neither of the two undefined predicates '$p_1$' and '$l_1$' which are, by assumption, formally equivalent. It follows further that, *if $S_1$ is extensional and if the thesis of elementarism is to hold, then it must be possible for $S_1$ to be adequate without containing any two undefined predicates of the first type that are, in fact, formally equivalent.* This and only this is the point I wish to make.

It seems to me that the argument I just proposed could also be made if an undefined predicate of the first type were, in fact, equivalent to the product, or any other compound, of two or more such predicates as in the familiar illustration

$$\text{human}(x) \equiv_x \text{featherless}(x) \cdot \text{biped}(x),$$

where 'human', 'featherless', and 'biped' are, for the sake of the argument, taken to be undefined. If this is so, as I believe it to be, then the condition for the possibility of an ele-

[2] P. 127 of "Notes on Existence and Necessity," *Journal of Philosophy*, 40 (1943), 113-27.

mentaristic and extensional language will have to be modified accordingly. One may further ask whether a similar situation would not arise whenever two compound expressions of the first type are, in fact, formally equivalent as in the illustration

$$\text{rational}(x) \cdot \text{animal}(x) \equiv_x \text{featherless}(x) \cdot \text{biped}(x),$$

where all four predicates are, for the sake of the argument, taken to be undefined. I am inclined to agree with those who are of the opinion that this last case would offer no difficulty, or rather, that whatever difficulties it offers are significantly different from the one pointed out with respect to pitch and loudness. As is to be expected, the issue depends in part on what is to be considered an adequate symbolic language. This, to be sure, is a difficult problem and goes far beyond what I proposed to discuss. But, on the other hand, I have no doubt that a language in which one would have to say that one and the same quality is both a pitch and a loudness is not adequate in any sense that is both reasonable and relevant.

# A NOTE ON ONTOLOGY *

AS I HAVE explained elsewhere,[1] I call "ideal language" a formally constructed linguistic schema that is complete, adequate, and, in a familiar sense, an idealization of our natural language. It is complete if "everything" can be said in it; it is adequate if, by informally discoursing about it in ordinary English, we can dissolve all philosophical puzzles. Since it is a schema rather than a language actually to be spoken, one may say that what is now coming to be known as syntactical positivism proposes to clarify the language we speak but do not fully understand by one which we understand but cannot speak. The idea of this approach is that the categorial features of the world reflect themselves in the structural properties of the ideal language or, in case there should be several such languages, in the structural invariants which they have in common. (Some philosophical puzzles and controversies may, in this case, be clarified by the circumstance that there is, among the several ideal languages, one that exhibits a certain structural feature.)

* *Philosophical Studies,* 1 (December, 1950), 89-92. Reprinted by permission.

[1] "Two Criteria for an Ideal Language," *Philosophy of Science,* 16 (1949), 71-74; "Logical Positivism" and "Semantics" in V. Ferm, ed., *A History of Philosophical Systems* (New York: Philosophical Library, 1950), pp. 471-82, 483-92, and also pp. 1-29 of this book.

## A NOTE ON ONTOLOGY

In what follows I shall assume that the ideal language of our world consists of the noncontroversial parts of *Principia Mathematica,* supplemented by undefined descriptive constants, both proper names and predicates, including relations. As I have stated on earlier occasions,[2] this permits assigning one possible precise meaning to the so-called ontological question by substituting for it the following query: Which are the undefined descriptive constants of the ideal language? It is the purpose of this note to eliminate an apparent difficulty of this formulation with respect to predicates, a difficulty which has recently, in a different context,[3] come in for some attention. In doing this, I shall restrict myself to a very simple nonrelational model world without particulars and a finite number of undefined descriptive predicates of the first type, '$f_1$', '$f_2$', . . . , '$f_n$', which I shall, for short, call primitive predicates or primitives. To simplify matters even further, I shall also restrict the grammatical apparatus by excluding quantification over the predicate variables.

The *non*formal idea behind that of primitive predicates is that, upon interpretation, they designate characters that are, in some phenomenological or psychological sense, not analyzable into simpler components. Thus, e.g., 'green' and 'blue' would qualify as interpretations of primitive predicates, while 'green' and 'blue or green' would not. The problem, then, is to find the formal correlate of this nonformal idea of the fixity, nonarbitrariness, or, if you please, givenness of the primitives. Its solution, I submit, requires the

[2] "Frequencies, Probabilities, and Positivism," *Philosophy and Phenomenological Research,* 6 (1945), 26-44; "Undefined Descriptive Predicates," *ibid.,* 8 (1947), 55-82.

[3] R. Carnap, "On the Application of Inductive Logic," *Philosophy and Phenomenological Research,* 8 (1947), 133-47.

formal reconstruction of our idea of *possibility*. This reconstruction or explication proceeds in two steps. First, we recognize that what is "possible" in *any* world for whose description a certain grammar or logic is adequate is determined by this grammar in the sense that every synthetic statement expresses a possible state of affairs. Second, if *one* such world is partially given to us by giving us its descriptive constants, then possibility in *this* world may be defined as the class of all synthetic statements that can be formed by means of these constants. In my simple model world, possibility in this sense is very easily defined by means of the class of all synthetic predicates—excluding, e.g., '$f_1 \vee \sim f_1$' and '$f_2 \cdot \sim f_2$'—that can be built from the primitives.[4] For if '$\phi$' is one of these predicates, then the two statements '$\phi = \Lambda$' and '$\phi = V$' and their negations are essentially all synthetic statements that can be formed from it.

To show, next, that by "replacing" one set of primitive predicates by another, one affects possibility, consider four predicates, '$f_1$', '$f_2$', '$g_1$', '$g_2$', so chosen that

$$f_1 \cdot f_2 = \Lambda, \quad g_1 = f_1, \quad g_2 = f_1 \vee f_2.$$

It is clear that in this case every class definable in terms of the f's is also definable in terms of the g's and conversely. Yet the two "worlds" determined by choosing once the f's and once the g's as primitive predicates do not contain the same possibilities. In the f-world '$f_1 \cdot f_2 \neq \Lambda$' is synthetic and expresses, therefore, a possible state of affairs. In the g-world the same state of affairs is expressed by '$g_1 \cdot (g_2 \cdot \sim g_1) \neq \Lambda$', which is a contradiction! Or, if one wishes to avoid reference to "the same state of affairs," one can say that the statement

---

[4] In order to enumerate them, one can use the terms of the so-called Schroeder normal form.

'$f_1 \cdot f_2 \neq \Lambda$ ', which is synthetic in the f's, cannot be obtained by means of the two translation rules '$g_1 = f_1$' and '$g_2 = f_1 v f_2$' from one that is synthetic in the g's.

Now it seems obvious to me that two worlds that differ in their possibilities are, indeed, two worlds and not one. Instead of speaking of two worlds I could, of course, speak of two languages. For the distinction, based as it is on a formal reconstruction of our idea of possibility, is itself purely formal. I conclude, therefore, that the undefined descriptive predicates of an ideal language are ontologically significant in a sense in which this could not be the case if they were "replaceable" by others, as in my illustration the g's replace the f's. For, as this illustration indicates, so to "replace" the undefined descriptive predicates of an ideal language means to propose the ideal language of what is, if possibility is taken into account, a different world. This, I believe, is the formal expression of the idea that the undefined descriptive predicates of the ideal language refer to "simples" which are "given" to us as such, so that we have no choice in the matter. Thus the apparent difficulty I mentioned before [5] is eliminated.

This fixity, as it were, of the undefined descriptive predicates warrants comparison between what I have proposed as a possible precise meaning of the ontological question and a not unsimilar proposal of Quine's.[6] Quine, if I understand him, wishes to say that, e.g., *properties of the first type exist* in a world if and only if quantification over the predicate variables of this type occurs *in* its ideal language, or, I would like to add, in case there should be several such

---

[5] Carnap, *loc. cit.*
[6] "Notes on Existence and Necessity," *Journal of Philosophy*, 40 (1943), 113-27; "On What There Is," *Review of Metaphysics*, 2 (1948), 21-38.

languages, in at least one of them. I should say that *proper-ties of the first type exist* in a world if in speaking *about* an ideal language of this world I find it to contain undefined descriptive constants that are substitution instances for its predicate variables of the first type. In both proposals the italicized phrase, 'properties of the first type exist', is to be taken as the explicandum, i.e., as the traditional ontological or, if you please, metaphysical assertion for which I, as a positivist, do not expect to find a literal correlate *in* the ideal language. This detracts, in my opinion, from what I take to be the main reason for Quine's proposal, namely, that expressions of the form '(∃f) . . . f . . .' are colloquially ren-dered by 'There is (exists) a property such that . . .'. In other words, I do not believe that the 'There is (exists)' in the quantifier has much to do with the "existence" which tradi-tional ontology tries to assert.

To show, on the other hand, an advantage of my proposal, consider a world whose ideal language contains undefined descriptive predicates of the first type only but which also contains and quantifies—say, for the sake of introducing mathematics—variables of higher types. Unlike mine, Quine's proposal makes no "ontological" distinction between such a world and one that contains, in addition, simple characters of the higher types. It seems to me that by making this distinction my proposal reconstructs what some nonpositiv-istic philosophers may try to express when they insist that while, for example, colors exist, numbers and grammatical categories merely subsist. In this sense, too, I believe that my proposal represents a more adequate analysis of the traditional ontological meaning of 'exist'.

# LOGICAL ATOMISM, ELEMENTARISM, AND THE ANALYSIS OF VALUE *

IN A RECENT essay [1] Miss Brodbeck quite correctly attributed the following opinion to me. To deny that such characters as goodness and beauty are objective or "out there," in the sense in which shapes and colors are, it is not necessary to deny that they are indefinable, in the sense in which most positivists insist that they are not. If this is so then one can, as I hinted and as Miss Brodbeck effectively argues, avoid the obvious shortcomings of so-called naturalism in ethics and esthetics and yet not be committed to what we are no more willing to accept than all those who did less than justice to whole areas of our experience because they thought that in order to avoid such commitment they had to deny more than is either safe or necessary.

But Miss Brodbeck's paper is not technical. Technically, I hold that the construction of an ideal language [2] is the proper tool of philosophical analysis. Thus, to adopt her and my view on values means, for me, to assert that the ideal

---

* *Philosophical Studies*, 2 (December, 1951), 85-92. Reprinted by permission.

[1] M. Brodbeck, "Toward a Naturalistic 'Non-Naturalistic' Ethic," *Philosophical Studies*, 2 (1951), 7-11.

[2] "Logical Positivism" and "Semantics" in V. Ferm, ed., *A History of Philosophical Systems* (New York: Philosophical Library, 1950), pp. 471-82, 483-92, and also pp. 1-29 of this book.

[243]

THE METAPHYSICS OF LOGICAL POSITIVISM

language contains at least one undefined descriptive term whose interpretation is the relevant root meaning of one of the English words that occur characteristically in ethical or esthetic judgments.

But then, I am a positivist; and this means more than to state the traditional philosophical problems in this "linguistic" manner. A positivist also believes that the ideal language has a certain syntactical structure, essentially that of the noncontroversial parts of *Principia Mathematica*. Thus one may ask whether the syntactical categories provided in *PM* for undefined descriptive terms can accommodate those which Miss Brodbeck and I believe to be indispensable for the analysis of value. In the first part of this paper I shall discuss this question and shall answer it in the affirmative. In its second part I shall explicate some of the reasons or intellectual motives that make the adequacy of the *PM* schema an issue of the highest significance and, as I see it, one of the pivots of positivism.

I

For the sake of simplicity I shall make all my points by considering various possible transcriptions of the sentence (S) that a certain dichord is beautiful ('This is beautiful'). Let 'a', 'b' be two particulars; let 'f₁', 'f₂', 's' be three descriptive predicates to be interpreted as 'middle $c$', 'middle $e$', and 'simultaneous' respectively; let 'ce(x,y)' be defined by 'f₁(x) · f₂(y) · s(x,y)'; and, finally, 'bt' the critical undefined descriptive term.

One way of transcribing S would be 'bt(ce(a,b))'; I shall call it the first (1) since, being the most literal, it suggests itself most readily. However, it makes 'bt' a *pseudopredicate*, i.e., a term that is a modifier or connector of sentences with-

[244]

out being a connective. *PM* provides no such syntactical category; its nonsentential variables mark the places of either particulars or predicates of the various orders and types. *Logical atomism* is the thesis that the ideal language is in this respect like *PM*. Thus, if logical atomism is to be maintained, for reasons I said I would discuss later on, then (1) is not a real possibility. Fortunately, there are three others.

Consider next (2) the formula 'ce(a,b) · bt(ce)'. Now 'bt' is a predicate; but it is of the second type. This violates the thesis of *elementarism*, which limits the undefined predicates of the ideal language to the first type. Historically the elementaristic thesis was and still is quite important; systematically it has been overrated. If it is true, as I believe it to be,[3] it states an interesting feature of our world; but its breakdown, unlike that of logical atomism, would not affect the grand strategy of a positivistic analysis. I shall briefly touch on these matters at the end. In the meantime we note that (2) remains a possibility.

A third transcription of S reflects the idea that the locus of value lies in specific acts, such as moral approval or esthetic appreciation, by construing 'bt' in analogy to 'it is known (I know)' in 'I know that . . .' and 'ce(a,b)' in analogy to what takes the place of the dots. As I have shown,[4] this can be done without abandoning logical atomism if one puts in the place of the dots the particular that in the ideal language is the name of the dependent clause. Then 'bt' becomes a predicate of the first type; and we have (3) as a further possibility 'bt('ce(a,b)')'.

As (3) corresponds in a certain sense to the ideas of

---

[3] "Conditions for an Extensional Elementaristic Language," *Analysis*, 8 (January, 1948), 44-47, and also pp. 232-37 of this book.
[4] "A Positivistic Metaphysics of Consciousness," *Mind*, 54 (1945), 193-226.

Brentano, so the next and last alternative (4) corresponds to those of Wundt who, as a psychologist, made the case for what he called affective elements and characters, assigning to these primitives a position coordinate, as it were, to that of sensation. Formalizing this pattern by means of an additional particular 'm' one obtains 'ce(a,b) · bt(m)' as a very schematic transcription of S, which makes 'bt' again a predicate of the first type.

An apparent difficulty concerning the adequacy of (4) needs clearing up. Assume that while I hear the dichord I also see a visual object, described by the sentence 'P', which is esthetically neutral. The text of this experience cannot be 'ce(a,b) · bt(m) · P' alone, since this formula does not indicate its "proper" reading, '[ce(a,b) · bt(m)] · P', if I may for a moment use a pair of brackets illegitimately, i.e., as if conjunction were not associative and commutative. The solution takes its cue from the analysis of perceptual judgments. The transcription of, say, 'This is a book' is a conjunction (A · B) of two statements.[5] A is molecular; B contains operators and, if I may so express myself, states what perception adds to its sensational core. Furthermore, A is almost always itself a conjunction. What "brackets" its factors, separating them from those of, say, a second object simultaneously perceived, are the universal and existential propositions conjoined in B. The "bracketing" of the 'bt(m)' factor in schema (4) can be accounted for in the same manner.

Another objection that might be raised against all four alternatives appeals to the configurational phenomena of which much is made, and quite rightly so, in the analysis of

[5] "Remarks on Realism," *Philosophy of Science*, 13 (October, 1946), 261-73, and also pp. 153-75 of this book.

value. Let me dispose of this objection in the case of (2). If 'p₁' and 'p₂' are two different predicates, then '[bt(p₁) · bt(p₂)] ⊃ bt(p₁ · p₂)' is not analytic. Hence, whether a whole of parts beautiful by themselves is itself beautiful is, as it ought to be, upon this analysis a matter of fact. Equally simple arguments lead to the same results for (1), (3), (4).

Philosophical analysis is analysis—or reconstruction, which amounts to the same thing—in principle only. I conclude, tentatively, that there are four ways, (1)–(4), of construing the value terms which are in principle adequate; an analysis being adequate if, among other things, the transcription of a statement we know to be true becomes either (a) analytic or (b) a deductive consequence of definitions and certain factual truths or laws after these laws have been stated in the undefined terms of the analysis. If, for the sake of an adequate analysis of logic, one insists on logical atomism, three possibilities, (2)–(4), are left; if elementarism, too, is to be maintained, there still remain two, namely, (3) and (4). Which then is the right one?

Some time ago I expressed the opinion [6] that this is not a question of fact and, in this sense, not a good question, just as it makes no sense to ask which of the several known axiomatizations of Euclidean geometry is the right one. Since then I have come to see that this opinion needs qualification. If, say, two analyses are adequate, it *could* be the case that the transcription of a certain English sentence falls with the one into category (a) and with the other into category (b). In this case, if possibility is taken into account, the two analyses describe two different worlds.[7] Which of

---

[6] "Professor Ayer's Analysis of Knowing," *Analysis,* 9 (June, 1949), 98-106, and also pp. 215-27 of this book.

[7] "A Note on Ontology," *Philosophical Studies,* 1 (December, 1950), 89-92, and also pp. 238-42 of this book.

[247]

these two is ours is a matter of fact, not of language. Specifically, I have no reason to believe that this phenomenon actually occurs with respect to (1)–(4). Generally, whenever it should occur, to choose the "right" analysis is to decide on what the phenomenally simple characters are, which is indeed a matter of fact.

But a few more words are needed at this point lest I seem to yield more than I intend on the crucial distinction between the analytic and the synthetic by grounding it in facts of this sort. Whether a statement of the ideal language is or is not analytic depends only on its form. Form in this sense does not depend on what is phenomenally simple. What does depend on it is merely the form the transcription of an ordinary English statement takes. And that we do not understand our ordinary language well enough to know in all cases whether what we assert to be true is also necessary is one thing on which we can all agree.

II

Logical atomism is an assertion about the syntax of the ideal language. If justified, it leads to a satisfactory explication of the idea that logical (analytic) truths are formal, or syntactical, or linguistic. If not, I know of no such analysis or explication. Let me explain by explaining and commenting on this idea of logic. Some express it by calling analytic a statement whose truth we can ascertain merely by inspecting the statement itself. Misunderstanding this formulation deliberately, one could, for example, first decide on a special shape for all color words and then "formally" recognize the truth of all statements obtained by substituting two different color words in '$(x)[f(x) \supset \sim g(x)]$'.

Obviously this is not what is meant. What is meant Quine

[248]

has expressed most felicitously when he said that in logical truths descriptive terms occur, if at all, vacuously. (It will not hurt my purpose to neglect those logical truths in which no descriptive terms occur. Also, it will be convenient to call only closed sentential expressions sentences, referring to open ones as schemata.) The familiar machinery of variables and substitution reflects this idea directly. Undefined *descriptive* signs are, by definition, undefined signs which, put in the place of the free variables of a sentential schema, yield a sentence. Each kind of variable represents a syntactical category which is also that of the indefinite number of expressions both undefined and defined that can be substituted for it. *Logical* or *structural* are, by definition, all other undefined signs and all expressions defined in terms of them only. *Analytic* is, by definition, every sentential substitution instance of each of a certain class of schemata none of which contains descriptive signs.

This is the *first* part of our idea of logic. Its *second* part is that one can, merely by attending to kinds and arrangements of structure signs, define a class of such schemata that realizes completely our preanalytic idea of logical truth. This, though well established, is not always well understood because of limitations that appear if one insists (a) on decidability or (b) on a certain kind of definition (demonstrability) or (c) on a certain kind of formalization of this definition itself. Requirements (a) and (b) merely refute certain oversimplified explications of analyticity. Requirement (c) is not philosophically a genuine limitation if one believes, as I do, that philosophical analysis is informal discourse in ordinary English (including arithmetic) about the ideal language which we formally construct for the sake of clarifying this very discourse. In this way analyticity can

[249]

be defined.[8] The *third* part of our idea of logic concerns the particular nature of this definition. Logical atomism, which has not been involved so far, comes in at this point.

According to logical atomism (and *PM*) undefined structure signs are essentially [9] either connectives or, together with their operators, variables that stand either for sentences or for particulars or for predicates. Connectives as well as what I call pseudopredicates are modifiers or connectors of sentences; but what distinguishes them from each other is not, of course, that the former are conventionally represented by special designs while we use letter symbols for the latter. The formal essence of connectives is that (a) they are, in the familiar sense, truth tables and (b) that logical truths depending on them alone are, again in the familiar table sense, tautologies and conversely. The mathematicians express this by saying that sentential logic has an *adequate matrix representation* (as do also *some* many-valued calculi which have no philosophically significant interpretation). Logical truth of this simplest kind has thus a purely combinatorial definition. In my opinion, this completes the analysis of all one could possibly mean by calling the truths of sentential logic formal, or syntactical, or linguistic.

This still leaves the truths of functional logic to account for. But these can be defined by means of the notion of *identical formula* and its generalization for the higher types. Assuming familiarity with this purely arithmetical notion

---

[8] R. Carnap, *Logical Syntax of Language* (London: Kegan Paul, Trench, Truebner & Co., 1937).

[9] For *PM* this neglects only parentheses. In "Semantics" I added two primitive signs for mention and designation. I am prepared to argue that (1) it makes sense to call them structural rather than descriptive and (2) the very limited nonextensionality they entail does not affect the argument in this paper.

which in a broader sense is also combinatorial I shall not, because I think I need not, argue that this completes the analysis of what we mean when we call truths depending on it formal, or syntactical, or linguistic. In other words, I consider these two notions of adequate matrix representation and of identical formula, together with what I called the first two parts of this analysis, a complete explication of that crucial phrase "formal, or syntactical, or linguistic." I, for one, know of no other. And since I believe that this phrase expresses, no matter how confusedly, the nature of logical truth, I must try to make shift with that explication. Let us now see once more what this implies for the ideal language which, being the ideal language, must embody this idea of logical truth.

1. For the ideal language to contain *undefined pseudo-predicates* means to contain certain kinds of variables, e.g., a variable '$\chi$' such that 'p$\chi$q', 'p' and 'q' being sentential variables, becomes a sentential schema. I know of no "combinatorial" criterion for the conditions under which a schema that essentially contains the new variable yields always truth. (A schema containing it unessentially as, for example, '(p$\chi$q) $\vee \sim$ (p$\chi$q)' offers, of course, no difficulty.) But it is part of our preanalytic idea of analyticity that every sentence that contains no descriptive sign is either itself analytic or the negation of one that is. I conclude that what I take to be an adequate idea of logical truth would not be adequate if undefined descriptive pseudopredicates occurred in the ideal language.

2. The *modalities* are often notationally assimilated to connectives by representing them through special designs. Yet they are really pseudopredicates; for it has been proved that the so-called modal calculi have no finite adequate matrix

[251]

representation. I conclude, then, that these formalisms, though quite interesting mathematically, have no philosophical significance. Nor is this particularly surprising, since one of their basic signs represents either the idea of necessity or one of its obvious derivatives. And surely this idea is in need of analysis. Moreover, one of its connotations, analyticity, is explicated by the construction of an ideal language with a nonmodal logic.

3. The criterion of identical formulas deals with predicates as classes of integers. Extended to higher types it commits us, therefore, in effect to an *extensional* ideal language. This deters some. I, for one, consider none of the known arguments against extensionality decisive. The one most weighty, perhaps, appeals to the notorious nonextensionality of ordinary language with respect to dependent clauses after expressions of propositional attitudes (acts). The difficulty disappears if one construes the act pattern as I have suggested before and mentioned above. Let 'P$_1$', 'P$_2$', 'bel' stand for two sentences and for 'belief that' respectively. Extensionality does not imply that '$(P_1 \equiv P_2) \supset [\text{bel}('P_1') \equiv \text{bel}('P_2')]$' be true; for ''P$_1$'' and ''P$_2$'' are two different particulars.

4. The anti-Humean side in the current debate on *counterfactuals* asserts essentially the indispensability of a pseudopredicate of causation. Conversely, logical atomists must argue the adequacy of formal equivalence and implication for the transcription of laws into the ideal language. I have made this argument elsewhere.[10]

[10] "Comments on Professor Hempel's 'The Concept of Cognitive Significance'," *Proceedings of the American Academy of Arts and Sciences,* 80 (July, 1951), 78-86, and also following this article.

The explicit or implicit commitment to elementarism is due, I submit, to the obsession with certainty that is so characteristic of our philosophical tradition. The "best" kind of certainty has indeed been proposed as an explication for analyticity. I should say that to know for certain is a kind of knowing, to be construed in the act pattern. That we do know analytical truths for certain is, therefore, even if we do so know them, which may be doubted for some, merely a fact about analyticity, surely worth mentioning particularly in discussing the historical tangles, but by no means the whole story. On the other hand, it is I think an adequate analysis of one meaning of 'certain' to say that what is held to be thus certain is what is analytic.

The "next best" kind of certainty is, I believe, best explicated as possessed by what can be expressed by an atomic or molecular statement of the ideal language, since what is so expressible is presumably "immediately given and wholly contained in the specious present." This is where elementarism comes in. For it seems to have been felt that as soon as undefined predicates of higher types are admitted then the atomic sentences that can be built with them express more than what is thus wholly given and wholly present. For some such predicates this is indeed so.[11] But however it may be, with certainty once dislodged from its central position by an analysis along the lines I just indicated, the truth or falsehood of elementarism is no longer a matter as momentous as it seemed to some.

One more word in conclusion. I have written this paper so that those who disagree with me can read it as a study

[11] "On Nonperceptual Intuition," *Philosophy and Phenomenological Research,* 10 (December, 1949), 263-64, and also pp. 228-31 of this book.

in intellectual motives, an exposition and dissection to show how the various parts of a philosophical position hang together. That the expositor happens to be swayed by these motives and, therefore, holds the position is incidental.

# COMMENTS ON PROFESSOR HEMPEL'S "THE CONCEPT OF COGNITIVE SIGNIFICANCE" * ¹

## 1. INTRODUCTORY

IT WILL BE best if I preface these brief comments by two statements of limitation concerning two matters Hempel mentions but which need not be taken up in discussing what

* *Proceedings of the American Academy of Arts and Sciences,* 80 (July, 1951), 78-86. Reprinted by permission.

¹ C. G. Hempel, "The Concept of Cognitive Significance," *Proceedings of the American Academy of Arts and Sciences,* 80 (July, 1951), 61-77.
Since I shall refer to several of my papers I list them here and cite them in the text by bracketing the numbers under which they appear in this list. 1. "Outline of an Empiricist Philosophy of Physics," *American Journal of Physics,* 11 (1943), 248-58, 335-42; 2. "A Positivistic Metaphysics of Consciousness," *Mind,* 54 (1945), 193-226; 3. "Remarks on Realism," *Philosophy of Science,* 13 (October, 1946), 261-73, and also pp. 153-75 of this book; 4. "The Logic of Quanta," *American Journal of Physics,* 15 (1947), 397-408, 497-508; 5. "Conditions for an Extensional Elementaristic Language," *Analysis,* 8 (January, 1948), 44-47, and also pp. 232-37 of this book; 6. "Contextual Definitions in Nonextensional Contexts," *Journal of Symbolic Logic,* 13 (1948), 140; 7. "Two Criteria for an Ideal Language," *Philosophy of Science,* 16 (1949), 71-74; 8. "Professor Ayer's Analysis of Knowing," *Analysis,* 9 (June, 1949), 98-106, and also pp. 215-27 of this book; 9. articles "Logical Positivism" and "Semantics" in V. Ferm, ed., *A History of Philosophical Systems* (New York: Philosophical Library, 1950), pp. 471-82; 483-92, and also pp. 1-29 of this book; 10. "The Logic of Psychological Concepts," *Philosophy of Science,* 18 (1951), 93-110. [1] and [4] are reprinted in H. Feigl and M. Brodbeck, *Readings in the Philosophy of Science* (New York: Appleton-Century-Crofts, 1953).

is customarily meant by a criterion of meaning. The first of these (a) is more fundamental and, therefore, systematically prior to the problems at hand; the second (b) is technical in a sense in which the core of these problems is not.

(a) Like Hempel, I shall make use of the distinction between *analytic* and *synthetic* sentences and, also, of that between *logical* (structural) and *descriptive* (extralogical) terms. But though I shall not explicate these two dichotomies here, I do not wish to give the impression that I share Hempel's diffidence as to the possibility of establishing "sharp dividing lines between statements of purely logical and statements of empirical significance"; that I do not consider as confusing an extension of the notion of analyticity which makes Carnap's reduction sentences analytic; or that I believe a philosophically significant notion of analyticity could and, perhaps, should be "relativized" in the sense indicated by Hempel. The gist of the matter, as I see it, is this. First, the two distinctions are completely clear and precise in that they can be made within pure syntax. Second, they can be made in a nontrivial manner in the sense in which, say, the setting aside of the logical terms by enumeration would be trivial. To say this is one thing. The familiar difficulties, how to decide whether in certain formal systems (language schemas) a given sentence is in fact analytic, or how we can ever be sure that such a schema is adequate for saying everything we want to say are another thing.

(b) Like Hempel, I believe that the technic known as the *partial interpretation of axiomatic systems* is useful in clarifying the logic or, if you please, the empirical significance of some terms. But I believe this to be true only for a relatively small class of highly specialized terms of theoretical physics such as 'electron' and 'nucleus' [1]. I suggest,

[256]

therefore, that we fractionate our problem by first looking for a criterion of meaning that works satisfactorily for a language from which these very special terms have been temporarily expurgated. One reason why this seems wise is that the "coordination" of, say, the "empirical" term 'pressure', defined by means of scales, barometric columns, etc., which would still occur in our expurgated language, to the term 'pressure', as defined in, say, the classical atomic model, can be construed as a purely syntactical affair in exactly the same sense in which a Finnish-Swedish dictionary is for me, who understands neither of these two languages, a matter of syntax. The difference is that in the case at hand the translation rules are very complicated as well as rather limited, and that they are established by explicit agreement for the familiar purposes of scientific explanation. Also, this time we happen to understand one of the two languages; thus we understand, within the limits set by the dictionary, the other.

An objection sometimes raised against this way of construing the particle notions of theoretical physics is that it introduces an invidious distinction between, say, 'chair' and 'electron' and therefore, presumably, between chairs and electrons. Not surprisingly, the intellectual motive behind this objection is, more often than not, some sort of realism, anxious to insist that electrons are as "real" as chairs, if not more so. The proper way of dealing with this objection is, of course, to show, by the usual discursive and indirect method of analytical philosophy, that the proposed technic for construing certain terms does not in fact imply what these objectors fear it does. Clearly, the task is beyond the scope of these comments. It is worth noticing, though, that one step of the clarification consists in showing that even the particle notions of classical physics could, in principle, be introduced by explicit definitions. This, by the way, is also true of all the concepts of scientific psychology [10]. On the other hand, it seems that the philosophical puzzles that have been raised concerning the Schroedinger-Heisenberg theory cannot be dissolved without the technic of partial interpretation of axiomatic systems. With it, I believe I have shown that they disappear [4].

## 2. THE PRINCIPLE OF ACQUAINTANCE

What Hempel now calls the *requirement of definability* is, if I understand him correctly, what analytical philosophers know as a *principle of acquaintance* [3]. I neglect, for this occasion, all problems connected with proper names; and I assume, without examining here the warrantedness of this assumption, what is part of the thesis of Russell's logical atomism, namely, that all descriptive terms of the ideal language are either proper names or predicates, including relational predicates. By ideal language I mean that formally constructed schema in which, when it is once "interpreted," we could, with the exception mentioned and provided for in 1 (b), say "everything" [7, 9]. This being understood, the principle states that all descriptive predicates belong to, or can be explicitly (contextually) defined by means of, a class of terms that "name" characters which are "immediately observable." Or, as I prefer to put it, the principle maintains that a descriptive predicate of the *ideal language* is *either* syntactically primitive (undefined) and in this case belongs to a class C whose members name, upon interpretation, immediately observable characters *or* explicitly definable by means of members of C.

It is well to distinguish questions about the *status* of this principle from those about its *desirability* and, again, from those concerning its *adequacy*, i.e., whether an ideal language can actually be constructed in accordance with it. Presently I shall make a few remarks concerning its status. As to its desirability, I shall only say that the principle is closely related to an idea of philosophical analysis which I, and not I alone, have found very useful, for which I know no substitute, and which I am, therefore, loath to abandon. Very roughly speaking, the idea is that the clarification, or an essential part of the clarification, of the philosophical puzzles raised in connection with a term consists in providing for each sentence which contains it another sentence which does not contain it, so that the statement of equivalence between these two sentences is analytic. The insistence on the exclusive use of explicit definitions serves to secure this *eliminability*, which is no longer guaranteed when one admits other methods, such as Carnap's reduction chains, for "introducing" rather than, literally, defining descriptive predicates. Two supplementary remarks are in order.

(a) Even if, accepting the principle of acquaintance, we restrict ourselves to explicitly defined predicates, we cannot be sure of their eliminability in contexts which are not extensional [6]. But, as I have argued elsewhere [2], there is reason to believe that the ideal language is on the whole extensional. The qualification "on the whole" is necessary because of the nonextensional properties of 'des', a nondescriptive symbol to be interpreted as 'designates' and which the ideal language must contain since it must provide for the clarification of all philosophical puzzles and because this (or a similar) term is needed to provide for those concerning 'truth' and 'designation' [9].

(b) Even in an extensional schema that admits only

[259]

explicit definitions, one would, unless a further condition is fulfilled, have to admit into the class $C$ predicates that belong to different types; for instance, in addition to such color words as 'green', 'blue', and 'yellow' also the word 'color'. The condition is that no two undefined descriptive predicates are coextensive [5]. But then, I know of no two characters that are coextensive and at the same time simple enough for their names to be likely candidates for the status of undefined descriptive predicates in the ideal language.

### 3. The Adequacy of the Principle of Acquaintance

Hempel holds that the principle is inadequate or, as he puts it, "too restrictive." The reason he gives is the alleged necessity of introducing the so-called disposition terms by means of Carnap's reduction chains rather than by explicit definitions. To join the issue once more by means of the old illustration, let '$f_1$' and '$f_2$' stand for 'put into water' and 'dissolves' respectively. The predicate '$f_3$' as explicitly defined by '$f_3(x) \equiv f_1(x) \supset f_2(x)$' is then not regarded as an acceptable analysis or, if you please, reconstruction of 'soluble (in water)'. If this rejection is at all justified, then it is of considerable importance; for, (1), it affects, at least, all definitions whose main connective in the definiens is '$\supset$', and (2), a very large number of concepts—all those which, as one sometimes says, are operationally defined—would, if they are to be introduced by explicit definitions from a reasonably limited basis $C$, be of this form.

I am prepared to maintain that the principle of acquaintance is adequate and, not unnaturally in the light of what has just been said, I shall argue my case by arguing that '$f_3$', *which I refrain from transliterating by the English word* '*soluble*', is all we need for an adequate analysis of this Eng-

lish word. Yet I know as well as the critics of explicit definition that '$f_3$' is not a synonym of 'soluble', if for no other
reason than that it could be truly predicated of a certain
match which has been burned before it was ever put into
water and of which nevertheless we wish to say that it is
(was) not soluble. It must be clear by now that, in my
opinion, the key to the problem cannot be found by more or
less formal ingenuity. What is needed is reflection on what
we mean by an adequate analysis or, to say the same thing
differently, reflection on the proper relation between our
ordinary language on the one hand and the ideal language
or schema by means of which we analyze it on the other.
But perhaps it is well to add here that, as I use the term and
as I think it should be used by philosophers, what scientists
speak and write is ordinary language.

Consider the English sentence 'If it rains and thunders then
it necessarily rains'. What we do in one stage of the analysis
of 'necessary', in the connotation it has in this sentence, is to
point out that in the ideal language sentences of the form
'$p.q \supset p$' are analytic. What we don't do is look for a
"synonym" of 'necessary' in the ideal schema. Again, in explicating the 'because' in the English sentence 'I have a headache because I smoked too much' we do not look for a
synonym of 'because' but point out that in the ideal language
three sentences of the same form as 'Whenever I smoke too
much I have a headache', 'I smoked too much', 'I have a
headache' respectively exemplify a syllogistic pattern. In this
case, we notice, the analysis requires a whole group of sentences in the ideal schema. Generally, we must expect that
what we call "translation" into the ideal schema is thus
indirect, complex, and dependent on the whole context of
this schema.

[261]

With this in mind, I propose to analyze the *particular* sentence 'The aforementioned match is (was) not soluble' by means of two sentences of the ideal schema, the first corresponding to 'This match is (was) wooden', the second to the *law* 'No wooden object is soluble'. At this point I shall be told that I have merely pushed the problem back one step since a law (whether or not one of the characters it conjoins is, as in this case, dispositional) cannot be adequately "translated" by a formal implication. In other words, I have run into the problem of counterfactuals which, as is well known and as Hempel again points out, is essentially the same as that of the disposition terms. Here is what I would reply to this criticism. What we mean when we state in ordinary English a law of nature conjoining two characters is indeed not adequately analyzed by '$f_1(x) \supset_x f_2(x)$' *alone,* even if, for the sake of the argument, we assume that '$f_1$' and '$f_2$' are undefined descriptive predicates and adequate "translations" of the English names of these characters. Such a law is adequately analyzed only by (1) giving a class of sentences of the ideal language that contains, in addition to '$f_1(x) \supset_x f_2(x)$', pairs of statements, such as '$f_1(a)$','$f_2(a)$', which correspond to *nontrivial positive* instances of the formal implication; and (2) by pointing out the deductive connections among the sentences of this class. But if this is so, then '$f_3$' may well be the second predicate in the formal implication that belongs to the class analyzing the English sentence 'No wooden object is soluble'. For it seems that the familiar deficiencies of '$f_3$' will be made up completely by such triples as '$w(b)$','$f_1(b)$','$\sim f_2(b)$', with '$w$' standing for 'wooden'. However, there are in this case still the *trivial negative* instances to be disposed of, as Hempel has pointed out to me in a private communication. In other words, something must be

[262]

done about such triples as '$w(c)$','$\sim f_1(c)$','$\sim f_2(c)$', all three of which may presumably be true and which yet jointly imply the negation of '$w(x) \supset_x \sim f_3(x)$'. We must therefore add that (3) such triples are excluded from the class of sentences which we consider as an analysis of the law. Similar measures to avoid the snares of material implication will have to be taken for laws conjoining disposition terms. If, in a still more complicated case, '$f_1$' and '$f_2$' are defined by means of operators, then the analysis is not yet complete; "instances" for the "instances" will have to be added and the procedure repeated as often as is necessary.[2]

I conclude that reduction chains serve no useful purpose, that the principle of acquaintance is adequate, and that the problem of counterfactuals which now causes so much discussion is a pseudoproblem. Nor do I mind saying how surpassingly strange I find the readiness with which Hume's fundamental insight is jettisoned in this discussion by writers who are more or less in the empirical tradition. Historically,

[2] In an interesting paragraph of a very recent paper Hempel himself argues substantially the reasonableness of such an analysis through *context*: "Problems and Changes in the Empiricist Criterion of Meaning," *Revue internationale de Philosophie*, 11 (1950), 59. However, 'context', as philosophers use it, is a very ambiguous term and provides the occasion for another remark that should, perhaps, be made in discussing a meaning criterion.

Some think that even if, say, 'mass' could be analyzed by explicit definitions in some such way as I propose, this would still not exhaust the meaning of 'mass'. The gist of this criticism is that the *laws in which a term occurs* are part of its meaning. E.g., the constancy of mass is, upon this view, a part of the meaning of 'mass' in Newtonian physics. This criticism can be disposed of by distinguishing between two of the many connotations of the English word 'meaning'. The one refers to the way a term is introduced; the other to the laws in which it occurs. I have repeatedly and again in a recent paper [10] insisted on this distinction. Idealistic and pragmatist positions attempt to absorb the first (introduction) of these two meanings of 'meaning' into the second (context); in discussing a "meaning criterion" we are concerned only with the first. See also M. Brodbeck, "The New Rationalism: Dewey's Theory of Induction", *Journal of Philosophy*, 46 (1949), 781-91.

this is perhaps a sign that, for better or for worse, a certain type of positivism has run its course.

## 4. THE STATUS OF THE PRINCIPLE OF ACQUAINTANCE

When a philosopher proposes a criterion of meaning, some other philosopher is likely to ask him: "Can your criterion be applied to itself? Is, in particular, 'immediately observable' a member of your class $C$ or, if not, can it be defined by means of it? If the answer is no, don't you convict yourself of talking nonsense? If the answer is yes, what does it prove? How can you be sure that your criterion is not too narrow? Is it not, therefore, at best a presupposition which you and your friends introduce dogmatically and sometimes, I fear, even unwittingly while, being such a presupposition, it can and must be argued?" Whoever poses such queries challenges the very idea of a meaning criterion rather than the adequacy of any particular one; to answer them is to clarify what I have called the status of our principle. Again, the right answer, or what I believe to be the right answer, is discursive and indirect. We arrive at it by reflecting on what we do, and why we do it, in philosophical analysis.

Its purpose is the clarification of the philosophical puzzles, those that are historically given to us and those we can think of ourselves. To achieve it, we begin by constructing *formally* that linguistic schema $L$ which I call the ideal language. Then, by *informally discoursing about L in ordinary English* (which, by the way, we also used, for what else could we do, when we formally constructed $L$), we convince ourselves, as well as we may, of two things. First, if we "interpret" $L$, then we can, in principle, use it instead of ordinary English to say "everything" we wish to say. Second, we can now unravel the philosophical puzzles. Informal discourse of this kind is, therefore, an essential part of philosophy; it is, at least for me, the part that justifies the whole enterprise.

The principle of acquaintance or, for that matter, any such criterion, belongs to this informal discourse about *L*. But this does not make it, in any sense I could understand, a premise or presupposition. What happens, rather, is this. I *discover* that I can construct an *L* which is otherwise satisfactory and which I can understand after I have "interpreted" only those of its descriptive predicates which "name" what is "immediately observable." And, of course, I also discover that this circumstance is of strategic importance in clarifying many traditional puzzles; which, by the way, is the only good reason for calling this sort of thing a criterion or principle. But all this is only part of what needs to be said in reply to the tangle from which I started.

I have throughout put certain expressions, such as 'immediately observable', 'naming', and 'interpreting', between double quotes. This was done to indicate that I used them in informal philosophical discourse. Now one may well ask whether *L*, which is supposedly comprehensive in the sense that in it we could talk about everything, must not itself contain "translations" of these terms and whether, if it does, this whole idea of philosophical analysis is not vitiated by circularity. Both questions deserve an answer; also, they are relevant for the problem at hand since every meaning criterion that has ever been proposed contains crucially some of these terms, e.g., 'observable'. Let me then begin with 'observable' or, rather, with 'observing', as the former adds to the latter nothing but that connotation of 'possibility' which can be independently explicated by saying that what is possible is what can be expressed by a synthetic sentence of *L*. As to 'observing', I would say that *L* must indeed contain

[265]

descriptive predicates [3] which allow for a "translation" of the ordinary English verbs for our perceptual and other mental acts [8]. And I also grant that these verbs are by no means unproblematic; for to analyze them by "correctly" translating them into L is, in my opinion, the main key to some famous philosophical puzzles that revolve around them [2, 9]. However, and this is the point, in our informal discourse we use these verbs not as they are used in the traditional puzzles but in their ordinary sense, which does not lead to any perplexity; and we find that by thus using them in talking about L we can dissolve the perplexities of these puzzles. There is, as far as I can see, nothing vitiatingly circular in this procedure. What goes for 'observing', goes also for such "semantical" words as 'naming' and 'interpreting'. But some may grant the force of these remarks and yet demur against my saying, even though in double quotes, that L can speak about "everything." For does it, or could it conceivably say what I just said about it? Thus pressed, I would not mind amending my statement to the effect that by talking about L we can clarify everything there is to be clarified, including this talking itself. The very idea of talking about something, for instance, is clarified by the "semantical" part of L. This much I would say to such a questioner. Silently I would wonder whether he has really grasped the distinction, which is to me a quite unproblematic matter of common sense, between using a symbol on the one hand and mentioning it on the other.

Historically, this account of the respective roles of formal and informal discourse in philosophical analysis is, it seems to me, only another explication of an old idea. G. E. Moore,

---

[3] 'Descriptive predicate' is here a purely syntactical term. See the remarks in section 1(a) above.

I believe, expressed it by his doctrine of common sense; Wittgenstein, in an unfortunately paradoxical and prohibitive manner, by his famous distinction between what can and what cannot be said. And I should also like to think that with his recent distinction between questions internal and questions external to a linguistic framework Carnap [4] approaches again, no matter how hesitatingly, this common ground. But I am not at all sure of this since he still disparages all external questions and thus also the two all-important ones of the comprehensiveness of the formalism and of its usefulness in clarifying the traditional puzzles, so that we may understand them and do not need to dismiss them by decree.

[4] "Empiricism, Semantics, and Ontology," *Revue internationale de Philosophie,* 11 (1950), 20-40.

# THE IDENTITY OF INDISCERNIBLES
# AND THE FORMALIST DEFINITION
# OF "IDENTITY" *

PROFESSOR BLACK has in a recent essay [1] stated his views on the so-called identity of indiscernibles. While I agree with part of what I take him to say, I do not think his discussion is a complete analysis of the problem traditionally known by this name. It is my intention to present the outline of such an analysis. Professor Black chose the attractive form of a dialogue. I shall make use of a more pedestrian device, numbering the steps of the argument as I think it should proceed.

1. I shall use 'identical (same)' and 'different' so that the one is synonymous with the negation of the other; but I shall not use ' = ' and ' ≠ ' as abbreviations for them. Generally, I shall until close to the end of this paper avoid all symbolic or quasisymbolic devices except the trivial one of using letters as proper names; and I shall up to that point make no reference or appeal to mathematical logic. For I quite agree with those who feel, as Professor Black does, that one cannot successfully apply this tool without first

* *Mind*, 62 (January, 1953), 75-79. Reprinted by permission.
[1] Max Black, "The Identity of Indiscernibles," *Mind*, 41 (1952), 153-64.

finding out what precisely the thing is to which one wants to apply it.

2. I shall assume, as I believe one must if there is to be anything to talk about, that we all know what we mean when we say, in ordinary language and in the ordinary course of events, such things as that the person known as Josephine Beauharnais is identical with the first wife of Napoleon the First, while Napoleon the First and the King of Rome were different persons.

3. As I understand it, the traditional problem is, not whether a certain proposition *P* is true but, rather, whether this proposition is analytic. There are thus at least two sources of disagreement and, in case it passes unnoticed, of confusion. One is the exact text of *P*; the other is what one means by 'analytic'.

4. There is, I believe, verbal agreement on the first point. *P* reads: *If* a *and* b *are different objects then there is at least one property such that* a *possesses this property and* b *does not.* There are two reasons for calling the agreement verbal. *First,* it seems that some who thought that they argued for or against the analyticity of *P* really argued that everyone of a certain class *S* of sentences, of which *P* is not even a member, is or is not analytic. *Second,* there are two disagreements about the meaning of 'property' in *P*. Some would exclude relational properties; the vast majority of contemporary students includes them. I shall, as Professor Black does, without further argument follow the majority. The other disagreement is more subtle. "Being identical with a certain thing" and "being different from a certain thing," if they are properties at all are, of course, relational properties. Some things some people have said about our problem can be understood only if one takes them to have meant that the two

[269]

phrases I put between quotation marks are not really the names of properties. This disagreement belongs to the heart of the matter. So I shall not prejudge it.

5. If, in order to clarify the traditional puzzle, one had first to examine the several notions of analyticity that have been proposed and then to decide which, if any, is adequate, I would not have written this paper. The subject is too large. Interestingly, it turns out that what needs to be done can be done without undertaking that task. One cause of this fortunate state of affairs is that in all those complex and multilateral disagreements about analyticity there is also an important core of universal agreement. Let $A$ be the conjunction of all the premises, $B$ the conclusion of a valid deductive argument. Everybody agrees that for a notion of analyticity to be adequate it is necessary $(a)$ that all sentences of the form 'If $A$ then $B$' are analytic; and $(b)$ that if $A$ is analytic, then so is $B$. Positively, this is all I shall use of the notion of analyticity. Negatively, I should like to mention that I am not satisfied with an explication of 'analytic' that is framed in terms of what we can "conceive" or "imagine." Consequently, I am also distrustful of proofs purporting to demonstrate that a specific sentence is not analytic because it would not even be true in an ingeniously invented "possible world," that is, I presume, in a world we could "conceive" or "imagine." Professor Black uses such arguments.

6. So far I have introduced $P$ and a class $S$ of sentences which I have not yet specified beyond saying that $P$ is not one of them. Presently I shall specify a third sentence, $D$, and a fourth, $P'$, obtained from $P$ by restricting the objects mentioned in it to certain kinds. Then I shall point out $(a)$ that $P$ follows deductively from $D$; and $(b)$ that $P'$ follows deductively from the conjunction of the sentences in $S$ (briefly,

from $S$). In order to understand many of the arguments that have been made for or against the analyticity of $P$ one must be aware of two things. ($c$) Some claim, implicitly or explicitly, that $D$ is analytic and conclude, by ($a$), that $P$ is analytic. ($d$) Some claim, implicitly or explicitly, that $S$ (more fully, every member of $S$) is analytic; infer by ($b$) that $P'$ is analytic; and believe that they can by certain reflections bridge the gap between $P'$ and $P$. Fortunately again, it will not be necessary for my purposes to inquire whether this bridge, too, is claimed to be a deductive inference.

7. The argument from $D$ (6c) presupposes that "being identical with a certain object" and "being different from a certain object" are considered relational properties. $D$ reads: *Nothing is different from itself.* The inference from $D$ to $P$ is familiar. Let $a$ and $b$ be two objects and consider the property of being different from $b$. The antecedent of $P$ states that $a$ has this property; that $b$ does not have it follows from $D$.

8. One may enquire why $D$ or, what amounts to the same thing, the proposition that every object is identical with itself should be thought to be analytic. Certain arguments begin like this. If one knows what 'louder' means and also that '$a$' and '$b$' are the names of two objects or, even, of two tones, one does not yet know whether '$a$ is louder than $b$' is true. If, however, one knows what 'identical' means and that '$a$' is the name of an object, then one knows also that '$a$ is identical with $a$' is true. I need not continue. The attempt to base in this manner an explication of analyticity on "meaning" is only too familiar. (I distrust it as much as the one I mentioned before, which starts from what one can conceive or imagine.) Curiously, the same felt difference between, say, 'louder' or 'later' on the one hand and 'identical' or 'different'

on the other also furnishes grounds on which the whole line of thought that argues from $D$, or even our problem itself, has been or may be dismissed. There are two variants of this. The first insists that 'identical' and 'different' do not really name two relations. Something like this may have been in Wittgenstein's mind when he rejected in the *Tractatus* the very notion of identity. The second variant, distinguishing between "logical" characters such as identity or difference and "descriptive" ones such as to be louder or later, amends $P$ to the effect that it speaks only of "descriptive" properties. However, I cannot at the moment think of anybody who argues this way.

9. The arguments from $S$ ($6d$) do not depend on the status of $D$. But I must now specify $S$. Each of its sentences asserts that one of a finite number of relations is asymmetrical. The condition $P'$ imposes on the objects mentioned is that of any two of them one stands either in at least one of these asymmetrical relations to the other *or* has a property which the other has not. Evidently, $P'$ follows deductively from $S$. 'If one of two objects is louder than the other then the latter is not louder than the former' and 'If one of two objects is to the left of the other then the latter is not to the left of the former' are sample sentences from $S$. Generally the idea is this. It is believed that there is a finite number of asymmetrical relations so that the class consisting of all objects which a familiar type of philosophy calls either sense data or elementary feelings fulfills the condition I just stated. This, by the way, is another premise needed by those who hope to establish the analyticity of $P$ in this manner. Thus, they would have to claim that this premise, too, is analytic. The way this kind of philosophy proceeds from $P'$ to $P$ is also

familiar. Broadly speaking, it claims (*a*) that everything one can say comes somehow down to statements about those simple objects; and (*b*) that after the "reduction" has been carried out *P* can be shown to follow deductively from *P'*. (I am, though with some serious reservations, quite sympathetic to this position. But that has nothing to do with the analysis I am trying to present.)

10. If one adopts the line of thought that starts from *S*, everything depends on whether *S* itself is analytic. Now it is common knowledge that whether the members of a certain group of sentences are or are not analytic constitutes in itself one of the major controversies of the last decades. Also, the answers to several other controversial questions depend at least in part on how one answers this particular one. All the sentences of *S* belong to that group. So do several comparable ones, such as 'Nothing is (all over) red and (at the same time all over) green' and 'If the first of three events is later than the second and the second later than the third then the first is later than the third'. The prominence and importance of this controversy is probably the reason why some believe that they talk about *P* when they really talk about *S*. Several chapters of Russell's *Inquiry* exemplify this tendency. Professor Black does not even mention sense data; he talks about iron spheres and possible worlds with a central symmetry. Yet, some of the things he says suggest to me arguments one might make against the analyticity of *S*. But I am quite willing to admit that nothing of the sort was in his mind. Nor do I wish to argue what the statements of one who can so well speak for himself may reasonably be taken to suggest.

11. So far I have not breathed a word about mathematical

logic. Now I must do so. For the discussion of the identity of indiscernibles has been affected by the so-called Leibniz-Russell "definition of identity." One major cause of confusion is that mathematical logicians use such words as 'analytic', 'logical', 'definition', 'descriptive', 'identity', and 'difference' in a manner of their own which as such, that is, *without further argument,* has no philosophical significance. I shall, therefore, whenever I use these words as they do, put the letter 'f' (from 'formal') in front of them. For instance, the two formulae

R $$(x = y) \;\underset{\text{Def.}}{=}\; (f)[f_x \equiv f_v]$$

and

R' $$(x \neq y) \;\underset{\text{Def.}}{=}\; \sim (x = y)$$

are, as everyone knows, the f-definitions of f-identity and f-difference given in *PM*. Certain confusions stem, as I just hinted, from uncritically mistaking f-notions for our ordinary ones. I mention in particular that f-definitions are f-analytic, and that f-identity and f-difference are designs of the kind called f-logical because no f-descriptive designs occur on the right sides of R and R'. Notice, too, that 'logical' and 'analytic' are used synonymously in the two phrases 'logical truth', 'analytic truth'. Also, that definitions are analytic is one more feature of analyticity on which everybody agrees. All these are temptations to mistake P for a definition (more precisely, since it is a conditional, for one half of one) and to infer that it is, therefore, analytic. Yet, P as we ordinarily understand it is certainly not a definition. For, to repeat, if we did not independently know what 'different' meant, what would there be to talk about?

12. Some philosophers who are at present not very popu-

lar in the British Isles believe that a formalism roughly like *PM*, or built around *PM*, can in certain ways be related to English and, so "interpreted," become a sort of "language" that is a help in philosophical discussion. I happen to agree with these "formalists." But this is again quite beside the point since I shall neither defend their thesis nor assume that it is defensible. The only question I shall ask, because these ideas have played a role in the discussion of our problem, is this. If for the sake of the argument the general thesis of the formalists is granted, are there then adequate grounds for their specific interpretation which relates 'identical' and 'different' to '$=$' and '$\neq$' respectively? I observe, first, that if this interpretation is tried out, what is correlated to *P* is

$$(\exists f) \sim [f_x \equiv f_y] \supset (\exists f) [f_x \cdot \sim f_y].$$

This formula is f-analytic, but is *not* a f-definition. But if the correlate of *P* is f-analytic, then *P* itself should, by the rules of the formalists' game, surely be true. Luckily for the interpretation, nobody in his senses really doubts that *P* is actually true—in our world, of course, not in some possible one of which I know nothing. That formalists sometimes call certain calculi the languages of possible worlds is merely a figure of speech, though admittedly a very misleading one. For, whatever it means, it has nothing to do with iron spheres and central symmetries or other things which we can or can't conceive or imagine. With respect to the formalists' interpretation of 'identical' and 'different', it seems that if one accepts their game at all, it may be as justifiable and successful as any.

I have finished this outline analysis of the so-called identity of indiscernibles. In conclusion, I venture to express my own opinion on some points. I hold that an adequate explication of analyticity can be given and that upon this explication *P* and *D* are analytic while *S* is not. But the argument I presented is completely independent of these beliefs.

# THE PROBLEM OF RELATIONS
## IN CLASSICAL PSYCHOLOGY *,[1]

---

### I

CLASSICAL PSYCHOLOGY [2] came to an end with the victory of the functionalist and behaviorist movements that arose in the last decade of the nineteenth century and by 1915 had all but conquered. What occurred in psychology during this brief transition period of about twenty years was nothing less than a major revolution, the virtually complete replacement of one style of thought by another. A corresponding date or short period to mark the rise of classical psychology is not so easy to choose. It has been said, quite aptly I believe, that the first volume of Hartley's *Observations on Man* (1749) is chronologically the first work that a

* *The Philosophical Quarterly*, 7 (April, 1952), 140-52. Reprinted by permission.

[1] It will be noticed that I have refrained from comments on Hume throughout this essay. The relevant Humean texts are in my opinion so difficult, not to say obscure, and have been the object of so many discussions on the part of historical scholars as well as of systematic philosophers that I thought it neither necessary nor prudent to add to these controversies.

[2] E. G. Boring, *A History of Experimental Psychology* (New York: Century Co., 1929; 2nd ed., New York: Appleton-Century-Crofts, 1950) is an excellent factual history of psychology from the Renaissance to the present. See also its companion volume, by the same author, *Sensation and Perception in the History of Experimental Psychology* (New York: Appleton-Century Co., 1942).

historically naive contemporary psychologist, though he would think it quaint, would yet recognize as a psychological treatise, both because of its subject matter and because of the manner in which the author deals with it. But the historical student knows that Hartley's *Observations* are already the consummation of earlier developments. Locke's *Essay* (1690) certainly contains psychological material and treats it in a manner continuous not only with Hartley's method but also with that which, for example, Thomas Brown used in his *Lectures on the Philosophy of the Human Mind* (1820). And Thomas Brown, like the other writers of the Scottish school, must of course be counted among the main figures of classical psychology. Classical psychology, then, extends over a period of about two hundred years, roughly speaking, from 1700 to 1900. Until some time after the middle of the last century it was substantially English and Scottish and, derivatively, French. Only towards the end did the German contribution, that is, primarily the work of Wundt, Brentano, and the schools that sprang up around them, come to the fore. But such chronological and national clusters, even if they be supplemented by the customary documentary evidences for dependence and influence, are not all I mean when I speak of classical psychology. My interest and, accordingly, my purpose in this paper is mainly structural or, if you please, logical, rather than in a narrow sense historical. The point, then, is that the authors I have so far singled out denotatively, as it were, do have something in common. They share a style of thought; they are concerned with the same problem; they merely disagree about its solution. Also, they all accept, disagreements "within the rink" [3] notwithstanding, the same method as the only proper way of arriving at a solution. The

[3] The phrase is Titchener's.

common problem is, in James Mill's phrase, the *analysis of the phenomena of the human mind;* the common method is *introspection.* This, let it be noticed, holds for the last, German phase as well. The only difference is that the Germans introduced experimental procedures and also gave a good deal of attention to the laws that connect mental phenomena with the environment on the one hand and with their physiological correlates on the other. (This is what Fechner called outer and inner psychophysics respectively.)

It is a measure of the change wrought by the functionalist-behaviorist revolution that contemporary psychologists, particularly if they are Americans, hardly know what their predecessors meant by 'mental analysis' and 'introspection'. And most contemporary psychologists are, for better or for worse, either Americans or under the spell of the massive American achievement in their field during the last two generations. I shall meet this challenge in two ways. First, I shall, before I even state my problem, explain the classical frame of reference. Second, I shall give this explanation by describing schematically some fictitious experiments in the language of behaviorism. The possibility of such translation, unnecessary as it may seem to some, is yet not without interest. For it is, as I hope to show, not a bad way of bringing out the logic of the old issues and, at the same time, avoiding some of the ambiguities that obscured them. On the other hand, this mode of presentation should go a long way toward destroying the prejudice, spawned, as all prejudices, by ignorance and intellectual sloth, that everything that was done in psychology before the advent of Watson is, in principle, unscientific. To be sure, by the time it collapsed, classical psychology had proved a scientific failure in that it could not, even by its own rather lenient standards of experimental reliability, discover the laws of "analysis" it was looking for. It also is arid or, at least, dated, in that contemporary psychologists, even if they could now establish such laws, would not be particularly interested in them. For functionalism and behaviorism have in the meantime taught them to search for another kind of laws, laws that state under what environmental and motivational conditions (bits of overt behavior and) mental phenomena, whatever their "analysis" may be, do occur. But to say all this is one thing. To say that classical psychology is in principle unscientific is another thing.

II

The classical psychologists proposed to "analyze (decompose)" by "introspection" all possible total "mental states (phenomena, conscious contents)" into "elements." These elements are themselves conceived as mental states or parts of mental states. They are called elements because, first, they themselves are supposedly not further decomposable by introspection and, second, all other mental states are thought to "consist" of them in that any mental state can presumably be "reconstructed (recomposed)" from its elements. Unfortunately, the precise meaning of the terms I just surrounded by quotation marks is rather obscure; many of the difficulties that plagued the classical psychologists stem from questions that have been raised about them. For instance, it is not at all clear in what sense a mental state $A$ can be said to consist of other such states, $a_1, a_2, \cdots\cdots, a_m$ when none of these $a$'s nor perhaps other states, $a'_1, a'_2, \cdots\cdots, a'_m$ similar to $a_1, a_2, \cdots\cdots, a_m$ respectively, are in fact parts of $A$. Again, what does it mean to reconstruct a mental state from the elements that occur in its analysis? Writers otherwise as disparate as Kant and Comte thought this particular objection to introspection so powerful that they rejected classical psychology completely and, since it was the only psychology they knew, denied the very possibility of this science. Presently I shall bypass these and other difficulties of the classical formulations by describing my fictitious experiment. But let me first insist on another point. Imagine two paintings, one a landscape and one, say, a reproduction of the *Mona Lisa,* which consist in the pointilist manner of the same numbers and kinds of small color patches differently arranged. Call *A* and *B* the percepts of an observer who views on two different occasions these two pictures and assume, for simplicity's sake, that his total mental states on the two occasions consist of these percepts only. The class of mental states consisting of his percepts of all the color patches could then not be offered as an analysis of either *A* or *B*, since such an analysis would not permit the unique determination of what it purports to analyze. Different states must yield different classes of elements, otherwise the analysis is not properly an analysis (a term which I use for the product of the activity as well as for the activity) or, as I shall sometimes say, it is not complete. This requirement is, rather obviously, an essential part of the classical idea of analysis; it may even be considered as a (partial) explication of the metaphorical verbs which I surrounded by quotation marks. Most of the classical writers accept the requirement, either explicitly or implicitly; but we shall see that some do, in fact, violate it.

Suppose now that a behaviorist shows to a group of subjects all kinds of things, books, fruits, pictures, and so on. The subjects are supposed to tell on each occasion what they see and in telling it to speak as they ordinarily would. Every time after one of these statements (*A, B, C,* etc.) has been made, the person is asked what he has seen. But on this occasion he is not free to speak as he ordinarily would. Before the experiment started the subjects were instructed (or, as psychologists now put it, they were given a set) to use in these their second responses only certain kinds of words and only sentences of a certain grammatical structure, e.g., only the names of so-called sensory qualities such as 'green' and 'red' and only sentences of the subject-predicate form such as 'this is green' or 'that is red'. Let us call $a_1, a_2, \cdots, a_m$ the class of statements elicited as such a second response following $A$. The purpose of the experiment is to discover sets of instructions that would enable one to find laws permitting one to infer unambiguously the $A, B, C$, etc., from the $a_1, a_2, \cdots, a_m$; $b_1, b_2, \cdots, b_n$; $c_1, c_2, \cdots, c_l$ etc. This is the schema of my fictitious experiment. Some comments are in order.

1. Obviously such experiments could be made. Nor are there any *a priori* grounds why they could not succeed, though we have ample reason to believe that they would in fact bog down. Such practical failure was, as I have hinted, one of the causes for the eclipse of classical psychology. 2. For the sake of expository convenience I have restricted myself to perceptual situations. The schema can be extended to all kinds of total mental states. 3. The special set induced in our subjects explains what was meant by introspection; the laws that would permit us to infer the first kind of verbal response ($A$, etc.) from the second ($a_1, a_2, \cdots, a_m$, etc.) explain the meaning and purpose of what was meant by 'analysis'. 4. How this behavioristic account avoids the difficulties involved in such traditional terms as 'consisting of', 'decomposing', and 'reconstruction' will, I trust, be evident without further explanation. 5. Demonstrating the significance of the uniqueness requirement in the direction from analysis to phenomenon, this account also shows why no such require-

ment operates in the opposite direction. To put it as psychologists do, in a manner which, though philosophically muddled, serves their purposes well enough, one and the same meaning may be carried by different contents. In our terms, A may in many cases read 'I remember Paris', yet the visual imagery revealed by analysis may be different in each case.

I said before that while they agreed on their problem, the classical psychologists disagreed about its solution. Loosely speaking, the main issue was how much could be built from how little or, if you please, how elementary the elements could be. To propose a solution or adopt a position meant, in our terms, to indicate the kinds of words and grammatical forms to be admitted into the language of the lower-case letters, *a, b, c,* etc. And, except for some of the later German work, it was indeed always a matter of kinds rather than of actual lists of admissible terms.

There was never any doubt among those "within the rink" that some relational judgments (or, as I shall briefly say, relations) can be analyzed. But it was highly controversial whether there was a hard core of relations such as, say, that of spatial contiguity which could not be further decomposed so that at least some names of relational characters such as 'contiguous' together with such grammatical forms as 'this is contiguous to that' would have had to be admitted into the language of the lower-case letters. To answer this question affirmatively is to take one of the possible positions. To answer it negatively is to be faced with the task of analyzing relations into nonrelational elements. This is the problem of relations in classical psychology. To understand the interest it commanded and the amount of controversy it aroused we must start on a new line of thought.

[283]

### III

Elementarism, as I intend to use the term in this paper, is the thesis that all mental contents can be completely analyzed into classes of punctiform elements of the kind exemplified by what we now call sense data or sensa. Thus, the only statements an elementarist familiar with my schema would admit into the lower-case language are either what some now call nonrelational atomic sense data statements or equally simple statements about equally minute affective states. I called these elements punctiform because I think this name helps to emphasize their nonrelational character. But in calling them so I do not wish to prejudge the status of extension as an unanalyzable character.[4] In other words, these elements are punctiform only in the approximate sense in which the Democritean atoms and the particles of modern physics are punctiform. And just as the latter occupy a definite portion of space,[5] so we find that Spencer, for instance, uses a spatial metaphor involving extension when he explains what he means by 'feeling', which is his term for sensum. A feeling is a "portion of consciousness which occupies a place sufficiently large to give it a perceivable individuality" while feelings of relation are "characterized by occupying no appreciable part of consciousness."[6] Titchener illuminates the same contrast by a kinaesthetic metaphor, calling palpable what I just called punctiform. The attractive image of the flights (relations) and perchings (qualities) which William

[4] Titchener, in one of his major disagreements with his master, Wundt, insisted on this irreducibility.

[5] At least, this is so as long as we describe physical space by means of real-number coordinates. In such a space mathematical points are, of course, the only real points.

[6] H. Spencer, *Principles of Psychology* (New York: D. Appleton Co., 1897), Vol. 1, p. 164.

[284]

James coined at the end of the classical period belongs to the same family of explanations.

Unless they are used with great care, some of these metaphors can be very misleading. The point is that only the particulars mentioned in statements of the forms '$f(a)$' or '$r(a, b)$' can conceivably be spoken of as punctiform, extended, or palpable. To say any such thing, either positively or negatively, about a character makes no sense; in this respect there is no difference between relational characters and qualities. Also, the gap between qualitied particulars and the quality they exemplify is logically just as unbridgeable as that between related pairs and relations. Because of their nominalism the classical psychologists from Locke on were rather vague, not to say confused, on these matters. On the one hand, their nominalism blurred for them the difference between the qualitied particular and the quality. On the other hand, the analogous transition from the related pair to the relation did not occur to them or, if it did, did not appear equally plausible. (This is, in fact, the only meaning I can attribute to the alleged impalpability of relations.) But if this is so, then it might appear that to be a nominalist one would have to embrace elementarism. This, I suggest, is one reason why elementarism seemed so attractive to some of the classical psychologists. More precisely, it is a reason in that it helps us to understand, in that specific sense in which a structural analysis can help one to understand historical facts. But there is at least one further reason for this emphasis on elementarism and, consequently, for the felt urgency of the relations problem. This second reason, I am inclined to believe, was also a potent cause and, with some authors, perhaps even a conscious motive. Let me explain.

[285]

Well before the end of the seventeenth century a new view of perception had found wide acceptance, even outside the antecedents of the movement with which I am directly concerned.[7] Though the basic logic of this view is that of the old atomistic doctrine, I call it new because it then supplanted Aristotelian thought, the sway of which in this matter had been virtually undisputed for centuries.[8] What I just called the basic logic of this view is not different from that of contemporary theories of perception. Physical processes in the object perceived affect, through changes which they cause in an intervening medium, the sense organs. The physical processes thus initiated in these organs cause, through the intermediary of the afferent neural mechanisms, another such process in the central nervous system. This process "corresponds" to the percept. How to account properly for this correspondence is, of course, one of the major problems or, as some of us now prefer to say, one of the major puzzles of our philosophical tradition. For surely not everybody accepted then or accepts now as a complete explanation Hobbes's formula that our mental contents are phantasms, since they are really nothing but internal motions of, as he put it, the innermost parts of our organs. But it so happens that for what I am about in this paper it is important to consider what people then did take for granted as well as on what they disagreed. I suggest that after the atomistic philosophy had come to its first British fruition in Hobbes it was taken for granted that *some* of its contents were impressed upon the mind *from without*. Controversial

---

[7] Even the Platonist Henry More embraced the new theory. For the emphasis with which Hobbes rejected the old, see the first (!) chapter of *Leviathan*.

[8] As is shown by Descartes's example, one did not have to be an atomist to hold the new views on perception.

was the ontological status of mind and, not unconnected with this, whether it was wholly passive in the sense that (1) *all* contents are of this kind, and (2) they are in no way affected or modified by mind. No great harm will be done if I yield to the temptation of extending the spatial metaphor where it does not belong. I shall say, then, that the issue was the contribution, if any, *from within*.

What will be accepted, uncontroversially, as impressed from without depends, at least in part, on what is held to be "out there." For this information we must turn to the physics of those days. If we do this, we find physics casting itself in the mould of atomism, not only during the period that set the pattern for classical psychology but throughout its course. To be sure, this claim must be carefully restricted to physics; in philosophy and psychology the story is quite different. Sometimes it even seems to me that the stark contrast between the physiologically oriented psychology of Descartes and his followers on the one hand and classical British psychology with its characteristic aversion to physiology [9] on the other is best understood as a shrinking away, in England and Scotland, from what were thought to be the materialistic implications of the new physics. But since British physics was in fact atomistic,[10] it stands to reason that what was thought to be out there and what, therefore, could

---

[9] The one noteworthy exception up to the time of Spencer and Bain was the physician Hartley. But even his most ardent disciple, Dr. Priestley, though rather notoriously not lacking in either courage or enthusiasm, thought it wise to jettison the physiological parts of Hartley's system when he tried to defend it at the height of the romantic reaction that coincides chronologically with the trough between the two crests of the associationist wave marked by the appearance of Hartley's *Observations* (1749) and James Mill's *Analysis* (1829).

[10] Boyle and some physical speculations of the Cambridge Platonists are exceptions. But this line soon became submerged and probably had no influence on the classical psychologists.

impress itself upon the mind, was implicitly determined by an ontology in the Democritean style. In such a world those "punctiform" and "palpable" elements, the atoms, are the only sort of thing that is really there, in a sense in which relations are not. Putting it this way, I probably succumb to the kind of overstatement that is so hard to avoid if one wishes to characterise broadly a style of thought. I might be told, for instance, that the spatial arrangement of the shaped and otherwise qualitied atoms, which is relational, is of the very essence in the atomistic ontology, since on this arrangement and on it alone all the differences among the things we perceive with our senses depend. But this is pointing at an inconsistency within atomism rather than a refutation of what I said. For the Greek atomists did not teach that (approximately) punctiform atoms and (relational) space are all "there is." Rather, theirs is a world of atoms that are, whirling in a void that is not. Failure to do justice to the ontological status of relations affects the whole of British empiricism.[11] It is, I suggest, an inheritance from the Epicurean line in its ancestry. In psychology it was probably the reason why only nonrelational elements seemed acceptable as impressed from without. And there is also the tendency among these psychologists to identify what is impressed from without with what is introspectively irreducible, since what is thus irreducible is, for them, of what our contents really "consist." The passage in which Hume compared simple impressions and ideas with atoms, association with gravitational attraction, and the program of classical psychology with that of Newtonian physics is too well known

[11] For a discussion of some implications of this weakness see "Undefined Descriptive Predicates," *Philosophy and Phenomenological Research,* 8 (1947), 55-82.

to require quotation. All this helps us to understand why elementarism was such a fundamental tenet of what I shall permit myself to call the left wing among the classical psychologists. For the only other alternative was, apparently, to have recourse to that contribution from within, which these authors were loath to admit.

So far as the relations problem is concerned, we have, I think, gained some understanding of its prominence. For if I am right in what I said about the impact of the atomistic ontology, then only two solutions seemed possible. Either relations can, in the elementaristic fashion, be analyzed into nonrelational elements, or a contribution from within—more specifically, as we shall presently see, an act—is necessary to account for them. Logically, there is, of course, a third possibility, namely, to treat some relational contents as both introspectively irreducible and impressed from without. But it took more than a century before Thomas Brown hit upon this simple solution.[12] Amazement that this possibility was so long overlooked is among the motives that led to the present analysis. Thomas Brown's example was, in 1855, followed by Herbert Spencer; Kuelpe in Germany took later the same position; and the ontological and introspective irreducibility of relations is, of course, at the very core of the more recent doctrine of *Gestalt*. But these very complex later developments lie beyond the scope of this paper.[13] I

[12] Brown stood in the center, as it were, between the left and the right wings. Insisting on the introspective irreducibility of relations, he was yet unwilling "to admit the variety of powers, of which Dr. Reid speaks"; i.e., he thought acts "to be susceptible of still nicer analysis." For some characteristic passages see his *Lectures on the Philosophy of the Human Mind* (Edinburgh, 1820) Vol. II, pp. 187-88; pp. 459-60; Vol. III, pp. 14-15; or, in the Philadelphia edition, 1824, Vol. I, pp. 432-33; Vol. II, p. 146; pp. 242-43.

[13] For some relevant comments on *Gestalt* see "Holism, Historicism, and Emergence," *Philosophy of Science*, 11 (1944), 209-21, and the review of Koehler's *Gestalt Psychology* in *Psychological Bulletin*, 45 (1948), 351-55.

[289]

turn now to some comments on the two other possible solutions.

### IV

The factual failure of elementarism is one thing; its logical possibility is another. For even when an idea is rightly rejected, it makes a difference whether or not it has been rejected on proper grounds. And in the massive onslaught under which the classical psychology fell at the beginning of this century the arguments often got badly scrambled. Two types of elementaristic solution of the relations problem, as of all other problems of "reconstruction," have been offered. One can be dismissed as inadequate on purely structural grounds; the other is logically possible. In discussing them I shall make use of the schema of $A$'s and $a$'s.

Let a subject be presented several times with a simple arrangement, two monochromatic spots, one green, one red, the green to the left of the red. According to what he notices on each occasion, the subject's first response $(A)$ will sometimes be 'This is green; that is red' $(A_1)$, sometimes 'This is green; that is red; this is to the left of that' $(A_2)$. The $a$-statement 'This is green; that is red' $(a_1, a_2)$ which, we notice, reads like $A_1$, can thus not be a complete analysis of $A_2$. For this would make it an analysis of $A_1$ as well as of $A_2$, which violates the uniqueness requirement. This is, of course, the point I have already made, less formally, when I spoke of the landscape and the *Mona Lisa*. Generally, we conclude that the qualitied particulars which are the terms of a relation cannot by themselves be a complete analysis of this relation. Such a proposal hardly deserves to be called a solution; it simply ignores the problem. Yet this "solution" has been offered, with laudable explicitness, by James Mill.[14] To put it as baldly as possible, to be aware of two sensa and to be aware of all the relations they exemplify is for him one and the same thing. The younger Mill, in his famous notes to his father's *Analysis,* criticises such naiveté rather bluntly and sides in effect with Thomas Brown. Whether Hartley must be counted with James Mill as another "naive" elementarist among the leading figures seems doubtful. What he actually says about relations [15] in his otherwise rather elaborate system is slight and not very clear. Perhaps the following conjecture is not too implausible. One of the main influences on Hartley was, as he himself avers, John Locke, who accounted for relations by an act of comparing. Hartley was bent on eliminating Locke's acts (ideas of reflection) as introspectively irreducible elements; but in this he was all but absorbed by the decomposition of the will. So it may have escaped him that without an act of comparing he was left with the problem of relations on his hands. However that may be, he did at least not explicitly embrace the doctrine later propounded by James Mill.

To consider the second type of elementaristic solution, the one that is logically possible, let the letters $A_1$; $A_2$; $a_1$, $a_2$ be used as before. $a_1$, $a_2$ is, of course, again offered as the analysis of $A_1$. But $A_2$ is this time analyzed into three elements, $a_1$, $a_2$, $c$, with the third letter standing for an atomic sentence about a third sensum. To fix the ideas, assume that $c$ is about a kinaesthetic datum supposedly corresponding to a minute eye movement from the left to the right. In one

---

[14] *Analysis of the Phenomena of the Human Mind,* Vol. II, pp. 7-11. For J. S. Mill's criticism see pp. 18, 19. (Page references from the second edition, by J. S. Mill and A. Bain, 1878).

[15] *Observations on Man,* Vol. I, p. 56. (Page reference from the 1791 edition by J. Johnson).

case ($A_2$) this kinaesthetic datum is presumably found in consciousness under the introspective set; in the other case ($A_1$) it is absent. The factual absurdity of this schematic illustration requires no comment; but logically, it seems, the problem of relations is solved. It looks as if relations among the particulars of nonrelational elements could, in principle, be analyzed into classes of elements containing, in addition to these elements, further ones that represent, in a logical sense, the relations. However, this is not all there is to it. For assume, next, that our subject sometimes makes the response $a_1$, $a_2$, $c$ in the ordinary course of events, that is, when he is not under the introspective set. In symbols, assume that there is an $A_3$ such that $A_3$ and $a_1$, $a_2$, $c$ read alike. Since $a_1$, $a_2$, $c$ can by assumption not be further analyzed, for otherwise it could not serve as the analysis of $A_2$, it follows that it would be a complete analysis of $A_3$ as well as of $A_2$. Thus the uniqueness requirement would again be violated. To exclude this vitiating possibility, one has to assume that states of the kind exemplified by $a_1$, $a_2$, $c$ occur only under the introspective set. That this *factual* assumption is necessary to make the elementaristic thesis a *logical* possibility has, as far as I know, not been noticed by any of the classical writers. Nor is this very surprising, since those minute mental states which the $c$'s presumably name have probably never been found at all, under any set, by *bona fide* introspection. Such states were never anything but the brain children of system-building elementarists.

The most elaborate of the later elementaristic systems and representative of all of them is Wundt's.[16] So I shall make it

---

[16] Wundt's *Outlines of Psychology*, trans. by C. H. Judd (New York: G. E. Stechert and Co., 1902) is concise and still readable. Concerning relations see pp. 278 ff.

the occasion for a few remarks. Wundt analyzes relations, elementaristically and in principle correctly, by means of representing elements. But what he actually does is vastly more complicated than the simple schema that served my own, mainly logical, purposes well enough. Instead of a single kinaesthetic datum he has a highly compounded thing amounting in effect to an act of comparing, only of course a decomposable act whose elements lie, if I may so express myself, side by side with those which they intend. The glue, as it were, that holds large numbers of elements together, so that they can become the analysis of such a thing as 'this is to the left of that', are the affective rather than the sensory elements among them. This is the core of Wundt's doctrine of apperception, once famous and now virtually forgotten. He himself emphasized this feature and insisted, rather self-righteously, that while his British predecessors had an unduly passive conception of mind, he was thus the first elementarist to do justice to mental activity. We, of course, realize that in the classical sense these tiny feelings or, as he also calls them, affective tones are in his system just as passively impressed from without as visual or auditory sensa. The only difference is that in their case the "without" are our bodies. *Habent sua fata verba.*

These little feelings by which Wundt tried to save elementarism have in his system a very peculiar property. A sensory element, say, a visual datum, can occur in all kinds of total states, by itself, in a simple arrangement, or in a very complex percept. A feeling element can occur only in states of the appropriate complexity, for instance, to choose an extreme illustration, the feeling characteristic of doubt only in (the analysis of) states of doubt. (It will be noticed that this is not the point made before about the necessity

[293]

of excluding the occurrence of certain states.) I mention this because it reveals the scientific sterility and triviality to which the classical psychology for all its unimpeachable logic had sunk before its course was run. For what Wundt does here is to smuggle into the jigsaw puzzle one piece that tells what to do with the rest of them. Such a piece is only in a very formalistic sense a piece among pieces.

Wundt's elementarism was rigid, emphatic, and doctrinaire. Yet, to connect it directly with the anti-relational bias of the Democritean ontology would be stretching the point beyond all reason. Like some other German elementarists Wundt came from physiology. So it is much more plausible to say that within the tradition in which he found himself when he turned psychologist he was rather attracted by the minute elements of the British left-wingers, since they reminded him of what he was used to from the laboratory; and, on the other hand, that he was somewhat repelled by the more dialectical and philosophical atmosphere in the writings of the right wing, that is, in the main, the Scottish school. There is, I believe, a structural point behind this historical conjecture. The physiologist may, and sometimes actually will, find it useful to analyze the stimulation from a perceptual object as it impinges on the sensory surfaces into "punctiform" elements, each tiny enough to be the adequate cause of the process in a single nerve or even a single fiber. Nor does he neglect the relational features of the stimulus object when he proceeds in this manner. For all the cues we receive from an object depend indeed only on which fibre is hit when and by what. But to conclude from this that corresponding and correspondingly minute elements can be found introspectively is to confuse two very different sorts of things with each other. I do not claim that this fallacy was explicitly committed by anybody. All I wish to say is that during the German phase an elementaristic suggestion from physiology had taken the place of that from the atomistic ontology. In fact, there was probably still another such suggestion effective during that time. I shall call it the genetic suggestion, since what I have in mind is the very foolish idea that an infant, if it could only introspect and report, would tell us that his world is a chaos of isolated sensa and feelings. But to analyze the impact of genetic and evolutionary thought on the last phase of classical psychology is beyond the scope of this paper.

v

The contribution from within on which the right wing insists is the indecomposable act or, in Locke's phrase, the simple idea of reflection. It has long been the fashion, particularly among psychologists even before the rise of behaviorism, to consider acts as philosophers' fancies. So I shall first of all briefly establish that this is a prejudice, as I did once before with respect to the ideas of introspection and mental analysis. Even the behaviorist cannot dismiss the act and, on the other hand, there is no reason why he could not account for it. For his subjects do sometimes say 'This is red' ($A_1$) and sometimes, on the same external occasion, 'I see that this is red' ($A_2$). Simply to neglect this difference, as again James Mill most explicitly proposed, is high-handed to say the least; and it certainly should not make psychological sense to a behaviorist for whom the verbalization is part of the mental state, if not the state itself. Thus, within the classical frame of reference, since $A_1$ and $A_2$ are different, so must their respective analyses be. To account for this difference by an additional irreducible constituent in

[295]

the analysis of $A_2$ that stands to the elements in the analysis of $A_1$ in that peculiar nexus which we express by the dependent clause after the verbs of awareness is, on the face of it, just as reasonable as anything else. Nor, by the way, would the admission of such a constituent imply that our minds are active in the sense in which this was at issue between the left and the right wing, particularly during the British phase. But it seems safe to say that this was not then realized. Had it been realized, one of the major points I have tried to make would indeed come to nought. It should also be noticed that I have in this argument restricted myself to the humble 'seeing' and not argued from those more conspicuous and undeniably significant acts that are now spoken of as the propositional attitudes.

The *Locus classicus* for the act solution of the relations problem is Bk. II, ch. 12 of Locke's *Essay*. Having finished his inventory of the several kinds of simple ideas and turning to those he calls complex, Locke lists there among the acts of the mind that of "bringing two ideas, whether simple or complex, together, and setting them by one another so as to take a view of them at once, without uniting them into one, by which way it gets all its ideas of relations." One could not wish for a clearer statement, not only of this solution of the relations problem but of the basic idea of the act doctrine as a whole, a doctrine that dissatisfied Hartley because, as he said, it assumed "an eye within the eye" and which, for the same reason, satisfied others. I shall restrict myself to two comments about the logic of this solution. 1. Psychologically it is indeed a possible solution since, in terms of the schema I have used, the irreducible act of comparing takes the place of the third element, the additional constituent in the analysis of $A_2$ which distinguishes it from

[296]

that of $A_1$. Philosophically or, if you please, ontologically this solution suffers, not surprisingly, from all the weakness of the classical nominalism. There are only two alternatives. Either a relation between, say, two particulars depends only on the mind or there is something in these particulars themselves which the mind perceives when "setting them by one another." The first of these alternatives is repugnant; the second takes us back to where we started. 2. I did not speak of indecomposable acts as elements, calling them constituents instead. The point is, first, that within the classical tradition they are, at least implicitly, conceived as relational and, second, that one term of the relations they exemplify is not a particular but itself one or several elements. The other term is, of course, what the philosophical psychologists had in mind when they entertained the idea of an Empirical Self. Thus it appears that this solution of the relations problem does not really get rid of all indecomposable relations but only of such relations within what is impressed on the mind from without. One may wonder whether this was always as clear as it might have been. As for Locke, I believe a case can be made that it was not clear to him, from the arrangement of the material in the second Book which I have mentioned and, also, from the circumstance that his Self, whatever else it may be, is not the kind of psychological datum it would have to be to serve as the other term of his acts. To say the least Locke was rather vague on the matter; and I incline to attribute this vagueness to that general neglect of relations within the main stream of the empirical tradition of which I have spoken. Only, in this case it was a failure to appreciate the logical rather than the ontological status of relations. However, I do not mean to assert that it is logically impossible to deal with the act so as to escape the relational suggestion of the active verb.[17] But it is safe to say that this possibility was not even thought of during the classical period.

The account Thomas Reid and his school gave of relations follows Locke. During the German phase Locke's view was held by Brentano and most of his students, the act psychologists, as the representatives of the right wing then came to be called. Yet there is also this important difference between Locke and Brentano that in the latter the Scottish tendency toward direct realism prevailed. For Brentano, acts and acts only are mental; contents, in that narrower sense which excludes acts, he considered as physical. In this Brentano stands alone among all the major figures of nineteenth-century Germany, where the preponderant Kantian influence certainly discouraged such views. This is but one sign of the intellectual courage and independence that were so eminently Brentano's. To return to the relations issue, it is worth noticing, I believe, that some of the later Germans on the right wing [18] advocated a pattern of analysis that had all three kinds of irreducible building stones, punctiform elements, acts, and relations among particulars. As far as the logic of mental analysis goes, this pattern is redundant. So we may inquire into the causes of such redundancy. One

[17] For such an attempt see "A Positivistic Metaphysics of Consciousness," *Mind*, 54 (1945), 193-226. It should also be noticed that, in the stricter usage of contemporary logic, relations obtain only among the referents of *terms*. Thus if acts in the classical sense are taken, correctly I believe, to intend the referents of *sentences* (e.g., in the terminology of this paper, elements) then they are not relations and their names belong to a different syntactical category than, say, 'to the left of'. See "Frequencies, Probabilities, and Positivism," *Philosophy and Phenomenological Research*, 6 (1945), 26-44.

[18] E.g., Carl Stumpf, who in 1906 published a monograph with the characteristic title *Erscheinungen und psychische Funktionen*. 'Function' was then a current term for acts, just as 'power' and 'faculty' had been a century earlier.

cause, I think, is the greater sensitivity as to what can actually be achieved by introspection which has always distinguished the right wing as well as the Brownian center. These authors felt indeed that, like some acts, some relations were simply there, given to consciousness, and that they could not as psychologists do anything about them by way of introspection. But then, it was not necessarily all a matter of psychology. For most classical psychologists, up to the very end, one cannot draw a sharp line separating their psychological from their philosophical interests. And philosophically relations belong indeed to the basic furniture of the world.

# IDEOLOGY *

MANY PHILOSOPHIES have come and gone within the span of historical memory; the very conception of the nature and function of philosophy has changed in the course of Western civilization. Yet it is fair to say that, whenever a philosopher addressed himself to a problem, he considered it his privilege and his duty to penetrate to the heart of the matter. Wherever he starts, he will, if he is a philosopher, soon arrive at those rather few fundamental questions which, once firmly grasped, help us to understand, though not necessarily to answer, all others. In this respect nothing has changed and nothing, I hope, ever will. One important change that did occur during the last half-century or so is, therefore, a change in method only. A rather large group of recent and contemporary philosophers insists that what they bring to their task—that perennial task of recognizing and clarifying the basic issues—is not any special knowledge—philosophical knowledge on a par, as it were, with zoölogical or geographical or economic

* This is, with very minor alterations, the text of an address delivered in the spring of 1950 at the University of Illinois before an audience of social scientists. I have tried to preserve as much of the livelier and less formal tone of the spoken word as was possible and seemed proper. Subsequently, it appeared in Ethics, 61 (April, 1951), 205-18. It is here reprinted by permission.

[300]

knowledge—but merely a special technic, the technic of *logical analysis*. Quite appropriately, these philosophers are known by the name of "logical analysts." What logical analysis is, is more easily shown by a concrete demonstration than by an abstract explanation. I shall present such a demonstration by attempting a logical analysis of the notion of ideology.

But there is also a sense in which I shall not speak as a technical philosopher. This requires a word or two to put myself at peace with my conscience and, if that is not hoping for too much, with my philosophical friends. These friends will notice that on this occasion I shall use the language of representative realism, though technically I am not a realist. Again, in ethics I shall sometimes sound as if I belonged to the garden variety of relativists, though I do hold that some ethical predicates are not reducible in the sense in which technical relativists must insist that they are. The reason for this, aside from the obvious demands of expository economy, is that I appreciate the common-sense core of both representative realism and ethical relativism. But, of course, I do recognize the assertions that go by these names for what they are, the nontechnical expression of (scientific) common sense; and, unlike the technical realists and relativists, I do not mistake them for what they are not, the solution of the epistemological puzzles which they pose but cannot answer. Only, these puzzles are one thing; the puzzlement sometimes caused by the concepts and problems of science, including the social sciences, is another thing. To dispel the latter, one does not need to dissolve the former. Again, I shall not undertake to prove that this is so; I merely hope to demonstrate it for the example of ideology.

If I were to play the analytical game strictly, I would now

[301]

have to start by considering the several ways in which we, laymen and social scientists, use the term ideology and to proceed from there dialectically, by raising questions, until we arrive at the fundamental issues involved. To save time I shall begin by stating and explaining what I believe to be the basic issue, not only for ideology but, to be quite blunt, for all social science. I refer, not surprisingly, to the dichotomy of *fact* and *value*.

Assume that, recently standing before a certain canvas, I exclaimed, 'This is Van Gogh's Berceuse'. What happened was that I had a percept which, as one ordinarily says, is a state of mind, a conscious content or *mental* object; and that my having had this percept was the ground for my then saying, truly, that there was in front of me what we ordinarily call a *physical* object, namely, the painted canvas known as Van Gogh's "Berceuse." Similarly, when I see a tree with seared leaves and broken limbs, there are, on the one hand, the leaves and the limbs and, on the other, my percepts of them. These two sorts of things stand, as it were, in the relation of original and picture to each other. (This is the common-sense core of representative realism.) Assume, next, that, having said, 'This is Van Gogh's Berceuse', I add, 'This is beautiful'. Or consider the case when, witnessing a certain action, say that of a friend courageously speaking his mind, I say, 'This is good'. How shall we describe these situations? We need not doubt—indeed, we would be very foolish to doubt—that in these two cases, that of an esthetic and of an ethical judgment respectively, there is in the speaker a state of mind or an aspect of his state of mind which is the ground of his judging 'This is beautiful' or 'This is good' in exactly the same sense in which his percept or an aspect of it is the ground for his saying about a tree, not about his percept of it, 'This is green'. What is doubtful is, rather, whether there is something not in his mind but, as philosophers sometimes say, "out there," in the canvas or in the act, that corresponds to these experiences in exactly the same sense in which the color of a tree corresponds to an aspect of the percept of a tree. The answer to this question is, to me quite patently, negative. (This is the common-sense core of ethical relativism.)

If we call such statements as, 'This is a tree' or 'This is Van Gogh's Berceuse' statements of fact and, on the other hand, such statements as 'The Berceuse is beautiful' or 'This action is good' value judgments, then the difference between these two kinds of statements can be put as follows: A statement of fact says something about the object or objects it mentions; and, depending only on the properties of these objects, it is either true or false. A value judgment is misunderstood if it is taken to ascribe a property to the object, act, or situation it mentions in the same sense in which a statement of fact is such an ascription; it is, therefore, literally neither true nor false. What it involves and misleadingly states as the property of an object, act, or situation alone is the fact that this object, act, or situation causes in the one who makes the judgment a certain state of mind, say, for instance, of positive esthetic appreciation or of moral approval.

To prevent misunderstanding, I shall next point out the comprehensiveness, in at least two directions, of the category of fact which I have thus set aside. First, a statement of fact is not necessarily so simple as 'This is a tree'. Galileo's law of falling bodies is also a statement of fact, and so is a whole theory couched in highly abstract terms, as, for instance, the modern theory of the structure of matter. I shall, of course, not tarry for a detailed justification of such whole-sale lumping together. Yet I hope it is not implausible. For, all subtleties apart, statements of laws, of theories, and the so-called "abstract" terms are in one sense merely tools we use to speak of and predict individual, immediately observable facts. Second, let me remind you that when I discussed value judgments I spoke of the fact of somebody being in a certain state of mind, whether this be a state of seeing green or, perhaps, of morally approving a certain course of action. That somebody is in a certain state of mind, then, is a fact. Call it, if you please, a "psychological fact." It follows that, while value judgments are not statements of fact, it is a statement of fact to say that a certain person makes a value judgment or, to put it quite unambiguously, it is a fact that a person now has the kind of experience which he may or may not verbalize as a value judgment.

But I notice that if I do not wish to be misunderstood when I speak in this common-sense manner about psycholog-ical facts, I must make one more digression. We cannot literally look into other people's minds. The difficulties and arguments to which this has led, both in philosophy and in the science of psychology, are notorious. The upshot of them, for all we need to care here, is this: All we know and, even more important, everything there is to be known about people's mental states can in principle be known from observ-ing their bodies and their overt behavior, including, of course, their speech. (This is the common-sense core of behaviorism.) Also, a person's mental states are nothing but certain parts or aspects of his bodily states, including his nervous system, seen, as it were, from within. (This is the common-sense core of the so-called "double-aspect" theory of mind. What goes for representative realism and ethical relativism goes for this "theory" as well. One gets hopelessly entangled if one mistakes it for the dissolution of the puzzles and absurdities which it yields under a little dialectical probing.) But since I am not at the moment concerned with these subtleties, I shall feel free to speak about people's minds in general, and about their values, ideals, and motives in particular, without further epistemological pedantry and without emphasizing apologetically again and again how little we actually know about people's minds if we apply those high standards on which the behaviorists so admirably insist in their heroic efforts to build a science of behavior that is both reliable and worth while. Such reliability is, after all, a matter of degree. Nor would it be wise to abstain from dealing as well as we can with matters that are both interesting and important to us merely because we cannot do better, as long as we pursue these difficult studies within the right frame of reference. Such a frame has, indeed, emerged from, or at least is implicit in, what I have said so far. Let me say explicitly, then, that the idea of an exhaustive and comprehensive science of behavior offers in principle no difficulties whatsoever. Like physical science, behavior science with its various branches—psychology, sociology, economics, and so on—deals with facts and with facts only. Like physical science, it tries to organize its facts by means of laws and theories which are of the same logical nature as those of physical science. Unlike physical science, it concerns itself with people's motives, values, and ideals and with those facts—institutional, historical, and so on—of which such psychological facts are important ingredients. But this does not mean either that behavior science makes value judgments or that the truth of its findings is in principle dependent upon value judgments.

Behavior science, since it is a science, tries to find laws. Laws, roughly speaking, predict what will happen if an object of a specified kind finds itself in a specified environment. To arrive at a just idea about the kind of law we seek in behavior science, let us take a glance at the white rat, that great totem animal and martyr of American psychology, which some of our friends chase so tirelessly through their mazes. For, however one may judge its eventual usefulness, experimental animal psychology is undoubtedly the simplest and at the moment the most successful piece of behavior science. Thus we are wise, I believe, if we turn to it for logical discipline. A historical analogy should make this plausible. The mechanics of rigid bodies to the extent that it was known to Newton is, to be sure, not the whole of physics. Yet this elementary fragment of physics may still be used to advantage if one wishes to explain the logic of the whole; how powerful a stimulus it has been historically for the first explicit formulations of this logic is a matter of record. Take, then, a white rat and put it in a maze in which food can be obtained if the right path is followed. What factors enter into the prediction that the animal will or will not, as the case may be, go down this path? Or, to say the same thing differently, what in addition to the characteristics of the environment are the causes that determine the animal's behavior? For to look for laws is, of course, the same as to look for causes. Very roughly and very schematically, there are two groups of such factors. The animal will go down the right path (1) if it is hungry or, as one also says, is motivated or has a need, and (2) if it "knows" the maze. As it must be if we are to have a genuine law, i.e., a generalization that allows for prediction, both these factors or groups of factors—let us call them

IDEOLOGY

"state variables," since they characterize the momentary state of the organism—can be ascertained in advance; the first one, e.g., by measuring the animal's blood sugar, the second from information concerning its past history. It is also worth our while to notice the difference in the role of these two groups of factors, the animal's needs and its knowledge. If it is not at the moment instigated by a need, the animal will not, even though it has the knowledge, go down the path that leads to food. If, on the other hand, it has the need without as yet having the knowledge, it will exhibit the kind of behavior, known as "learning," that will eventually lead to the selection of the right path and thus to the temporary satisfaction of the need and, simultaneously, to the (as a rule more permanent) acquisition of the relevant knowledge.

These, then, are the three groups of causal factors that must in principle be represented in all laws of behavior science: the environmental conditions on the one hand, and, on the other, the two kinds of state variables, the individual's needs and his knowledge. There is, in addition, a further group of variables, biologically determined and known as "individual differences." For our purposes it will suffice to mention them. This general schema, it seems obvious, applies to man, as an individual and in his society, as well as to the white rat. But there are, of course, also important differences or, as I had better say, complications. These I shall now briefly discuss, in three steps, by explicating one after the other the following three statements: Man is a propositional animal. Man is an ethical animal. Man is an ideological animal.

The first of these complications, which is at the root of the others, is involved in the full meaning of the verb "to know." When we say the rat knew at the end of which path food was to be had, we do not mean all that is meant by saying, for instance, that I knew how to get into this room in time to deliver this lecture. Both of us, the rat and I, do, when the need arises and under a certain range of conditions, which in my case is rather wider than in the rat's, display the appropriate behavior. In this respect there is no difference. The difference is that I, unlike the rat, have, upon this as upon other such occasions, a certain mental state, which is best called "verbal" whether or not I explicitly verbalize it either to myself or to others. If so verbalized or tagged, as it were, this kind of state variable takes the form of a proposition or of a series of propositions. This is what I mean by calling us "propositional animals." But by calling us so I wish to imply more than that we are afforded the luxury of some sort of inner light by which we can watch ourselves act where the dumb creature merely acts. The presence or absence and the kind of propositional states make a difference, or, as some like to say, a dynamic difference, in that, all other things being equal, the course of our behavior still depends on them. In other words, our propositional states are themselves among the causal factors that determine our behavior. Also, some propositional states represent, and some, to put it quite bluntly, are, needs. To avoid at this point the colloquial ambiguity of "knowing" that appears in such phrases as "We know what we need," permit me to introduce some new terms. Let me from now on call the system of a person's actual and potential propositional states his "rationale," and let me also discard the clumsy phrase "propositional state" in favor of "proposition." We can say, then, that bits of skill are not the only things that can become parts of a person's rationale; the same may happen with his

[308]

needs. These latter propositions we call "motives" or, somewhat redundantly, "conscious motives." This clarification of terms which we often use quite loosely and, I fear, quite carelessly helps one to grasp firmly the peculiar dynamic significance of our rationale. For we know well—the psychoanalysts, but not they alone, have brought this home to us— that there are very important differences between the behavior of two persons who find themselves under exactly the same circumstances and who are, for the sake of the argument, assumed to be in all other respects alike, if the one is, as one ordinarily says, aware of his needs while the other acts automatically or, perhaps, under a different motive.

It will not take quite so long to explain the remaining two formulas: man is an ethical animal; man is an ideological animal. To begin with the first, it is safe to say that every man's rationale contains certain propositions which combine in themselves two characters: they are value judgments, and they play the role of very powerful motives. In the form in which they actually occur in consciousness, they are known by various names; we call them a man's standards, his ideals, the rules of conduct he tries to follow, or his moral code. More often than not they are what we mean when we speak of a man's philosophy, for only technical philosophers reserve this name for their more recondite pursuits. To deny the power of these motives, the influence they exercise upon our actions, is like denying that water flows downhill. In this sense man does not live by bread alone and has, indeed, a higher nature. But to insist that man is thus, quite uniquely, an ethical animal does not commit one to deny that these peculiar motives and the influence they have on our actions are as ineluctably causally determined and therefore in principle as predictable as, say, our tissue needs. It could even be, as the psychoanalysts and, again, not they alone, tell us, that the rise of our higher motives can be genetically traced to these very tissue needs. Whether or not this is so is, relatively speaking, a matter of scientific detail. Whatever the answer to these intriguing causal questions may be, the sway of ethical motives among men is universal. To take pride, for instance, in rejecting the standards that prevail in one's society is, as we use the term, itself a standard. Nor does it make any difference whether such a private or minority standard is, as one ordinarily says, one of cynical opportunism or, perhaps, one of self-sacrificing reformist zeal.

As we survey man's history, we cannot, I believe, escape the following conclusion. *The motive power of a value judgment is often greatly increased when it appears within the rationale of those who hold it not under its proper logical flag as a value judgment but in the disguise of a statement of fact.* A statement of this kind, that is, a value judgment disguised as, or mistaken for, a statement of fact, I shall call an "ideological statement." A rationale or an important part of a rationale that contains in logically crucial places ideological statements I shall call an "ideology." And, finally, I call man an "ideological animal" because, at least up to this point in his history, his rationales were more often than not ideologies and because, whether we like it or not, the motive power of his standards is, at least sometimes, greatly increased if they take the form of an ideology. Take just one obvious example, the doctrine of natural law which inspires our classical constitutional documents. It is, I believe, open to serious doubt whether the effect on the people would have been the same had the text read "These we hold to be self-evident value judgments" instead of the clarion call

"These truths we hold to be self-evident." What goes for the people goes also, I believe, for most of the founding fathers and perhaps even for a man of the intellectual pre-eminence of Thomas Jefferson.

Having defined my terms, which always takes the philosopher a long time, I can now turn to the problems that have been raised in connection with "ideology" and "ideological." But it seems proper that I first mention the name of the late Karl Mannheim, who started these terms on the present, second phase of their career in the social sciences. (A first brief popularity they owed to their inventors, those *idéologues* who were the last flower of the great eighteenth century and whom, therefore, Stendhal admired and Napoleon so heartily disliked.) The experts will easily recognize where I follow Mannheim as well as where I deviate and, by implication, criticize. So I shall not, as a rule, bother either to give or to claim credit beyond this general acknowledgment. Perhaps this is not the worst way to do justice to both the stimulation and the confusion that may be traced back to this vigorous writer.

Systems of ideas as they are actually held by people and social groups, or, as Mannheim would say, ideas existentially considered, are facts. As such, we know they are potent causes. But what is a cause is of necessity also an effect. In other words, rationales themselves are causally determined; accordingly, it is the business of social science to discover their causes as well as their effects. Students devoting themselves to this task hope to build a scientific foundation for those variegated and interesting pursuits that have long flowered in our civilization and which are now, somewhat self-consciously, known as the sociology of knowledge and the history of ideas. More important than any such names is one point that must be kept clearly in mind. What a person knows and believes is in principle predictable from the two classical factors, his needs and his environment, his environment being essentially his society. This goes for the factual part of a rationale as well, and for its truths as well as for its errors. In other words, we must in principle be prepared to explain why a person knows what he knows truly as well as why he errs when he errs, as Ptolemy erred when he propounded the factual falsehood known as the geocentric system. In fact, these two things cannot be separated from each other any more than one can separate the recognition and diagnosis of disease from the physiology of the healthy organism. Again, if a rationale happens to be an ideology, the fact that this is so, the particular form the ideology takes, and the kind of defective logic involved are, on the one hand, all causally determined and, on the other, amenable to explanation. Nor do we need to know many such laws or explanations—it may, in fact, be doubted whether we know any that are really satisfactory—in order to realize that it makes a difference whether a proposition that was actually held is a factual truth, a factual falsehood, an ideological statement or, perhaps, a complex mixture and, in the case of an inferential belief, by what "logic" it has been "established." This leads to some questions which, I suspect, have been uppermost in your mind for quite some time. So let me ask them myself. How can I be sure, in the light of what I have just said, that my own rationale is not an ideology? How, in particular, can I be sure that the distinction between fact and value, on which everything I have said and shall say rests, is not itself an ideological distinction? Who shall guard the guardians? Now, in one sense, which is a human and practical sense, I myself would insist that there is not much of which I am certain. In fact, I am so impressed with this that I have come to think the analysis of this very confused and difficult idea of certainty is one of the more important tasks of systematic philosophizing, just as the tracing of its vicissitudes is, in my opinion, one of the challenges in the history of philosophical ideas. But if this is once understood, it must be admitted that the questions I just raised deserve an answer. Permit me to approach them by means of a historical analogy which, as will soon transpire, is more than just an analogy.

"Sociological subjectivity" is, perhaps, a suggestive name for our puzzle. At any rate, I shall call it so, since the older puzzle, of which I shall make use in my analogy, is known as the problem of "epistemological subjectivity." During the seventeenth century physics, physiology, and the psychology of perception reached a stage in which one could, in a careless and misleading language, argue like this. What a person sees, hears, or smells is not the "real" object but his own percepts or, perhaps, his brain states; hence the possibility of perceptual error or even of systematic delusions produced in his subjects by a scientist who is familiar with the laws of physics, physiology, and perception. But then, one may pursue, how does this scientist himself achieve anything but a "subjective" picture of the real object or, to put it as radically as possible, how does he know that there is any real object at all? The history of philosophy from Descartes to Kant and J. S. Mill is in a sense the history of all variations on this theme. The decisive turn, also known as the "positivistic turn," occurred when it was recognized a generation ago that the original questions (How do we know that there is a real or objective world? Assuming there is one, how could we ever know what it is like?) are not good questions but, in a certain technical sense which I cannot stop to explain, mere verbalisms, and that, therefore, if we accept them uncritically, we enter a dialectical squirrel cage that has indeed no issue. The task of epistemological analysis is, therefore, not the impossible one of answering these questions in their original intent but that of doing whatever can and needs to be done about them by means of logical analysis. If this is done, then we see that we know perfectly well what we mean when we speak, in the ordinary non-philosophical sense, of truth and falsehood, of physical objects, percepts, and illusions. And not only do we know this in general, we know also in each case how to apply these terms, using, as we do and must, the methods of science. These methods are, to be sure, subject to doubt and error; but these are merely doubt and error in the ordinary self-correcting sense, not in that sterile "philosophical" sense which commits us to the squirrel cage. The structural similarity between the problem of epistemological and sociological subjectivity is, I trust, by now obvious. There is also a historical similarity. As the one has been created by the development of physics and physiology, so the other has been precipitated by the rise of the social sciences.

Like the problem of epistemological subjectivity, though for different reasons, the problem of sociological subjectivity is, I submit, a pseudo-problem. There appears to be a problem only as long as one fails to distinguish between value judgments and statements of fact, treating some of the former like statements of perceptual error or, more significantly, like systematic delusions due to one's social circumstances. If one does this, then the notorious subjectivity of our value judgments may mislead him into believing, as Mannheim does, that the discovery of their causal dependence has reopened the epistemological question. In contradistinction to this I and, I believe, most analytical philosophers would insist that the distinction between fact and value, which explains this notorious subjectivity, is as clear and unproblematic as those between a physical object, a percept, and an illusion. Moreover—and this is the crucial point—all these distinctions are matters of logical, not of sociological analysis, just as they are systematically prior to and independent of all sociological considerations. Who denies this must, if he is to be consistent, also maintain that Locke, who in a quite obvious sense called green a simple idea, has since been proved wrong by the scientists' discovery of the very "complex" physical and physiological events on which the perception of a "simple" hue causally depends. And, obviously, whoever maintains this confuses two very different sorts of things.

Mannheim, as I have hinted, did not and, as we shall presently see, could not within his own rationale accept this dissolution of the alleged puzzle of sociological subjectivity. But he had at least the courage of his convictions, for which we may admire him. As some of the classical philosophers, accepting their predicament, with quixotic heroism denied the existence of the physical universe, so Mannheim accepts his and, greatly impressed as he is with the conflict among the partly ideological structures that passed and still pass for science, denies in principle the possibility of an objective social science. Or, to say the same thing by means of the familiar terms as I use them and he, naturally, doesn't, he insists that every rationale is an ideology. This formulation has the merit of revealing, in a pattern only too familiar to the historian of philosophy, the intrinsic difficulty of a position like Mannheim's. If this proposition that every rationale is an ideology is itself objectively true, how can he know it? If it is not, why should we pay any attention to it? And what, in particular, is the value of a social science thus construed? To this last question Mannheim gives, in his famous theory of the "free intelligentsia," an answer that is surprising and, besides, of some logical interest. Social scientists who, as members of the intelligentsia, circulate rather freely among the various social groups are, he suggests, by this very fact as well as by their own group interest led to collect and compare all kinds of ideologies. From these they construct, very roughly speaking, a new composite ideology which, by virtue of being such a composite (and often compromise), finds acceptance and achieves progress. To expose the weakness of this argument, one merely needs to ask: Progress toward what? Permit me a comparison. If I show you a snapshot of a person you do not happen to know, it is hardly fair to ask whether you think it a good likeness. The question remains unfair, no matter how many portraits of this person I show you—snapshots, water colors, oil paintings, or even a montage (composite or synthesis) of all of them. As it is meant, the argument is therefore without force. A subjectivist cannot in this manner define progress and, in particular, approximation toward an objective truth whose very existence he in principle denies. But one may insist on this and yet think that as a sociological *aperçu* about the way certain groups function Mannheim's so-called theory of the free intelligentsia is, perhaps, a brilliant insight. I, for one, believe that it is. Let us further note, for later reference, that it assigns to the social scientist qua scientist a rather spectacular part in the social drama.

Such internal difficulties indicate what I am indeed prepared to maintain: like many other logically similar approaches, Mannheim's original doctrine of ideology is itself an ideological structure. And it is of logical interest that within a rationale of the type I have proposed one can at least consistently maintain that this rationale itself is not an ideology. But consistency as such is no criterion of truth, so this remark adds nothing to what I have so far attempted, namely, to demonstrate that the other side errs. Crude and sketchy as it is, this primary and central part of my case must be left to speak for itself, by its logic and by what it adduces to be the case (facts). Yet it should help us to grasp the total dialectic of the situation if we realize that such demonstration, no matter how complete, is not the only sort of thing that can be done. I should also be able to explain causally why the other side errs and why that which is happily my own beholds the truth without ideological distortion. But, to be sure, what is needed is a sociological explanation. To say simply that the one side is brighter than the other would not only be most ungracious; it would not be true. Personal ingenuity, or so at least I sincerely believe, is, by and large, quite evenly distributed among the several sides of the great controversies which together constitute the intellectual history of our civilization.

For the idea of the desired explanation we can amusingly draw upon another brilliant *aperçu* by Mannheim. For he takes pains to explain why my side, those who believe in objective (factual) truths and in the possibility of an objective nonideological social science, have come to hold their views. He suggests that the objectivist rationale is a survival from earlier times when the functions of the intelligentsia were exercised by an essentially conservative priestly caste that claimed privileged access to eternal verities, verities that stood immutably above the "ideological" strife of the

[317]

day and thus secured to their professional beholders a similar enviable exemption. Primarily interested as I am in what I just called the "total dialectic" of the situation, I wish to point out that I could without any intellectual embarrassment accept this explanation or, more accurately, this *aperçu*. For I do believe that there are causes that make some of us see the truth, just as other causes make others fall into error. So, if sociological factors enter, as they probably do, though they are very likely not the whole story, why couldn't it be as Mannheim suggests? This is, after all, merely a matter of detail—I would say scientific detail if we were not, all of us, limited to *aperçus* rather than to scientifically trustworthy explanations. Even so, I am inclined to think that Mannheim's explanation is a little lopsided; so I shall make my next point by using a part of his idea to propose an alternative that deals simultaneously with both sides. Let me, then, remind you of the two classical factors, needs and knowledge. As for needs, I believe both objectivists and subjectivists, like all other intellectuals, provide, incidentally and for the most part unconsciously, an argument to bolster the social status of the intelligentsia.[1] In this respect there is no difference between them. The difference is that the objectivistic temper craves the spectator safety as well as the intellectual and emotional delights of the neutral expert and critic, while the subjectivist rationalizes his desire for social leadership. (You remember what stellar role Mannheim assigned to the social scientist as a social leader.) Knowledge, in cases like this, means primarily intellectual ambience and tradition. In this respect, there is again a difference. Objectivism takes

---

[1] For an elaboration of this idea cf. W. P. Metzger, "Ideology and the Intellectual: A Study of Thorstein Veblen," *Philosophy of Science,* 16 (1949), 125-33.

its inspiration from the natural sciences and the empiricist philosophies of the last century. Subjectivism stands in the tradition of Hegelian idealism, which is history-centered, could not accept the "positivistic" distinction between fact and value, and even denies that there is any such thing as objective self-contained truth in the sense in which all non-idealistic philosophers, realist and positivist alike, insist that there is such truth. Mannheim as an individual certainly stems from Hegel; so, by the way, does Dewey, who in many respects holds structurally very similar views.

In nonacademic discourse 'ideology' and 'ideological' are nowadays almost terms of abuse. This is why I feel I should stress again that value judgments as such are not ideological. Nor is there anything wrong with them because they are not logically the same sort of thing as statements of fact, including those of science. We could not for one moment live without making value judgments, and who, even if we could, would want to? But if one is so overimpressed with science that he deprecates all value judgments as ideological simply because they are not scientific, he will perhaps also reject as futile that reflective, critical, and, in an obvious sense, highly rational discourse about values without which life is not worth living. Unfortunately, such a person does not cease to make value judgments; he merely tends to make them unreflectively. One danger of this attitude is greatest in our rulers and those who assist them or wish to assist them as experts. They may think that they still act as scientists when, in fact, they act as policy-makers. This, as we all know to our sorrow, is the soil in which callousness and fanaticism thrive. Loathe as I do that smooth-faced "well-adjusted" new barbarism, I regret one implication of the way I defined my terms. (But then, no terminology is perfect.) If I am to be consistent, I must call ideology every rationale, no matter how explicit and articulate on the fact-value issue and other fundamental questions, that assimilates facts and values to each other in a way in which the tradition in which I stand insists that this cannot be done. Clearly, this is a special case, and the application to it of what is popularly almost a derogatory term is rather unfortunate. So let me set it aside by speaking about such systems of thought as "philosophical ideologies."

Most systems of social thought and of what passed or still passes for social science are not philosophical ideologies. This sort of literature is, by and large, not concerned with the basic philosophical issues and, therefore, even though sometimes inspired by and congenial to a technical philosophy, in the technical sense philosophically naive. But such systems often show another interesting feature that one may well call ideological, in a somewhat extended sense of the term, which I shall indicate by speaking of "scientific ideologies." What I have in mind is this. We sometimes find in the scientific and methodological discussions of writers whom we otherwise greatly admire passages which are so obviously either factually false or logically inadequate that we cannot help wondering how they passed the censorship of their authors' self-criticism. In themselves these passages are not necessarily ideological. What marks them is either fallacious logic or statements of fact and theory extremely implausible on the evidence that was available to the author. These trouble spots, I submit, these lows where the argument drops, as it were, beneath its own level, are more often than not the results of motivational pressure. More specifically, while these bits of rationale are not literally either value judgments or ideological statements, they yet assert facts or, rather, alleged facts and logical connections or, rather, alleged logical connections which the author, if he has or had consciously attended to the matter, has or would have thought congenial to his values. Permit me again an illustration. Imagine a small boy very fond of fruit who is told that he may take as many apples as he wishes from a certain basket, provided only he leaves four. The basket contains six apples; the boy reasons hastily "$6 - 3 = 4$" and takes three apples! '$6 - 3 = 4$' is not an ideological statement but, to use Pareto's term, a logico-empirical falsehood. I don't think we shall be very wrong if we attribute, at least in part, this error in arithmetic to motivational pressures of the kind that operate in scientific ideologies. Only, the worth-while and historically important cases are not always quite so transparent as the little boy. A few examples should be of interest.

As my first case I take an opinion of J. S. Mill, a thinker whom I greatly admire; but uncritical hero worship is pagan and, I am convinced, one of the great sources of evil. Mill insists that "human beings in society have no properties but those which are derived from and may be resolved into the laws of the nature of individual man." Put as we would put it today and also as conservatively as possible, this means that the laws governing the behavior of (individuals in) large groups can be deductively derived from the laws that govern their behavior in isolation or in very small groups, just as all geometrical theorems can be derived from the axioms of geometry. The point at issue is thus, as we would say, the methodological relation between psychology and sociology. This, as you know, is still an issue. Now for analysis. The assertion that sociology is in this sense reducible to psychology is indubitably of a factual nature. As to its truth, I incline to believe on the basis of the evidence now available that it may well be true, though one can never be too sure about such a sweeping prognosis concerning the future results of science. This, however, is not the point. The point is that Mill mistakenly offered his thesis not as a factual prognosis but as a logical truth, i.e., as the result of a purely logical analysis of the subject matters of the two disciplines. The value involved is, I submit, Mill's commitment to the dignity of the individual and to the pre-eminence of individual ethics over social expediency and the so-called *raisons d'état*. The verbal bridge, as it were, leads from individual to individualism.

My second case is a rather notorious argument Herbert Spencer made against poor relief, purporting to show that such public charity was bound to produce evils even greater than those it was designed to prevent. The gist of the argument is that such measures are unnatural in that they futilely attempt to interfere with inexorable laws of nature, namely, those of a free-market economy. The factual error involved is nowadays, after the rise of institutional economics, obvious. On the other hand, it is only fair to say that, for all we know, overreliance on the economic bounty of an unlimited welfare state could well produce social phenomena which some of us would agree with Spencer in considering most undesirable. But again, this is not the point. What concerns me is the stupendous logical blunder. Spencer says, in effect: Do not interfere with the laws of nature. As if anybody conceivably could! It is logically like exhorting water not to flow uphill. On the other hand, in what sense do we interfere with the law that it does, in fact, flow downhill when, say, we pump it up? Do we not, rather, utilize this law, in conjunction with others, to produce by proper arrangement a desired result? (These other laws correspond, of course, to the noneconomic dynamisms that operate in every institutional structure.) The motive behind this particular piece of scientific ideology is, I suggest, Spencer's fierce nonconformist devotion to freedom of the individual from all interference by the state, including even benevolent interference.

As my third case I take one part of the argument the classical marginalists made for the distribution of the social product among the several so-called factors of production, land, capital, and labor, in proportion to their marginal productivity. Very roughly, this part of the argument runs as follows. The proposed distribution is at least just, in that each factor receives what it has actually produced, i.e., what it has, in the sense of "cause" that occurs in science, caused to exist. As for the appeal to justice, it is either a frank value judgment or manifestly ideological. For justice in its relevant root meaning is a value. Accordingly, my concern is with the other part of the thesis, the part which says that in this manner each factor receives what it has actually produced. The fallacy is, very simply, that all factors are necessary conditions for the existence of the product; and if A, B, C, D, etc., are all necessary to produce the effect X, then it makes no sense, either empirically or logically, to ask for which quantitative part of X each of the several joined causes is responsible.

My fourth and last case deals not with an individual writer or school but with a general difficulty caused by our relative ignorance in the area of the social sciences. We know today that the volume of a given quantity of a gas depends in a certain manner, which is expressed by a certain formula, on its pressure, its temperature and, within certain limits, on nothing else. Within these limits, pressure and temperature are a complete set of relevant factors or, as one also says, variables. Boyle in the seventeenth century knew only of the dependence on pressure and proposed for it a formula that yields correct predictions only as long as the temperature happens to remain constant. His formula is, therefore, literally false, though historically it was quite an achievement and though it does hold under certain conditions which we know but which the formula itself does not mention. The import of this (rather oversimplified) illustration is, I trust, obvious. In the social sciences we not only often do not know the laws (formulas), we do not even know a complete set of relevant variables. (In fact, one is not likely to discover the former without discovering the latter.) In such situations many Boyles may arise, each with his partial truth which is, literally, a falsehood. If this is so, as I believe it to be, then the laws proposed and even the variables entering them may well be determined, at least in part and either consciously or unconsciously, by the values of the author. Practically this is, I believe, one of the most important mechanisms by which scientific ideologies establish themselves as social science, sometimes dangerously and with disastrous consequences, as in the case of Marxism, which—let us be just—brought home to us the relevance of the economic variables as it had never been brought home to us before. Burdensome as this phenomenon is in practice, logically it is merely a by-product of our ignorance. It is not, as, for instance, Max Weber thought, an objection in principle against the possibility of a nonideological social science.

I have come to the end of this string of comments which, if I am not too mistaken, amount to a logical analysis of the notion of ideology or at least to the outline of such an analysis. In conclusion, I should like to say a few words about two questions of a very different sort. *Is an ideology-free society possible?* More precisely, can a society recognize its values for what they are, without any ideological support and

[324]

yet with reasonable stability remain committed to them? This is clearly a matter of factual prognosis, not of logical analysis. Our ignorance being what it is, the most honest answer is, in my opinion, that we do not know. The positive answer appeals more to the radical-optimistic temper, the negative one goes by and large more readily with a conservative-pessimistic outlook. Each side can point to some evidence; each side tries to make its case from what we believe we know about human nature. The evidence is, naturally, inconclusive; though surely the historical record as well as the soul-shaking experiences of our troubled present should keep anybody's optimism from growing too sanguine. Nevertheless, the arguments on both sides are more often than not themselves ideological. So my first question, which is one of fact, remains open and I turn to the second. *Is an ideology-free society desirable?* To answer this question is to make a value judgment. Now, naturally, one cannot prove values, but you remember I insisted that one can reason about them. I would say, then, that by the standards of classical nineteenth-century liberalism, which, freed from some historical dross, happen to be my own, the ideal of an ideology-free society is a consummation devoutly to be desired, if for no other reason than the humanity, the intelligence, and the courage it takes to bear life without the support of ideological illusion. To me such a world is the only one worth living in and therefore, if necessary, worth dying for. Perhaps we shall be called upon to die; I have no easy optimism to dispense. But then, again, we may increase our chances if we can learn to stand by our values without clutching at an ideology.

## AUTHOR'S NOTE

The papers in this volume appeared originally as follows:

I. "Logical Positivism" in V. Ferm, ed., *A History of Philosophical Systems* (New York: Philosophical Library, 1950), pp. 471-82.

II. "Semantics" in V. Ferm, ed., *A History of Philosophical Systems* (New York: Philosophical Library, 1950), pp. 483-92.

III. "Logical Positivism, Language, and the Reconstruction of Metaphysics" in *Rivista Critica di Storia della Filosofia,* 8 (July-August, 1953), 453-81.

IV. "Two Cornerstones of Empiricism" in *Synthese,* 8 (June, 1953), 435-52.

V. "Two Types of Linguistic Philosophy" in *The Review of Metaphysics,* 5 (March, 1952), 417-38.

VI. "Bodies, Minds, and Acts" originally scheduled to appear in *Philosophy and Phenomenological Research,* but withdrawn for this volume.

VII. "Remarks on Realism" in *Philosophy of Science,* 13 (October, 1946), 261-73.

VIII. "Sense Data, Linguistic Conventions, and Existence" in *Philosophy of Science*, 14 (April, 1947), 152-63.

IX. "Russell on Particulars" in *The Philosophical Review*, 56 (January, 1947), 59-72.

X. "Professor Ayer's Analysis of Knowing" in *Analysis*, 9 (June, 1949), 98-106.

XI. "On Nonperceptual Intuition" in *Philosophy and Phenomenological Research*, 10 (December, 1949), 263-64.

XII. "Conditions for an Extensional Elementaristic Language" in *Analysis*, 8 (January, 1948), 44-47.

XIII. "A Note on Ontology" in *Philosophical Studies*, 1 (December, 1950), 89-92.

XIV. "Logical Atomism, Elementarism, and the Analysis of Value" in *Philosophical Studies*, 2 (December, 1951), 85-92.

XV. "Comments on Professor Hempel's 'The Concept of Cognitive Significance'" in *Proceedings of the American Academy of Arts and Sciences*, 80 (July, 1951), 78-86.

XVI. "The Identity of Indiscernibles and the Formalist Definition of 'Identity'" in *Mind*, 62 (January, 1953), 75-79.

XVII. "The Problem of Relations in Classical Psychology" in *Philosophical Quarterly*, 7 (April, 1952), 140-52.

XVIII. "Ideology" in *Ethics*, 61 (April, 1951), 205-18.

# INDEX

Abstract entities, 12, 74, 116 f., 119-31

Abstract vs. concrete, 123, 127

Acquaintance, principle of
adequacy of, 259, 260-64
behaviorism and, 20 n.
convention and, 184 f.
desirability of, 259
disposition terms and, 260-63
empiricism and, 6 f., 77, 146, 279-86
existence and, 53, 104, 143-45, 158-60
meaning criterion and, 53, 100, 158-63, 184 f., 279-86
minds and, 142, 266
phenomenalism and, 43 f., 54 ff., 104
physical objects and, 54, 104, 158, 163-71
positivism and, 7

Act, mental
analysis of, 15 f., 54-57, 98 f., 132-52, 215-27, 252, 253, 266
certainty and, 98 ff.
empiricism and, 33, 77, 130 n., 195, 211, 291, 295 ff.
existence of, 220
irreducible, 149, 222 ff., 295 ff.
meaning and, 57, 63
psychology and, 221
value and, 245-47

Analysis
adequate, 224, 232 f., 234-36, 247, 256, 260 f.
Cambridge School of, 1 ff., 107

casuistic, 4, 14, 33, 68-73, 107-15
logical, 2, 301, 314
metaphysics and, 2, 133
of language, 2, 6 ff., 182 ff., 224 f., 260 ff.
operational, 4 f.
purpose of, 79 ff., 84, 88, 264 f.

Analytic-synthetic dichotomy, 45, 78, 82 f., 86, 99 f., 119, 256

Analyticity. See also Truth
"absolute," 46, 49 f., 73
and semantics, 66 f.
"certainty" and, 45 f., 51, 79, 83, 87, 97, 100, 228 f., 253, 261
convention and, 14, 182-83
definition of, 8 n., 14, 25, 37 ff., 45 f., 66 f., 90-93. 248-51, 270 ff.
grammar and, 14, 73, 186 f.
"knowing that" and, 55
logical atomism and, 89, 93, 248
"meaning" and, 73, 271
Quine and, 78 ff., 249 f.
Ryle and, 74 f.
tautologies and, 45, 91-93
vs. formal truth, 39, 46, 92
Wittgenstein and, 49 ff.

Arithmetic, reconstruction of, 14, 129

Arithmetization, 24 f., 38, 46, 92

Atomism, 123, 288 ff.

Aufbau. See Ideal Language; Reconstruction

Awareness
as particular, 55, 99, 151
as undefined predicate, 10, 15 f., 54 ff., 98 f., 149-51